On That Point!

On That Point!

An Introduction to Parliamentary Debate

John Meany

Kate Shuster

International Debate Education Association

New York • Amsterdam • Brussels

On That Point! An Introduction to Parlimentary Debate

Published in 2003 by
The International Debate Education Association
400 West 59th Street
New York, NY 10019

Library of Congress Cataloging-in-Publication Data:
Meany, John.
    On that point! : an introduction to parliamentary debate / John Meany,
    Kate Shuster.
    p. cm.
    Includes bibliographical references and index.
    ISBN 0-9720541-1-1
    1. Debates and debating. [1. Debates and debating.]   I. Shuster, Kate,
    1974– .   II. Title.
PN4181.M43 2003
808.53--dc21
            2002155338

Printed in the United States of America.

Table of Contents

Preface

All students can benefit from training in oral communication and argumentation. A course in debating is a course in practical knowledge, critical thinking, research, and public speaking. These are all essential skills for students who wish to succeed in school or in the workplace. We sincerely hope that this book will be of use to teachers and students who desire an introductory course in debate and argumentation.

This book is designed for use in a secondary school classroom or as part of an extracurricular debate program. It begins with an introduction to public speaking and argumentation and proceeds to discuss many advanced concepts in argument theory and the finer points of competitive and noncompetitive debating. Although there are many different formats and kinds of debating used around the world, this book primarily discusses the practice of parliamentary debating. The parliamentary debate style is the fastest growing and most widely used style of debate in the world, with parliamentary debate societies in such diverse countries as Indonesia, Russia, Chile, Ireland, Romania, Korea, and the United States. Although English is the primary language for international parliamentary debating, there are debate events in many languages held all over the world.

The parliamentary style of debating is easily learned and extraordinarily adaptable. You will find that the flexibility of the format is such that it supports both competitive events and public discussions on just about any topic. Parliamentary debate is the ideal format for debate by secondary students, because it emphasizes research at the same time that it emphasizes the development of performance and speaking abilities.

We have included all of the basic elements of public speaking, critical thinking, critical listening, and research skills for new debaters. The text also contains exercises aimed at helping experienced practitioners to develop sophisticated argumentative skills. You will also find speeches, excerpts, and resources, as well as a glossary and several hundred potential debate topics. All these resources are useful for novice and experienced debaters as well as debate trainers and coaches. The best way to learn how to debate is through constant practice. The exercises in each chapter are meant to help you learn how to use the vocabulary and concepts in parliamentary debate gradually, rather than all at once. Some exercises may be profitably repeated with different topics and in different groups of debaters.

The text presents some technical jargon associated with debate, but whenever jargon is used, a common or plain meaning description of the same concept is also given. Our goal is to help debaters communicate with inexperienced or experienced judges or a diverse array of audiences. Jargon is not meant to substitute for elegant rhetoric in parliamentary debates. We have included some jargon associated with other debate formats including policy and Lincoln-Douglas debate because many debaters learn their skills from textbooks or online sites that use those formats as models. Also, parliamentary debaters frequently participate in multiple formats—international or American and others—as part of their debating experience. Policy and Lincoln-Douglas formats are used in several countries, so there is substantial overlap between debate communities. Debaters need to understand the jargon and techniques of other formats to counter students with that experience effectively. We keep this information related to policy debate and Lincoln-Douglas debate to a minimum and always place it in the context of parliamentary debate.

This book is designed to be read and studied over a period of time, rather than to be absorbed in a single sitting. While you read the text, you may encounter vocabulary terms that you do not immediately understand. Take notes on these vocabulary words and closely examine their accompanying definitions or explanations.

We have included information on debate and argumentation theory and practice to allow practitioners to innovate the thinking, practice, and craft of parliamentary debate. No community can remain static for long. Debate is particularly dynamic. Debaters and coaches continuously reinvent the norms and practices of debate. We hope that this book will aid, rather than hinder, this process of growth and change in the debate community. We encourage readers to use the text to develop their own exercises.

This book includes four sections labeled "On That Point." These sections are designed to teach different styles of debating and speaking other than parliamentary debate. The sections include reprinted articles from major news publications. These articles are meant to serve as resources for students investigating the recommended topic for those sections. However, the exercises in those sections can and should be repeated using other topics and other resources. We hope that these sections will encourage teachers and students to use different and diverse forms of debate.

Acknowledgements

The authors wish to thank IDEA and Noel Selegzi for their support of debate and of this textbook's production in particular. The authors also wish to thank David Chamberlain of Claremont High School, Robert DeGroff of Colton High School, and other coaches of the Citrus Belt Speech Region for providing helpful reviews of the text.

John Meany wishes to thank Robert Branham, the former director of debate at Bates College, an inspirational teacher of debate who introduced this author to parliamentary debate. Bob was a brilliant debate theorist with a commitment to debate education. John also wishes to thank his son, Jake Meany, for his sacrifices, patience, and support during the production of this book, as well as current and former members of the Claremont Colleges Debate Union, who have shared with him in learning the art and practice of parliamentary debating.

Kate Shuster wishes to thank her grandparents, Jack and Catherine Dulaney and Don and Helen Shuster. They worked tirelessly to give her the foundation of support she required in secondary school and has built on ever since. She would also like to thank Jon Sharp, whose merciless wit and intellect have helped hundreds of high school and college debaters succeed. Finally, Kate would like to thank all of the high school debaters she has had the privilege to coach, including Anne Marie Todd, Justin Wilson, and David Poline (Pace Academy), Alex Berger & Matt Ornstein (Georgetown Day), and Wally Eastwood & Ryan Scoville (Centennial High).

Chapter 1

Introduction to Debate

We all engage in argument every day, on a variety of issues. Sometimes we are the people making the arguments. For example, you may argue with your friends over what movie to see, with your parents about adjusting your curfew or with your employer about getting a raise. At other times, you are part of the *audience* for arguments that try to persuade you to believe a certain thing or to take a particular action. You may not realize it, but you spend the majority of every day surrounded by arguments:

> "I need a hall pass."
>
> "The Red Sox will win the World Series this year."
>
> "We should order a pizza."

All of these are arguments. When you think of the word *argument*, you probably think of its negative use. We often characterize uncivil or otherwise disagreeable confrontations as *arguments*, saying things like: "Don't argue with me," or "I don't want to get into an argument about this." While these phrases use one sense of the word argument, another way to think about an argument is simply as a *claim or statement that attempts to convince an audience about some idea*. We make arguments about the world in order to *persuade* an audience to adopt a specific point of view about something. When you say, "I need a hall pass," you are most likely trying to persuade your teacher to allow you to leave the classroom for some reason. When you say, "We should order a pizza," you may be trying to convince your friends or family to have a specific kind of meal. Arguments can also be about facts or predictions, as in the case of the above claim about the Red Sox. It is not necessarily true that the Red Sox will win the World Series this year. Thus, when you claim that they will, you are making an argument to convince a listener that your prediction will prove to be correct.

We make arguments to persuade other people to take our side on a particular issue. What are some arguments you might make in everyday situations? What kinds of arguments might you make to your friends? How about to your parents or guardians? What kinds of arguments might you make to your teachers?

Just as we make arguments to others, they also make arguments to us. Most of your day, whether you realize it or not, is spent being an audience to the arguments of others. What are some of the arguments you hear from your teachers, siblings, or parents?

You consume arguments, just as you consume products like toothpaste and video games. We are used to thinking of ourselves as consumers of goods and services, but we may not think of ourselves as consumers of information and argument. Yet we are constantly bombarded by arguments in the form of advertisements. All advertisements are arguments because they try, however indirectly, to persuade you to take a course of action—to buy a product.

Arguments are the driving force of everything from science to politics. A scientific hypothesis is a kind of argument that must be proven through testing or other kinds of experimentation and research. Public policies are made and continued on the basis of argument. Public transportation, such as buses and subway systems, didn't just come into being by accident. Public transportation exists because someone (or, more likely, a group of people) decided that it would be a good idea to have a bus system and made persuasive arguments for funding and maintaining mass transit. People buy health insurance because they have been persuaded by arguments that it is a good idea to have health insurance. Elementary schools have recesses or play breaks because educators made arguments that it would be beneficial for elementary school children to have play breaks or recesses.

As you can see, argument is serious business. It is your business, because you navigate your life and your social relationships with others by convincing them of your opinions or being convinced by theirs. In democratic societies, argument is the lifeblood of politics. Citizens or their elected representatives argue all the time about how to best make policy that represents the interests of the people. These conditions mean that those who do not know how to make effective arguments are often left behind or left out, because they cannot advocate on behalf of their interests or the interests of their family, co-workers, or other groups to which they might belong. If you learn how to argue effectively and persuasively, you will be able to overcome these obstacles and become a participating citizen in the global culture of argument.

The purpose of a course in debate is to become better at the business of argument. Everyone knows how to argue, but few people know how to argue well. As you study the practice of debate, you will become more competent at making arguments as well as listening critically to the arguments of others. Both skills are necessary for success in debate and life. In this chapter, you will learn some basic debate skills and practice developing those skills using several different exercises.

What Makes a Debate?

Debating is, of course, as old as language itself and has taken many forms throughout human history. In ancient Rome, debate in the Senate was critical to the conduct of civil society and the justice system. In Greece, advocates for policy changes would routinely make their cases before citizen juries composed of hundreds of Athenians. In India, debate was used to settle religious controversies and was a very popular form of entertainment. Indian kings sponsored great debating contests, offering prizes for the winners. China has its own ancient and distinguished tradition of debate. Beginning in the 2nd Century C.E., Taoist and Confucian scholars engaged in a practice known as "pure talk" where they debated spiritual and philosophical issues before audiences in contests that might last for a day and a night.

In medieval Europe, debate was critical to the teaching in the universities that arose around the 12th century. At Oxford, in England, instruction in debate and argumentation occupied whole years of the education of the average student. Around this time, debate became increasingly popular in Christian monasteries, where monks would engage in formal public debates that would often last for days. Thomas Aquinas was said to be one of the most celebrated debaters in all of Europe, able to simultaneously debate ten opponents on ten different topics.

Modern parliamentary debating has its roots in all of these types of debating as well as the formal parliamentary debates that got their start in the House of Commons in the 14th century British Parliament. As Parliament gained more influence in the course of British governance, so too did the debates that occurred among its members. This process of government by debate made its way to England's American colonies. Debate flourished within these colonies, and after America's Revolutionary War, debate became one of the primary forces driving government and the course of social policy.

One of the most widely debated topics in the history of the United States of America was slavery. The famous debates between Abraham Lincoln and Stephen Douglas on the issue of slavery in new territories made Lincoln famous throughout the nation. Later, Frederick Douglass became one of the most powerful debaters in the history of the United States, and was renowned for his eloquence in advocating the abolition of slavery.

Organized and informal debate occurs all over the world and plays an important role in just about every human society. Students study and engage in debate in Sierra Leone, Indonesia, Mongolia, Japan, Romania, Chile, Korea, Mexico, Ireland, and Ukraine, just to name a few countries. By studying debate, you are joining a global community engaged in one of humanity's oldest pursuits.

While millions of people all over the world enjoy a good debate, they do not all debate in the same way, in the same format, or even in the same language. In this book, we teach many different ways of debating and encourage you to come up with your own. Most formal debates have two characteristics in common:

• Participating debaters try to persuade a third-party audience or judge.

• Debates are usually on a fixed topic or proposition.

When we argue with our friends or parents, we are usually trying to convince them of our viewpoint, and vice versa. We say that someone wins an argument when he or she convinces the other side to agree with a particular viewpoint. Debate does not work this way. One important way that debate is different from simple argument is that in a debate, you are not trying to convince your opponent or opponents that you are right. Rather, you are trying to convince some third party that is watching the debate. This third party is usually an audience, but it might also be a judge or a panel of judges who have been specially assigned the job of deciding the winner of a debating contest.

Both public and competitive debates are normally on a fixed topic or motion. The topic might be broad and undefined, such as "school safety" or "affirmative action." The topic might also suggest a direction for the debate, such as

"School safety should be improved," or "Affirmative action should be abolished." The function of a topic for debate is to constrain the issues that will be debated—generally, judges and audiences expect that debaters will stick to the assigned topic. Debate topics usually deal with controversial issues. These can be international issues such as global warming or local issues such as scheduling or dress codes at your school. One of the great things about debate is that once you learn how to debate, you can debate about any given topic.

In this chapter, you will learn about the components of an argument. Once you have learned these components, you should practice making arguments to your fellow students. Of course, debate is not just about making arguments—as a debater, you must also learn how to *refute*, or answer, arguments. The last section of this chapter teaches you basic techniques in argument refutation. At the conclusion of this chapter, you should be able to engage in debating with your friends and classmates.

What Makes an Argument

Arguments are the most basic building blocks of debate. To debate, you will need a sophisticated understanding of how arguments work. Arguments are like automobiles: if you understand how they work, you are likely to get more service out of them, understand what went wrong when they break down, and fix the problem before your next outing.

Debates are made up of arguments, but argument is distinct from debate. An argument is an attempt to influence someone else in some direction. In debates competitors present many arguments, all of which can serve different functions in a debate. Of course, in debate as in life, not all arguments are created equally. Some arguments are more successful than others. The question for debaters is how to make successful arguments and how to make these successful arguments work in debates.

Often, arguments are not successful because they are incomplete. It is important to remember that an argument is different from a simple *assertion*. An assertion is a claim that something is so:

> "The death penalty is justified."
>
> "Hyacinths are better than roses."
>
> "*The Simpsons* is the best television show."

"The USA should eliminate its nuclear arsenal."

"Economic growth is more important than environmental protection."

Most topics for debate are assertions. They, like the preceding statements, are simple claims about the world. This means that topics are not arguments in and of themselves. When debaters take up a topic, their job is to flesh out the arguments for and against a particular topic. Assertions are only the starting point for argumentation and debate.

In everyday situations, many people mistake simple assertions for their more sophisticated cousin, argument. This error leads to disputes like those had by children: "Is too." "Is not." "Is too." "Is not..." This method of argument is similar to the method of conflict resolution used by warring mountain goats, where both parties simply lower their heads and butt horns until one of them falls off the cliff and dies.

An argument is more than an assertion. An assertion says that something is so, but an argument attempts to prove *why* that thing is so. There are three basic parts to any argument, easily remembered as **A-R-E**:

Assertion: A claim about the world.

Reasoning: The reasons why that claim is true.

Evidence: Proof, usually in the form of data or examples.

Simply speaking, all arguments contain an *assertion*, which is simply a statement that something is so. Arguments also include *reasoning*—the reasons why the assertion is true. Reasoning is the "because" part of an argument. Finally, arguments have *evidence*—the proof for the validity of the reasoning. A complete argument must contain all three components. A novice debater might simply offer claims to prove her point:

"The death penalty is justified."

A more sophisticated debater knows that her argument will be more persuasive with reasoning:

"The death penalty is justified because it deters crime."

Better yet is the technique of the advanced debater, who offers proof for her argument:

"The death penalty is justified because it deters crime. Studies conducted across the nation strongly point to this deterrent effect."

For successful debating, it is critical that you understand and deal with all of the components of your arguments and the arguments made by your opponents. Many people argue by simply answering assertions with other assertions. This is not a sophisticated or persuasive way to argue. Good debaters know that an assertion should be refuted by answering the supporting *reasoning* and *evidence*.

Suggested Exercises

1. Examine the editorial page of your local newspaper. Take each editorial and figure out what arguments are being made by the author. What is the author's major argument? What other arguments does she make? What reasoning does she use for these arguments? What kind of evidence does she offer as support?

2. Practice providing reasoning for your arguments with the "because" exercise. There are several assertions listed below. For each assertion, generate three reasons why each assertion might be true, like this: "School uniforms should be required in schools *because* they cost less money than other clothes, and *because* they stop competition over how nice your clothes are, and *because* they would stop students from wearing gang colors." After you have finished with the following assertions, generate your own.

- School should be year-round.
- Violent television should be banned.
- The voting age should be lowered to 16.
- Police are necessary for safety.
- People should eat meat.
- Books are better than video games.
- Math is more important than English.
- There should not be curfews for high-school students.

Refuting Arguments

When you advance an argument, you are making an assertion, and, it is to be hoped, you are supporting it with reasoning and evidence. Remember: arguments are not just claims. Arguments explain *why* something is so. Making an argument is just the beginning of a debate. To engage in a debate, you will have to answer the arguments of others, and then in turn answer their answers to your answers, and so on. Debates are a complicated business. Debates can't be composed only of initial arguments, because then they wouldn't be debates, but rather exchanges of unrelated ideas, like the following exchange:

> Speaker 1: Bananas are better than apples because they contain more potassium.

> Speaker 2: Circles are better than squares because their shape is more pleasing to the eye.

What this "discussion" is missing is what in debate we call *clash*. Both speakers are advancing arguments, but their statements are unrelated to each other. Clash is one of the fundamental principles of good debate. Unless arguments clash, there is no way to compare and judge them. Debate deals with arguments that oppose each other directly.

To dispute an argument effectively, you must master the skill of *refutation*. Arguments of refutation serve as answers to arguments already in play. Refutation is necessary in debates because it promotes direct clash between arguments.

Arguments have answers just like questions. There are many ways to answer an argument that has been advanced. Of course, some methods are better than others. The first, and unfortunately most common, way of refuting an argument is simply to provide a counter-assertion:

> Speaker 1: Bananas are better than oranges because they contain more potassium.

> Speaker 2: Speaker 1 says that bananas are better than oranges, but I disagree. Oranges are better than bananas.

Speaker 2 has simply provided an assertion to counter the assertion of the first speaker. Who wins this debate? Clearly, Speaker 1 has the edge, since she is the only debater to have actually provided reasoning for her assertion ("because they contain more potassium"). Good reasoning always trumps no reasoning at all.

A more advanced method of refutation is to provide reasoning for your counter-assertion:

> Speaker 1: Bananas are better than oranges because they contain more potassium.
>
> Speaker 2: Speaker 1 says that bananas are better than oranges, but I disagree. Oranges are better than bananas because they contain more vitamin C.

What makes this rejoinder better than Speaker 2's previous attempt? Here, she is providing reasoning for her assertion: "because they contain more vitamin C." Imagine that you are asked to judge this debate. How will you decide who wins? You find that Speaker 1 has proven conclusively that bananas contain more potassium than oranges. You also find that Speaker 2 has proven that oranges contain more vitamin C than bananas. Neither debater really has the edge here, do they? Notice that while there is direct clash between the assertion and the counter-assertion, there is no direct clash between the reasons for each. Speaker 2 has not yet succeeded in completely refuting her opponent's argument.

Complete refutation is important to win decisively when arguments clash against each other in debate. In order to refute an argument, you must include what we call a "therefore" component. The "therefore" component of an argument of refutation is where you explain *why* your argument trumps the argument of your opponent. Observe:

> Speaker 1: Bananas are better than oranges because they contain more potassium.
>
> Speaker 2: Speaker 1 says that bananas are better than oranges, but I disagree. Oranges are better than bananas because they contain more vitamin C. You should prefer oranges because while many foods in an ordinary diet contain potassium, few contain an appreciable amount of vitamin C. Therefore, oranges are better than bananas.

Speaker 2 wins. She has completed the process of refutation by including a "therefore" component in her rejoinder. Notice how this last part of her argument works. She compares her reasoning to Speaker 1's reasoning, showing why her argument is better than that of her opponent. Almost all refutation can follow the basic four-step method demonstrated above. As you practice your refutation skills, consider starting with this model:

Step 1: "They say...."   It is important to reference the argument you are about to refute so that your audience and judges can easily follow your line of thought. Unlike the bananas/oranges example above, debates contain many different arguments. Unless you directly reference which of these arguments you are dealing with, you risk confusion on the part of your audience and judge, and confusion is seldom a good technique for winning debates. Good note-taking skills will help you track individual arguments and the progression of their refutation. We'll discuss how to take notes in the specialized form demanded by debates in the "Skills" chapter.

One important thing to remember here is that when you refer to your opponent's argument, you should do so in shorthand. In formal debates, speeches are given in limited time. If you were to repeat all of your opponent's arguments, you wouldn't have any time to advance arguments of your own. So try and rephrase the argument you're about to refute in just three to seven words to maximize your speech time: "They say that reducing welfare benefits helps the economy, but...;" or "They say Batman is better than Superman, but....;" "On their global warming argument...."

Step 2: "But I disagree...."   In this part of your refutation, you state the basic claim of your counter-argument. This can be, in the case of the banana/orange controversy, simply the opposite of your opponent's claim. It can also be an attack on the reasoning or evidence offered for your opponent's claim. The important thing is to state clearly and concisely the counter-argument you want the judge to endorse. You can elaborate on it later. For now, it is important to phrase your argument as concisely as possible. This tactic helps your judge, audience, and opponents to remember it and get it in their notes.

Step 3: "Because ...."   Having advanced your counter-argument, you need to proceed to offer a reason. Arguments of refutation need to be complete, just like the arguments they answer. Your reason can be independent support for your counter-assertion, as in the case above. It can also be a reasoned criticism of the opposition's argument.

Step 4: "Therefore...."   Finally, you need to draw a conclusion that compares your refutation to your opponent's argument and shows why yours effectively defeats theirs. This conclusion is usually done by means of comparison, either of reasoning or evidence or both. You need to develop a variety of strategies for argument comparison and evaluation. This is a critical skill for success in competitive debate. What you need to accomplish here is to show that your argument is better than their argument because....

- **It's better reasoned**. Perhaps their argument makes some kind of error in logic or reasoning.

- **It's better evidenced**. Maybe your argument makes use of more or better evidence. Perhaps your sources are better qualified than theirs, or your evidence is more recent than theirs. Maybe your examples take more people into account than their examples.

- **It's empirical**. When we say that an argument is *empirically proven*, we mean that it is demonstrated by past examples. Perhaps your argument relies on empirical proof, while theirs relies on conjecture or speculation.

- **It takes theirs into account**. Sometimes your argument may take theirs into account and go a step further: "Even if they're right about the recreational benefits of crossbows, they're still too dangerous for elementary school physical education classes."

- **It has a greater expressed significance**. You can state that your argument has more significance than their argument because (for example) it matters more to any given individual or applies to a larger number of individuals.

- **It's consistent with experience**. Perhaps your argument is consistent with experience over time, in a different place, or in different circumstances. This technique is particularly effective with audiences: "Hey, this is something we can all relate to, right?"

These are only some examples of techniques you can use for argument comparison. In this book and through your debate education, you will find others.

Suggested Exercises

1. Play a game of "I disagree." Generate a series of claims of various types. Then refute each claim using the four-step method ("They say...", "but I disagree...", "because...", "therefore..."). Try this exercise with a partner. Have one person generate claims, while the other person refutes them. After ten repetitions, switch roles.

2. Analyze the following excerpted arguments using the tools you have acquired.

- What is the main assertion each author is advancing? What reasons do they offer to support their claims? What evidence do they advance to back up these warrants?

- Construct two different refutations each argument. Choose either the author's main assertion or some other part of the argument.

a) The United States of America should end its trade embargo against Cuba. The embargo violates the International Covenant and, arguably, the 1994 General Agreement on Tariffs and Trade (GATT). The embargo is a policy of starvation that offends the moral sensibility of the world. In other situations, the USA claims to be working against starvation and international isolation. Why, then, does it persist in its trade embargo toward the people of Cuba? Alfredo Duran, of the Cuban Committee for Democracy, has said that "the embargo hasn't worked and everyone knows it. The starvation in Cuba is what the embargo has created."

b) Education is vital for any civilized society. If citizens are not adequately and properly educated, they cannot be expected to participate meaningfully in important decisions that affect their lives. Education also provides long-term economic benefits, both to individuals and to their society at large. This does not mean that education should be mandatory. In democratic societies, citizens should not be forced to attend school if they choose not to do so. We do not require our citizens to quit smoking, even though that behavior would be beneficial. Likewise, we do not require our citizens to work at a job, although they clearly suffer if they do not do so. Education should be treated in the same way. If we are truly a society committed to ensuring choice for our citizens, we should end mandatory school attendance.

3. Using the four-step refutation model, refute each of the following simple claims:

- School should be year-round.
- Sunbathing causes cancer.
- Drug testing violates individual privacy.
- Environmental protection is more important than economic growth.
- Televised violence causes social violence.
- Military spending is bad for society.
- You don't need a weatherman to know which way the wind blows.
- The debt of the third world should be forgiven.

- Secondary schools should require their students to wear uniforms.
- Video games are better than books.

Performance and Speaking Fundamentals

Parliamentary debaters must be good public speakers. It is not enough merely to have the right argument at the right time. To be persuasive, you must present your arguments with authority and credibility. You must win over the good will of your audience. How can you accomplish this? Public speaking, like argumentation, is more of an art than a science. Good public speakers have many practices and habits in common; however, they also embrace their own unique and individual styles. Think of the good public speakers you may have seen or heard. Barbara Jordan and Winston Churchill were both powerful, inspirational speakers. They had different ideas and different persuasive techniques. They sounded and gestured differently. Their speeches were organized in different ways to different effects. Yet both were able to motivate groups of people to act on their ideas.

Public speaking is an exercise in both content and performance. You may have the best arguments, the best examples, and the best evidence to substantiate your side in a debate, but if your performance is poor, you may still fail to persuade an audience. Likewise, you may be a fantastic speaker, but if you do not know what you are talking about, you will fail to persuade an audience. Just as you should research and think critically about your arguments, so you should practice and think critically about your performance.

Initially, you should endeavor to speak clearly and at an appropriate volume. Speakers who mumble or otherwise mutter incomprehensibly may puzzle or annoy an audience, but will rarely be able to persuade them. Just as you should not mumble under your breath while speaking, so too should you not YELL AT THE JUDGE AT THE TOP OF YOUR LUNGS. Audiences do not like to be yelled at by speakers. Try to use an appropriate volume when speaking. Articulation is also important. If you want to be understood, try not to run your words together or otherwise fail to pronounce clearly. Try recording yourself while delivering a speech and then listening to or watching the tape. This will easily help you diagnose and correct any speaking problems you might have.

A good speaking performance requires good *delivery*. You will have to use vocal variety, appropriate gestures, and good word economy to deliver your speeches effectively. By "vocal variety" we mean that you should vary the tone, pitch, rate, and volume of your speech to cultivate and maintain the audience's interest. Few things are more likely to induce instant sleepiness than a speaker who delivers her presentation in a monotone.

You will also need to use appropriate nonverbal communication. We do not communicate only with our voices. Our bodies are also vital tools for communication. Some debaters are notorious for using overly expressive gestures—they wave their hands about in a manner more appropriate for guiding airplanes into their gates. If your hands seem to be out of your control or serve to fan or otherwise air-condition the room, you should rethink your use of gestures. We recommend that you gesture sparingly, using your hands to emphasize important points or transitions, and not to keep time during your speech. Be conscious of how you use your hands—consider using a three-part gesturing method: first, get ready to gesture, then gesture, and then put your gesture away in a graceful manner. Do not hold a pen or other object in your hand while you speak. It appears to be a security blanket and communicates to the judge that you are insecure about speaking. Such props are also distracting. Sometimes a debater, holding a ballpoint pen during her speech, will unconsciously and repeatedly click the point in and out while she speaks.

Do not pace, shuffle, dance, or otherwise move your feet in a distracting manner. Try to plant yourself and remain planted throughout your speech (although subtle, slight, natural movement is of course acceptable). Debates are enough like tennis matches without the audience having to follow you with their eyes constantly. Some debaters try to implement a method of using steps to signal transitions. Do not do this. It is distracting and appears amateurish. The judge will be left wondering why you cannot restrict your waltzing to the dance floor. Our best advice for nonverbal communication is to appear confident at all times. Do not cross your arms or appear to hug yourself. Remember: you are good enough and smart enough.

Make good eye contact. If you are nervous about your speech or about public speaking in general, you are not alone. Most people rate public speaking among their top fears. Do not stare at your notes, the ceiling, or just over the judge's shoulder while you speak. You should make eye contact with the judge or audience during your speech. If you have trouble doing this, you should consider practicing in front of a mirror. If you can make eye contact with yourself, you can make eye contact with other people. A bit of advice: if you are speaking in front of an audience, particularly a large one, you should try to make eye contact with individuals at different points in the crowd; you should not simply scan the crowd with your eyes.

While speaking, debaters often look at their opponents. This is a terrible idea and is generally considered to be an amateurish mistake. You are not trying to convince the other team of your side of the issue. Even if you are the most gifted debater on the planet, they are unlikely to agree with you—it is, after all, their job to oppose you. You are trying to convince the judge or audience. Therefore, you should look at the judge or audience. Looking at the other team while you are speaking can also put you at a major disadvantage, because you seem to invite interruption or points of information (a feature of parliamentary debating discussed in later chapters). If you appear to be insulting or otherwise criticizing the other team in a direct manner, they will pop up repeatedly for points of information. Just as you should not look at the other team while speaking, so you should not address the other team directly by prefacing your arguments with "you..."

> "You just don't say anything about our case."

> "We're beating you on this argument."

> "You bring shame on this House."

> "You are ridiculous, wrong, and absurd. You are abusive. You
> don't have a prayer of winning this debate."

If you engage in this kind of boorish chest-pounding, you will most likely get what you deserve. You should not only avoid addressing the other team as "you," but you should also *avoid hostility at all costs*. Of course, good-natured humor is a vital part of parliamentary debate. *Debate is adversarial, but debaters should not be adversarial with each other.*

It is particularly important that you are never adversarial or hostile toward your own partner. EVER. Even if you are convinced that your partner is the worst debater in the history of the activity, even if you are prone to compare yourself to Job for being saddled with such a terrible partner, you should NEVER, EVER talk badly about or behave in a disrespectful manner towards your partner. Your relationship with your debate partner is professional. You must conduct it in such a manner. Never discuss conflicts with your partner with anyone except your partner or your coach, and always in private. Meanness to your partner will make you look like the worst sort of jerk, damage your competitive prospects, and undoubtedly hurt your partner's feelings.

Sometimes debaters confuse hostile behaviors and confident behaviors. The two could not be more different. Hostile debaters are mean, rude, irritable, and often so insecure that they must make others feel badly in order to feel good about themselves or about their own performances. Confident debaters are forthright when explaining ideas. They speak in a convincing way and command attention without having to demand attention with cruelty. You should always appear confident, calm, and collected in debates, even if you are losing. Be careful that you do not accidentally invite opposition to your arguments by engaging in nervous behaviors like lowering your voice or trailing off at the end of your sentences.

Good debaters speak in a civil and confident manner. They also make efficient and effective word choices. There are two critical considerations for debaters in this area: word economy and word choice.

Word economy   In a formal debate, you must perform under time constraints. Speech time is always limited by the rules set by your particular format, so you need to choose your words carefully. Debaters who exhibit good *word economy* use the minimum number of words necessary to present their arguments. Economical word choice allows them to present the maximum number of independent arguments and examples possible in their limited speech time. If you use a lot of filler words, you will not be using your speech time to its maximum advantage.

Think about how you speak in everyday conversation. You will find that you use lots of filler words that do not contribute to your statements. In America, people often use "like" ("And then I was like, dude, we're *totally* disproving the motion," or "Like, are you going to eat that burrito?") or "you know" ("So, you know, I was wondering if you, you know, wanted to get some coffee or something?" or "This movie is completely, you know, terrible."). Interjections, such as "um" and "er," are also used.

Debaters use these filler words plus all kinds of others, some of them more debate-specific. They punctuate their remarks with phrases such as:

- "remember" (Used once, it's completely suitable, even desirable. Used repeatedly, it's highly annoying, massively redundant, and a terrific waste of time: it takes a whole second to say, and if you say it 15 times in a speech, you are in effect sacrificing 15 seconds of your speech time.)
- "in fact" (This phrase places in doubt the speaker's overall grasp of the facts by the 30th time she has used it. She does, perhaps, protest too much.)

You most likely use all these verbal fillers and many more. What's worse, you may not even realize that you, like just about everyone who has ever debated, have bad word economy habits. Try to diagnose and repair these bad habits. We suggest that you tape yourself debating—videotape, if possible, and then pay close attention to how you phrase your arguments. Once you diagnose a word economy problem, it is relatively easy to solve. If you remain conscious of the word(s) you are trying to fix, you will try to avoid them normally. Practice speaking more slowly and deliberately, and focus on the individual words as they come out of your mouth. This practice will allow you to become more efficient in the long run.

Word choice   Just as you should use an economy of words, so too should you respect the admonition offered in *Indiana Jones and the Last Crusade* and "choose wisely." In the section on impact assessment, we will explore more how important it is to use vivid language to persuade judges and audiences. In debate, we talk a lot about the concept of "power wording." The words you use will shape the reality that the judge perceives. Do you describe a decline in the stock market as a "correction" or a "crash"? Do you describe discrimination by the state as "inequality" or "slow-motion genocide"? Is a military invasion a "police action" or a "war"? Consider that your words matter, and directly affect how your arguments will be perceived. Strong wording will always make your arguments seem more credible. There is one caveat to this rule, though: If you routinely use "power wording" to frame arguments that are obviously weak, you will lose credibility. For further reference on this subject, see: "The Boy Who Cried Wolf."

There are many other word choice decisions you can make in debates to improve your effectiveness as a speaker. For example, consider using selective repetition to emphasize your most critical arguments. Or, quote your opponents when appropriate. Often you can take their dubious statements and turn them to your advantage.

Suggested Exercises

1. Give an impromptu speech. Ask another person to pick a topic for you or pick a topic out of the list at the back of this book. Take five minutes to prepare a two-minute speech on the topic. Structure your speech in a simple manner: have an introduction, three major points, and a conclusion. Repeat this exercise often, gradually reducing your preparation time.

2. Practice developing word economy. Write a one-page argument for a topic of your choice. Make sure that you include all steps of the A-R-E format. Give three reasons to prove the topic. Then, take out 1/4th of the words in the paper, making sure that you keep the best parts of your argument intact. After you have rewritten the argument, do it again. This time, take out half of the words in your argument, still keeping the basics of your position. Why did you take out the words you took out? Why did you choose to leave certain words in? How did you know which words were the most important and which could be removed?

3. Get some feedback. Give a short speech on a topic of your choice in front of your group or class. Have everyone in the class fill out evaluation forms that rate your eye contact, volume, and gestures. The forms should say two things you did well and two things you could improve upon. Study the forms for help in improving your speaking.

4. Name two speakers (teachers, relatives, community figures, politicians, etc.) that you have seen on television or in person who impressed you with their abilities. Why did their speaking impress you? Name two speakers who did not impress you. Why did you think they could use improvement? What habits did they need to develop or change?

On That Point!

Persuasive Speaking

Most public speaking experiences are not in the form of debates. In fact, most of the times you will have to speak in public, you will be delivering brief speeches on issues of importance to you. Most of these speeches will be *persuasive* speeches where you try to persuade someone to believe something or to do something. When you interview for a job, you will be engaging in persuasive speaking. When you negotiate the purchase price of a car or a home, you will be engaging in persuasive speaking. You may at some point have to argue a consumer complaint about a defective product or poor service—this will require persuasive speaking. If there are social or political causes you feel strongly about, you will require persuasive speaking skills to get your point across and make yourself heard.

The best way to persuade someone of something is to make an informed argument confidently. However, this is not as easy as it may seem. What seems confident or credible to some people may not seem very appealing to a different audience. You probably speak differently to different audiences already. How do you speak to your friends? How is this different from the ways you speak to the administrators of your school? If you speak differently to different audiences, you are already engaging in one of the most fundamental principles of persuasive speaking, which is *audience adaptation*. Audience adaptation simply means adapting your speech content and style to the way that best persuades the audience you are addressing.

Generally, you should learn to observe some basic guidelines about public speaking. Many of these are described in the "Performance" section of Chapter 1. For example, you should always:

- Have good non-verbal communication
- Make active eye contact
- Speak at an appropriate rate and volume
- Avoid vocalized pauses

On That Point!

There are other aspects of persuasive speaking that are important. One critical issue is organization. You should always try to be organized when you speak, even if you have just been given the topic or have been called upon to offer an opinion. This will require practice. Very few people are born with the natural ability to organize a speech.

Most good speeches, whether they are 30 seconds or 30 minutes long, follow a basic structure. They have an introduction, a main body, and a conclusion. This structure may be very much like the models for basic essay writing you have learned in your other classes. Try to have an attention-grabbing introduction. This should be the part of your speech that interests the audience in what is to follow. If your introduction is poor or nonexistent, you risk having the audience simply tune out or otherwise not listen to the important content that follows.

The body of your speech should be structured with several major points. We recommend that you try to have three major points in persuasive speeches that you deliver in class, but this number is certainly not set in stone. Your speech as a whole should make an argument. You should be able to identify the *purpose* of your speech before you deliver it. The purpose of your speech is a short statement of about one sentence that explains why you are giving the speech and what you hope to accomplish: "The purpose of my speech is to persuade my class that George Lucas makes better movies than Steven Spielberg;" "The purpose of my speech is to persuade my audience to protect themselves against skin cancer."

Your speech makes an argument to fulfill its purpose. In order to prove this larger argument, you should make a few smaller, more specific arguments. Each of your major points, therefore, should be a self-contained argument. For example, if the purpose of your speech is to persuade your audience that school should be year-round, you might make the following three basic points:

1. Year-round school would allow for more student choice in electives and other classes.
2. Year-round school would improve test scores.
3. Year-round school would allow schools to serve more pupils.

These basic points lack reasoning and evidence. You will have to develop these other components so that you can create a full outline for your speech. What

On That Point!

you see happening here is that a basic persuasive speech nests arguments within arguments to create a solid case for a larger argument.

One critical organizational issue remains. You should try to plan your transitions between points. If you change topics too quickly, you may confuse or annoy your audience. Have transitions, even if they must be brief, e.g.., "If you learn to swim, not only could you save your own life, but you could also save the lives of others." Remember that listening to a speech is not like reading a book. When you read a book, if you lose concentration while reading sentence you can always go back and re-read. When you are listening to a speech, if you stop paying attention for a sentence, you cannot go back and re-hear. It is therefore important for you, as a speaker, to help your audience follow what you are saying by using good verbal cues to mark your transitions.

Finally, you will need a conclusion. The simplest kind of conclusion briefly summarizes the content of the speech and restates the argument of the speech, e.g., "So, in conclusion, everyone should learn to swim because it could save their lives, it could save the lives of others, and it's just good exercise." This kind of conclusion, while very basic, is certainly better than nothing. You might also conclude a speech by urging the audience to take action. You might finish with a moral lesson or a warning. When in doubt, however, you can just summarize your speech. Try to avoid trailing off or otherwise showing a lack of confidence.

Exercise

Prepare a persuasive speech that will last for four minutes. The purpose of your speech should be "To persuade the audience that there are three major ways my school should be changed." Create an outline for your speech, planning for an introduction, conclusion, and three major points. Fill out your major points by elaborating on the reasons for your suggested reforms. Be as specific as you can and provide as much evidence and as many examples as you can. Practice your speech at home so that you know it meets the time requirements. Then perform it in front of your class using minimal notes. Do not read your speech from a script. You do not, however, have to memorize it. Practice will help you strike the appropriate balance between these two extremes.

On That Point!

We have included two articles on the subject of school reform from two different sources. These articles should serve as resources, and give you some ideas about what other students have suggested as reforms in their school.

After you and your classmates have given your speeches, discuss the results. What was most difficult about the exercise? What was easiest about the persuasive speech assignment? What were some characteristics of particularly good speeches?

This exercise can be productively repeated using all kinds of topics.

Middle School Students Suggest School Improvements

What kinds of classes, activities, resources, or facilities (etc.) would middle school students like their community to provide for them in school or after school? Learn what some middle school students had to say!

What kinds of classes, activities, resources, or facilities would middle school students like their community to provide for them in school or after school?

"My students had many interesting ideas," says teacher Linda Haskell, who posed that question to her students at Williams Junior High School in Oakland, Maine. The thoughtful responses she got from her students ran the gamut.

"Many thought the school athletic fields needed improvement or the sports teams needed new equipment and uniforms," Haskell told Education World. "Others suggested buying tour buses for field trips. Still others suggested larger lockers, wider hallways, homework on alternate nights, or adding a rock-climbing wall or a pool to the school. One student wanted a jazz band, another a magic class, and another wanted to chew gum during the day. A few asked for a longer lunch period or having fast-food such as McDonalds. One student asked to repaint the interior with brighter colors."

But the most common add-on requested by students in Haskell's classes—and in many other schools where teachers posed this question for Education World—was an after-school program.

If you think about it, the desire for after-school programs is not at all surprising. After all, middle school students *love* to socialize! But their thoughtful responses indicate that such programs would meet needs beyond socialization.

"School is a wonderful place for kids to learn, play, have fun, and stay out of trouble," wrote Lisa B., one of Haskell's students. "What about after school, though? How can kids stay out of trouble and have fun? That is why an after-school activity program should be put into action. An after-school program could allow kids of all ages to make new friends, stay away from drugs and television, and experience new things."

Amanda R., an eighth grader in Kathy Foster's class at St. John Vianney School in Orlando, Florida, agrees that an after-school program might solve many problems for young teens. "Many students come home from school to an empty household, with no one to share their thoughts of the day," wrote Amanda. "Others come home to busy parents who take no interest in them. Still others wander the streets until dinnertime. Why should this be? An ideal solution to these problems would be a teen community center, a place where teenagers could find a safe haven among peers, finish homework, provide company, and generally have fun."

"I think there should be an after-school club," added Amanda's classmate, Kenny S. "It would be nice to have an activity area where the junior high students could play ping pong, foosball, or just relax amongst themselves. This would not have to be an everyday kind of club, but even once a week would be nice—like every Wednesday."

"Is your child sick of coming home after school to do nothing? Well...I have a solution!" wrote Daniel S. in his essay. A student in Donna Thomas's class at Heritage Prep Middle School in Orlando, Daniel added that his community could create "a play place, or as the older kids would say...a place to hang out. This place will have a pool table, Fooseball, a pool to swim in, football, and a T.V. with a PlayStation."

Homework is on Kids' Minds!

Homework—the amount of it, the organization of it, and the need to support it—is another topic occupying the minds of many middle schoolers. Students had no shortage of suggestions for ways schools might help them deal with "the homework problem."

"Homework! Homework! Almost every day!" said Jerome S., one of Donna Thomas's students. "Kids get tired of it sometimes!...It would be nice to have an after-school homework program so the kids who want to do their homework can do it before they get home."

"A homework club is needed to help students with their homework," agrees Katrina M., a student in Beverly Maddox's class at Henderson Health

Sciences Magnet Middle School in Little Rock, Arkansas. "We could meet two days per week. High school students or parents from PTA could come and help students with their homework....The homework center would be most helpful to students that have low grades in their classes. It would be helpful to the parents who have to work late."

"Another important suggestion would be to separate subjects' homework so the homework isn't all in one night," wrote Maria L., a student at St. John Vianney. "For example, Monday would be English homework night, Tuesday would be Math, etc. This would be better because we wouldn't have a pile of homework on one night and our bookbags wouldn't be so heavy on our backs. Each subject would have a night."

Having less homework, or having a chance to complete it before going home, might help improve life at home too. Kristen T., a student at Heritage Prep, addressed her essay to parents: "This year we are also going to give your child less homework, because we know how hard it is when you get home and your child is packed with homework, and you are already stressed out since you've already had a hard day at work. We want you to go home...maybe rest, or plan something with the family."

Order in the Court!

Rita P., another student at St. John Vianney, wrote about an idea she'd like to see implemented-a Student Court!

"The Student Court is a court made up of students, for the students," she explains in her essay. "The Student Court makes up rules and consequences for breaking those rules, for all the students, so the students can live safely at school."

"If someone has broken one of the rules," Rita continues, "they must attend a Student Court session to learn their consequence for breaking the rule. The student is then given a pink sheet with their consequence to give to the teacher who is serving their consequence. (An example of this might be when a detention is the consequence, the student must give their pink sheet to the teacher who is serving the detention.) I think this is a great idea for a school because the students are allowed to make the rules and get suggestions for rules from the rest of the Student Body, the teachers, and the principal."

Ideas Worth Follow-Up!

"My kids worked on the assignment, enjoyed it, and we'll be following up with more analysis of the school and its needs," reports teacher Beverly Maddox. Among the other ideas her students had were these:

"I think we should have more activities. Students misbehave because they know they don't have any privileges to lose," wrote Anastashia R. "If we had pep rallies, dances, or school spirit days, students would behave so they can participate in those activities instead of staying in class and doing work."

Randy H. thinks a community newsletter would be a great idea. "A community newsletter would let the community and parents know about what goes on in school. This type of newsletter gives parents and other potential sponsors details about what goes on in Henderson Middle School. The community might get involved with what we write about and might get involved with the PTA too."

Joanna H. thinks that changing the school day to a block schedule format would be a good thing because she wouldn't have to remember homework assignments for seven classes! "Having three classes one day and four on another day means we wouldn't have to worry about seven classes every day!," she wrote. "Teachers say they never have enough time to work 'hands on' with students. The block schedule would allow teachers to spend more time with

their students. If students need extra or special attention, they would have the extra time."

Ideas by the Dozens!

Ideas came in by the dozens from teachers who used the Lesson Plan offered by Education World. Among the other students we heard from were those in Tracy Miller's classes at the middle school of the American School Foundation in Mexico City, Mexico: "Considering the in-school facilities, the snack bar would be just wonderful if we could have different kinds of foods," wrote student Nelly G. "We already have chips, cookies, and molletes, but we could also add fruit. Fruit plates would be ideal, and also cucumber, carrot, and jicama sticks would make an improvement."

Student Alexis K. had ideas for improving the school's exploratory program and for making recess time more fun. She expressed her ideas in an essay titled "Middle Schoolers M.A.D. (Making A Difference)." Among her thoughts: "There should be a bigger variety of exploratories, like a job exploratory to show kids how different jobs work. Kids should be able to choose exploratories they like to do....During recess, there should be more activities besides sports. Computer labs should be opened, as well as the art room and the music room..."

And the students in Corrie Rosetti's classes at Lincoln Middle School in Clarkston, Washington, had some great ideas too!

"I think school would be a lot better if they had more funds for visual aids and props," wrote Gaylene C., an eighth-grader at Lincoln. "People learn more effectively when they can see what is being discussed....Not everyone can create a picture in their mind by hearing words only....With more money for school, teachers could get more props and visual aids and help students understand."

Leanne K., another of Rosetti's students, wrote an essay that spoke to the crowded conditions at Lincoln Middle. "I think making periods between classes longer would help," she wrote. "It's so hard for some students to get to their crowded, small lockers. Also, it's so stressful to [have to] get to class so fast...I don't think we should be rushed like that."

Reprinted with permission from the St. Louis Post-Dispatch, copyright 1992.

Valley Park Pupils Offer Suggestions

by Virginia Hick, March 23, 1992.

We know what the adults have in mind to improve schools, but what do the pupils say? More than 200 teachers, school administrators, business leaders and representatives of non-profit groups worked on subcommittees for the Metro 2000 proposal for schools of the future for the St. Louis area. A member of one of the subcommittees asked some pupils what kind of school they would make. Seventh- and eighth-graders in Valley Park were asked, "What would you change or add to make school better? Assume that the goal of school is for you to learn the skills you need to be a successful adult and effective citizen." Some of their responses: Have teachers that make learning interesting; challenge pupils to learn as much as they can. Do not make pupils learn the same thing over in several subjects. Have teachers coordinate topics so it takes less time to cover the material. Go to school three hours, then leave school to go to a job that uses what pupils are learning. Make learning relate to the world. Throw out the textbooks. Use more hands-on activities. Let pupils do things. Give pupils time. For instance, pupils wanted more time between classes and an hour for lunch, so they could study or do research in the library. Hold classes everywhere-outside, in theaters, at the science center or the art museum, at jobs-where the topic is real. Make sure rooms are air-conditioned and heated.

Chapter 2

Parliamentary Debating

Introduction

There are as many different ways to debate as there are topics to debate. This text, however, concentrates on one basic style of debating, known as the *parliamentary debate* format. Parliamentary debate is the most popular and fastest growing form of debating in the world. As you learn to debate in the parliamentary format, you will join a global community of thinkers and competitors with whom you may engage in argument.

There are, in fact, many kinds of debate that go under the name "parliamentary debate." In the USA and internationally, the fastest growing style of parliamentary debate is the four-person, or "American," format. The eight-person British format, which is often called "Worlds style" debate, is another popular style of debating. These formats are essentially similar, and you will most likely use both in your debate class or club as you learn to debate. The purpose of this chapter is to introduce you to the basic rules of the four-person format for parliamentary debate. We will explain the rules and conventions of debating in this style, and show the responsibilities of each participant. There is information on debating in the British style in Appendix 2.

One of the best features of parliamentary debate is that there are very few official rules that constrain debate and the creativity of debaters. The format, like most of life's best pursuits, is easy to learn and difficult to master. The rules govern four basic areas:

- Number of teams and debaters
- Order of speeches
- Limits on speaking time

- Decision making procedure

In parliamentary debate, one side makes a case for the proposition, while the other side opposes the proposition team. For this reason, we call one side the **proposition** side and the other side the **opposition** side. The proposition team always opens the debate by delivering the first speech. Remember that the debate is centered on the motion for debate; thus, it makes sense that the proposition team starts the debate by advocating adoption of the motion.

Four-Person Debating

The topic for debate is usually directional—that is, it proposes a change in action or policy. In this respect, debates are different from everyday discussions. You may have a discussion with friends or classmates about topics of controversy, but those topics probably do not suggest a direction for debate. Consider the difference between these two topics:

- Affirmative action.
- The government should promote affirmative action.

The first topic suggests an area for debate but does not suggest a direction for debate. The second topic is more similar to topics you may encounter in competitive or classroom debates, as it clearly points towards a direction for debate.

The standard American parliamentary debate is a contest between two debate teams, one on each side of a debate topic. Each team has two members. The proposition team's job is to support a **motion** for debate (the motion is also known as the **topic, proposition** or **resolution**). The proposition team has the burden to prove that the motion for debate is more probably true than false. In other words, the proposition team must convince the judge that it has successfully supported the motion.

Since the proposition team must defend the motion, if they had to debate the second topic listed above, what kind of arguments would you expect them to make? On the second topic, the proposition team would have to argue that the government should promote affirmative action.

The other team in the debate is known as the **opposition**. The opposition team argues against the proposition's support for the motion. If the proposition team argues that the government should promote affirmative action, the opposition team must then argue against that proposal. Listed below are some sample topics for debate. On each topic, what would you expect the proposition team to argue? What would you expect the opposition team to argue?

- Advertising should be banned in schools.
- School newspapers should be allowed to publish whatever they want.
- Nations should eliminate their nuclear arsenals.
- Television is a bad influence.
- Citizens should be allowed to carry concealed weapons.
- Governments should respect the rights of animals.

To succeed in debate, you will have to get used to thinking about the way that topics divide up arguments between the proposition and opposition teams. As you will learn in the next chapter, the meaning of a topic is often not as obvious as it might seem. However, with these examples you can at least see how the direction of the topic divides responsibilities between the two teams. One thing you might notice immediately is that the proposition team will usually argue that a course of action *should* be done or a value position *should* be endorsed, while the opposition may simply disagree with the "should." The opposition can argue that a course of action should *not* be done or a value position should *not* be endorsed.

The topics for parliamentary debate are flexible and may take many different forms. To get an idea of what kinds of topics are used in parliamentary debate competitions, consult the sample topics listed in Appendix 1 of this book. In the course of a debate competition, or tournament, topics are announced before every round of debate. Once teams have learned the motion for debate, they will have a period of time to prepare for the debate. Usually, teams will have fifteen minutes or more to prepare for the debate. After this "prep time" has ended, the debate begins.

There are six speeches in a four-person parliamentary debate. The first four speeches are known as **constructive** speeches. The constructive speeches are used, as you might imagine, for both teams to construct arguments for their side and to respond to arguments made by the other side. The proposition and opposition constructive speeches establish the core arguments for each team's side of the motion.

After the constructive speeches are over, the rebuttal phase of the debate begins. Every four-person debate has two **rebuttal** speeches. In these speeches, each side summarizes the major arguments for their side and proposes the reasons why their team should win the debate.

Parliamentary debates should have six speeches in this order:

First proposition constructive speech	7 minutes
First opposition constructive speech	7 minutes
Second proposition constructive speech	7 minutes
Second opposition constructive speech	7 minutes
Opposition rebuttal	5 minutes
Proposition rebuttal	5 minutes

The time limits for these speeches are flexible, and may vary from region to region. In college parliamentary debates in the USA, the time limits are a bit different, but we feel that the times listed above are the optimal times for high school parliamentary debates. When you stage public debate events, you may choose to shorten the speech times to keep the audience interested or to provide more time for input or questioning by the audience or the panel of judges.

The proposition team opens and closes the debate. The opening speaker for each side presents two speeches in the debate—the opening constructive speech and the rebuttal speech. The second person on each side delivers one speech—the second constructive speech for her team. There is no preparation time for speakers during the debate. This means that there are no breaks between speeches for debaters to prepare their remarks. When it is her turn to speak, the next speaker should rise and immediately follow the previous speaker.

Suggested Exercise

Practice the order and roles of the speeches. Have a "mini-debate" with shortened speech times. Try 1-minute constructives and 30-second rebuttals on a topic you choose randomly or one that is assigned by your teacher. Then, switch sides and debate that topic again from the other side.

Points of Information

One unique feature of the parliamentary debate format is not accounted for in the above order of speeches. A parliamentary debate is not just a series of speeches in succession. In addition to using their designated speech time, debaters may present **points of information**. When a debater is speaking, she is said to "hold the floor." In governing legislative or parliamentary bodies, there are so many potential speakers that only one person can hold the floor at a time. That person is usually recognized by a Chair, or by the Speaker of the House. In parliamentary debates, when you are speaking you are said to hold the floor. This means that anyone else who tries to speak or present a formal point without being recognized is **out of order**. A point of information is a question or statement offered by a debater who *does not currently hold the floor*, presented to the debater who currently holds the floor. If another debater wishes to present a point of information, she cannot present her point until you recognize her. The way this works in debates is usually something like this:

> You: "....And so, as you can see, it is a good idea to let fast food franchises into our public schools to provide lunches for students."
>
> Your Opponent: [rising] "On that point."

By rising and stating "On that point," your opponent is signaling that she wishes you to yield the floor to her so that she can make her point. You have two options here: you can accept her point or reject her point. If you reject her point, you are refusing to yield the floor and she must sit down. Points of information are easily rejected, like so:

> You: "...And so, as you can see, it is a good idea to let fast food franchises into our public schools to provide lunches for students."
>
> Your Opponent: [rising] "On that point."
>
> You: "No, thank you."

If you accept her point, she may speak for up to 15 seconds and may ask a question or present a statement, like so:

> You: "....And so, as you can see, it is a good idea to let fast food franchises into our public schools to provide lunches for students."
>
> Your Opponent: [rising] "On that point."

You: "I'll take your point."

Your Opponent: "But those fast food lunches will be less nutritious and therefore less healthy for the students who will eat them."

The time used for making and responding to points of information comes out of the total speaking time allotted for the speaker. Points of information are a valuable and critical part of the process of parliamentary debating, and are discussed at length in Chapter 12, Points of Information. They are only allowed during the constructive speeches in the debate, and then only in the middle five minutes of every constructive speech—that is, not in either the first minute or the last minute of those speeches.

The first and last minute of every constructive speech are known as **protected time**. Protected time is time that the speaker has to introduce and conclude her speech without interruption by points of information. Any opponent who attempts to make a point of information during protected time is **out of order**, and should be told so:

You (in the first minute of your speech): " I would like to introduce our case for the proposition by quoting Homer Simpson, who said that..."

Your Opponent: [rising] "Point of information."

You: "I'm sorry, but you are out of order. As I was saying..."

The timekeeper or judge in the debate should signal the ends and beginnings of protected time.

Suggested Exercises

1. In a small group, analyze daily news press clippings or an article from a weekly periodical on a public policy issue or other current event. Everyone in the small group should analyze the story and propose areas for questions. How can the information be explored or challenged? Every participant should explain her criticism of the issue.

2. One debater should present a three- or four-minute extemporaneous speech on a narrow topic. All others assembled should prepare a point of information and make attempts during the speech.

3. Play a game of "Twenty Questions." One person should think of a person, place, or thing. Other club members should ask questions to try and identify the item. Only twenty questions are allowed. Contestants may try to guess what the item is during this period, but if they guess incorrectly, they are out of the game. The first person to guess the item gets to think of the item for the next round.

Managing the Debate

There is often a judge or designated evaluator for each debate. In many debates, there are panels of judges, typically three or five judges per panel. If there is a panel of judges, they may decide the debate individually, allowing the majority opinion to decide the outcome of the debate.

A debate may also have a designated timekeeper to track preparation time and speaking time. In the absence of a timekeeper, the judge usually keeps time. The timekeeper announces the end of preparation time. Technically, the debate officially begins immediately at the end of preparation time. The timekeeper signals time to the speakers during the debate with hand signals or a series of cards that indicate the remaining time. For example, if a speaker is delivering a seven-minute speech and has used three minutes of her time, the timekeeper should signal "four," the remaining time for the speech. The timekeeper should never signal elapsed time in a speech. It is challenging enough to try and deliver a winning debate speech without having to do the math to determine your available speaking time. The person keeping time should signal the remaining time to the speakers at the passing of each full minute and at the half-minute mark of the final minute. The timekeeper should also note when the speaker has no remaining time.

The timekeeper announces available time for points of information during the constructive speeches. After the first minute and before the last minute of each constructive speech, the timekeeper will "knock;" that is, rap her knuckles on a desk or table, slap a table with a gavel or palm of her hand, ring a bell, or make some other appropriate noise to signal the end or beginning of protected time.

The Topic for Debate

Each round of tournament debating has a different topic. In competitive parliamentary debating, the motion for debate is announced just before the debate begins (usually, 15 or 20 minutes). There are two major, different approaches to the announcement of the topic. They are listed in the order of their popularity.

- The topic may be attached to the ballot presented to each judge to complete regarding the outcome of the debate. When the two teams and judge arrive at the assigned location for the debate, the judge announces the proposition to the teams and begins preparation time.

- The tournament may have a central gathering place. At that site, a tournament representative makes a verbal announcement of the motion for all participants.

In the next chapter, you will learn much more about topics and topic analysis in parliamentary debate. Bear in mind that parliamentary debaters must speak on a variety of topics with very little time to prepare. This practice mirrors and anticipates most of the public speaking opportunities you have in school, work, and other social settings. Normally, when we are called upon to speak in public or otherwise express our thoughts or opinions on a subject, we do not have much (if any) time to prepare. This is why we learn to debate—the training you will receive as a debater will help you keep your cool and succeed in the many speaking opportunities you will have in your lifetime.

Speaker Responsibilities— Walking Through a Parliamentary Debate

In parliamentary debates, participants are presented with a motion for debate and have a scant 15 minutes to prepare. Parliamentary debaters do not read published material or argument briefs gathered prior to preparation time during their presentations; in fact, almost all competitive parliamentary debate leagues prohibit the use of quoted evidence in debates. In almost all parliamentary debates, debaters speak from notes they've made *during the preparation time* prior to the debate *or* from notes they've made *during the debate*. This way, debaters can speak from their own authority about the issues for debate. This does not mean that debaters should feel free to make up information about the topic; on the contrary, this means that debaters are responsible for accurately communicating facts based on their knowledge and their research to the audience, the judge, and the other team.

Because of the constraints of debate, each speaker has specific responsibilities for his or her part of the debate. The four debaters in a parliamentary debate occupy four different *speaker positions*, one debater to each speaker position:

- The first speaker for the proposition, or First Prop;
- The first speaker for the opposition, or First Opp;
- The second speaker for the proposition, or Second Prop; and
- The second speaker for the opposition, or Second Opp.

Each speaker position in parliamentary debate involves responsibilities for effective presentation, defense, and refutation. In addition, parliamentary debaters are members of teams and some responsibilities of speakers involve shared efforts with a colleague.

This section on speaker responsibilities identifies the fundamental strategic and tactical roles of speakers. Subsequent chapters offer more complete commentary on preparing and delivering the full text of each speech in a debate. Each speaker is known by one or more references to the speech she will deliver in the debate. The opening speaker for the proposition team is variously known as "first prop," or "1PC." The latter is a code for the title of the speech itself—it literally translates as "First Proposition Constructive," but it can be used as a title for the speaker as much as a reference to the speech. The other speakers in the debate are known in a similar manner:

- First speaker, proposition: first prop, 1PC
- First speaker, opposition: first opp, 1OC
- Second speaker, proposition: second prop, 2PC
- Second speaker, opposition: second opp, 2OC
- Opposition rebuttal: opp rebuttal, OR
- Proposition rebuttal: prop rebuttal, PR

We will discuss the duties of each speaker in turn, concluding with some general remarks about the responsibilities of debaters.

First Speaker, Proposition (a.k.a., " first prop constructive")

The opening speaker in the debate makes a **case** for the proposition. To make a case, a speaker offers a logical proof, a demonstration that the proposition for debate is more probably true than false. The first speaker for the proposition interprets the topic for debate, defining any unclear terms or otherwise clarifying the foundation for argument. The speaker may establish additional frameworks for the discussion, including setting up decision making criteria or offering other evaluation tools to assist the judge.

This first proposition speaker may offer a history of the debate's subject matter. Parliamentary debate topics come from all academic disciplines and fields of study: current events, economics, philosophy, cultural studies, the sciences, the law, politics, social studies, women's studies, media studies, immigration, race relations, education, human rights, national defense and social welfare. Your judges or audience will probably not have precisely the same knowledge base as you. If you provide a history of the issue in controversy, you will assist the judge so that everyone in the debate is on the same page or has the same background information. Providing a brief history of the issue in controversy may also inform the judge so that she appreciates all of the argument claims from the proposition team.

The first proposition speaker must prove the proposition for debate. As Raymond Alden explained in his 1900 book *The Art of Debate,* there is an "obligation resting upon one or other parties to a controversy to establish by proofs a given proposition, before being entitled to receive an answer from the other side." This responsibility rests, he concluded, "upon the side that would be assumed to be defeated if no progress at all were made in the consideration of the case." This means that the team that speaks for the motion for debate must prove the motion—if they do not provide a proof, then they have not met their burden.

After the opening speaker provides a clear foundation for the debate, she presents a case, that is, a detailed exposition of arguments in support of her interpretation of the motion. The case for the motion typically consists of three or four main arguments with corresponding examples or other forms of contemporary or historical evidence. You make a case for different topics in everyday discussions but have probably never thought of your arguments in these terms. How do you convince your friends to go and see a particular movie? You offer several lines of argument, or reasons to prefer your choice of movie. This is called making a case for your position.

For example, on the motion, "This House would abolish affirmative action," an opening speaker might organize her main arguments in the following manner:

> 1. Affirmative action has failed to address race and gender issues over time.
>
> 2. Affirmative action policies undermine community reform by forcing the best and brightest of marginalized communities to be assimilated into mainstream culture.
>
> 3. Alternatives to affirmative action are more likely to deal with the root, or underlying, causes of racism and sexism.

These arguments might serve as a simple outline for the case. The opening speaker would need to provide reasoning and examples to make concise, complete, and compelling arguments on each of these issues. The speaker would offer a summary of her speech to demonstrate the manner in which the arguments met the burden of proof for her interpretation for the motion.

First Speaker, Opposition (a.k.a. "first opp constructive")

The opposition team provides **clash** in the debate. Clash, one of the fundamental principles of any kind of debate, is simply what happens when arguments directly oppose each other, or clash against each other. The opposition team provides clash when they attempt to undermine the logic of the proposition team's case. The opposition argues that the proposition, as interpreted by the proposition team, does not hold.

The first opposition speaker uses tactics of direct and indirect refutation to counter the proposition team's case. The opening speaker for the opposition may challenge the definition of the motion or the proposition's decision framework of the debate. (See the chapter on topic interpretation for more on arguing these issues). The first opposition speaker may also challenge the main arguments of the proposition's case.

Refuting the main points of the case, that is, disputing the argument analysis or fact claims of the opening speaker, is called **direct refutation**. The opening speaker for the opposition should critically evaluate the first proposition speaker's arguments, pointing out inconsistencies, gaps in logic, argumentative fallacies, improper causal chains and exaggerated claims. This speaker might also offer counterexamples to offset the examples presented in the proposition case.

The opposition could also promote clash with the proposition case through **indirect argumentation**. You practice indirect argumentation when you bring up critical issues that are not formally included in the proposition team case. For example, if the first proposition speaker makes an argument for massively increasing funding to schools nationwide but fails to deal with the potential impact such a policy might have on the finances of the nation, you might bring up the problem of deficit spending or other fiscal irresponsibility in your first opposition constructive. Arguments of indirect refutation include disadvantages, counterplans and critiques. These are discussed in detail in later chapters on opposition strategy.

The best first opposition speakers know that they should present some combination of direct and indirect refutation. They must carefully select opposition arguments that will be relevant and effective for proving that the proposition, as interpreted by the proposition team, is more likely false than true.

The opposition does not have to disagree with every argument that the proposition team makes in their case. This strategy is not effective and can be tiresome for a captive audience. Often, it is a good idea if the opposition team agrees with one of the proposition arguments. This practice, called **strategic agreement**, can help the opposition team focus the discussion on those points that they feel are critical for winning the debate. Also, strategic agreement can be used to support a different and more powerful position for the opposition team. You will learn much more about the possibilities for strategic agreement throughout this book.

In the opening speech, opposition debaters should at least account for all the major arguments of the proposition case. The opening opposition speaker should do this in a forthright and formal manner, making it obvious to the judge that they have dealt with all the major elements of the proposition case. The first opposition speaker should say *something* about each of the major issues of the case. You can do this by directly or indirectly disputing the proposition claims. Make sure that the first opposition speech communicates to the judge that the opposition team has a credible and strong strategy for defeating the proposition case. First impressions matter in debate as well as in life. Even if you are unsure of your arguments, it is important that you always sound credible and effective. This confidence may not come easily at first, but with practice you will sound more and more confident.

Basically, the opening opposition speaker should try to identify and flesh out two or three main lines of argument against the proposition case. For example, you might advance two lines of argument to address the core issues of the case (direct refutation) and one new argument that could undermine the proposition position in the debate but, at the same time, is not an idea articulated in the opening speech (indirect refutation). Using the example of the affirmative action case given above, an opening opposition speaker might advance the following three lines of argument:

> **1.** Affirmative action has made important steps to improve diversity in universities and in the workplace. We should not abandon affirmative action.
>
> **2.** Affirmative action is a necessary remedy to counter centuries of discrimination based on ethnicity, gender, and economic circumstances. Without affirmative action, minorities will continue to be victimized and marginalized.
>
> **3.** Affirmative action is not responsible for cultural assimilation. Assimilation is enforced by other factors, like media images and economic conditions.

Compare these sample lines of argument to the proposition's lines of argument advanced earlier. Which are direct refutations of the proposition's case? Which are indirect? If you concluded that 1 and 3 are direct refutations of the proposition team's claims, you are correct. Both arguments directly counter claims made in the case for the proposition. Line 2 is an indirect refutation of the proposition's case because it makes an offensive argument *for* affirmative action. Look at it this way: arguments 1 and 3 play defense, because they say that affirmative action is not bad in the ways that the proposition team has claimed. Line 2 plays offense, because it advances an argument *for* affirmative action.

The opposition speaker might then let the judge know that these three issues are of greater import than the other matters in the opening speech; in other words, the other major arguments for the proposition team are not as important in evaluation of the motion.

Second Speaker, Proposition (a.k.a., "second prop constructive")

The second constructive speech for the proposition team is that team's last opportunity to introduce new arguments and issues. The only stand on the floor for the proposition, after this constructive speech, is the final rebuttal speech in the debate. This is a particularly important speech for the proposition, as it immediately precedes two consecutive opposition speeches, called the *opposition block.* The "opposition block" is composed of the second opposition constructive speech, and the opposition rebuttal speech. Those speeches give the opposition team 12 consecutive minutes to advance their arguments. Therefore, the second proposition speaker must convincingly prove her side's case to withstand the serious forthcoming opposition assault.

The second speaker for the proposition must answer all of the major objections to the case offered by the opening speaker for the opposition. In addition, this speaker must reestablish the principles of the case as initially presented by her colleague in the first proposition speech. In doing so, she might supplement her colleague's reasoning, offer additional examples, or otherwise amplify the opening presentation. The second proposition speaker must address the opposition's claims *specifically and in order.* This means that she should try to employ the four-step refutation process outlined in the introductory chapter.

Let's imagine that you were the second proposition speaker in the hypothetical affirmative action debate we've been following for the last few pages. How would you go about answering the opposition's arguments and rebuilding your case to prepare for the coming opposition arguments?

First, you would begin your speech by *briefly* summarizing the arguments that your side has already made for the proposition. After this introductory phase of your speech, you would then proceed to answer the arguments made by the opposition, using those arguments as opportunities to further solidify and expand your case. You might begin this process by saying: "They say that affirmative action has improved diversity in the workplace and at schools, but...." After you provide a response to their first argument, you should move to their second: "They say that affirmative action is a necessary remedy, but we think that there are better ways to solve this problem because...." You can see from this example how your refutation of the opposition's arguments might proceed. You will learn more about this process later in chapter 4. It is important to make sure that you correctly allocate your time in this speech. Make sure that you allow yourself enough time to appropriately address all of the opposition's arguments.

After refuting all of the arguments advanced by the opposition, the second proposition constructive speaker should remember to close with an appropriate conclusion. This usually includes some sort of summary of the debate thus far, where the speaker explains why the proposition should win the debate despite all of the arguments made by the opposition up to this point.

Second Speaker, Opposition (a.k.a., "second opp constructive")
This is the final constructive speech in the debate for the opposition team. No new arguments or issues may be introduced after this speech by the side opposing the proposition.

The second speaker for the opposition has several options for her speech. She may continue the objections of the first opposition speaker to the proposition team's case; she may present new arguments against the proposition team (these arguments may be either direct or indirect refutation); she may defend and expand the opposition's counterplan, disadvantages, critiques and other indirect argumentation if they have been presented; and she may evaluate inconsistencies between the arguments of the first and second proposition speakers.

Although the speech is known as a constructive speech, debaters should be cautious about presenting information as if the second opposition speech were a constructive speech. Although it may be tempting to start the debate fresh for your side with a whole slate of new opposition arguments, this is not an optimal use of the second opposition constructive. This speech should function like an opposition rebuttal speech. It is vital to expand the arguments from the first opposition speaker. It is equally important to answer or account for the key issues of the second proposition speaker. The opposition team, in their second speech, should be careful about introducing new arguments or unnecessarily expanding arguments in the debate.

If the second opposition speech functions as a rebuttal, then the opposition offers an integrated front of 12 minutes of argumentation, an effective tactic to overwhelm a final proposition rebuttalist's five-minute speech. Opposition speakers should share rebuttal responsibilities, with each speaker managing a section of the debate.

Opposition Rebuttalist

This part of the debate is the summary speech for the opposition team, and the last opportunity this side will have to explain why its arguments mean that it wins the debate. *Rebuttals* should be used to compare and contrast the major lines of argument from both sides in the debate.

The opposition's rebuttalist should select from among the issues of the debate. It is not possible to cover every argument in the debate. There are likely to be too many argument points from the constructive speeches in the debate, and the rebuttalist has about one-half the allotted time of the constructive speakers.

The opposition's rebuttal speaker should focus attention on two to four major critical issues that might tip the debate to the opposition side. It is important to select more than one issue. Multiple, independent, winning arguments will increase the probability that the opposition will win the debate.

These arguments must have a foundation in the constructive speeches. *New arguments may not be introduced in the opposition rebuttal.* The opposition rebuttalist should:

• Carry through important issues from her opening speech in the debate, as well as from her partner's constructive speech.

• Show why these important issues mean that the opposition wins the debate.

• Identify potentially winning proposition arguments and show why those arguments do not significantly damage the case for the opposition.

In other words, the job of the opposition rebuttalist is basically to *play both offense and defense*. The speech should have an offensive part, as the speaker must show why her side should win the debate. The speech should also have a defensive part, as the speaker shows why the other side should not win the debate.

The opposition's rebuttalist should be careful that she does not simply repeat her partner's speech. Many opposition rebuttalists merely repeat the issues from their partner's speech, but this is a bad idea. Simple repetition is not the best way to make a presentation. Simple repetition is not the best way to make a presentation. Simple repetition is not the best way to make a presentation. (That last bit should just about settle the matter.)

Proposition Rebuttalist

The proposition has the final speech in the debate. This speech should effectively summarize the entire debate. The final rebuttalist should:

- Extend the proposition's most effective arguments from the constructive speeches.
- Refute the opposition's claims about why they win the debate.
- Establish the reasons why the proposition team wins the debate.

This speaker must take care to answer the major arguments from the opposition speakers, particularly those arguments made in the opposition's rebuttal. The proposition rebuttalist should offer multiple, independent proofs of the motion for debate. This strategy increases the probability that any single idea will be enough for a victory. This means that the proposition rebuttalist should point out several ways that they should win the debate, hopefully taking the other side's points into account, e.g., "Even if they win this argument, we still win the debate because this other argument is more important..."

For this speaker, there may be a narrow exception to the "no new arguments in the rebuttal" rule. The proposition rebuttalist is entitled to answer new arguments made in the second opposition constructive speech, because the final rebuttal is the first opportunity in the debate that the proposition team has to refute these issues. Although the answers to the new arguments of the second opposition speaker may appear to be "new," they are not new arguments in the debate. They have their foundation in a constructive speech.

Concluding Thoughts on Formats

Although there are substantial differences between parliamentary debate formats, the major styles are quite similar in substance. The process of argumentation and refutation to determine winners and losers of debates varies little from debate to debate. The proposition team will, invariably, make a case for the topic. The opposition team will refute or otherwise undermine the proposition team's case. As the debate progresses, both teams will develop lines of argument to prove why their side wins the debate. At the end, both sides have a chance to summarize their arguments and refute the major issues raised by their opponents. Finally, the judge or judges will render a decision about the debate, assigning either ranks or a winner and a loser. They will assign speaker points on a fixed scale to individual debaters. After these decisions are made, the judge will offer oral and written critiques of the debate.

Regardless of the specific format used for debate, good debate requires ethical practice. We advise you to consider the seriousness of the event when you practice debate. In the interest of pursuing open debate and discussion, all participants must respect each other and create an environment free of intimidation. All debate formats create space for dynamic, engaged, and informed discussion. One of the only major variables to change from debate to debate in parliamentary debating is the topic. Teams should expect to debate a different topic in each debate. In Chapter 4, we discuss the types of topics and explain the process of topic analysis that debaters should employ.

Chapter 3

Taking Notes

Good listening and note-taking skills are critical elements for consistent debate performances and successes. Since debate is, in large part, about refutation and responsive or reactionary argumentation, it probably goes without saying that in order to debate, you're going to have to learn to listen critically. Critical listening is different from simple listening. Simple listening is the process of hearing information and perhaps (if the speaker is lucky) storing it in your mind or notes. Hearing is passive. Critical listening is just what it sounds like: listening with an eye towards criticism. It is an active process of engagement with the speaker. You must be able to understand and evaluate your opponents' arguments in order to respond adequately and appropriately. Good listening, like good speaking, takes practice. We learn terrible listening skills in many parts of our lives. Television and radio train us to be passive receptacles of information. To counter this training, debaters must work on their concentration skills.

You *must* learn to take notes effectively in order to succeed in debates. There are so many arguments made in the course of a given debate that even if you have an encyclopedic memory, your chance of recalling all of them is effectively zero. You probably have extensive experience in taking notes, but the note-taking process in the classroom or business arena is very different from the note-taking process in debate. When you are taking notes during a lecture at your school, for example, you are trying to write down as much as possible of what the teacher says, for later use. When you take notes in a debate, you need those notes for much more than effective recall. You also need them for effective refutation. To refute an argument effectively, you need to refer to it before you refute it. This is the "they say..." part of the four-step refutation model.

You may use notes during your speech. In fact, you should use notes during your speech so that you will be able to organize and deliver your speech effectively. In a debate, notes *track* the development of arguments. This is why we refer to the process of taking notes in a debate as *flowing*. Arguments *flow* during the course of a debate, and refutations pile upon each other throughout speeches by both teams. For the American parliamentary debate format, we recommend that you use one or more sheets of paper. Each piece of paper should be divided into five columns, like so:

1st prop constructive	1st opp constructive	2nd prop constructive	2nd opp const/ opp rebuttal	prop rebuttal

Notice that we've put the second opposition constructive and the first opposition rebuttal into the same column. The proposition team must refute the content of both speeches in the same speech, so it's practical to put them in the same column.

Flowing helps debaters to refute arguments effectively. Flowing promotes direct clash in debates. A flowsheet also allows debaters to track the arguments of the opposition so that they can answer them specifically and in order. When you flow, you take notes in the column appropriate to the speech. That way, you'll know what you need to refute when it's your turn to speak. When you take notes in a debate, you need to follow a few basic precepts listed below:

- **Abbreviate whenever possible**. Debates proceed rapidly, with remarkable density of information and argument. It is not physically possible for you to write everything down that is said in a given debate. Therefore, you will have to be selective about what you choose to write down, and abbreviate when you do. Develop a list of abbreviations that works for you. Try using standard abbreviations for debate terminology, such as "CP" for "counterplan," "DA" for "disadvantage," "T" for "topicality." Use abbreviations that make sense to you. Your notes are for your use and not for the ages.

- **Try to write legibly**. Although your notes are primarily for your own use, your partner may need to refer to them from time to time, so you should try to write legibly. Some debaters find that cannot read their own handwriting. If this happens to you, take steps to correct the problem.

- **Don't stop writing if you get lost**. Sometimes, debaters will get confused about what their opponent is saying or what part of the debate they are addressing. The appropriate response is certainly not to stop writing, stare into the ether, or hide under the table whimpering. Just keep taking notes, lest you miss some critical argument or example. Debaters should not lose debates because their opponents are disorganized.

- **Make notations of "dropped" or "unanswered" arguments**. If an opponent fails to answer your critical arguments, you will be able to tell at a glance by looking at the flow. Circle arguments that have gone unanswered so that you will be able to point out that the other side has effectively agreed with certain contentions you have made.

- **Practice routinely**. You will only learn to flow well if you practice. A lot. Practice flowing your classes, the evening news, radio broadcasts, or debate meetings. Use abbreviations and try to track argument references and refutations with arrows.

- **Use plenty of paper**. Don't try to cram an entire debate onto one piece of paper. You will not only fail, but will also create a tremendous mess in the process. Use multiple pieces of paper. Many people use separate pieces of paper or separate sections of their notes to track the development of "off-case" arguments, such as counterplans or disadvantages.

- **Space out**. Here we are not talking about the time-honored practice of navel-gazing; rather, leave plenty of vertical space between individual arguments that you write down. Space ensures that your flow will not become cramped and illegible later in the debate.

- **Use relational symbols to track argument development**. If you make an argument in your speech that is subsequently refuted, you need to visually represent that refutation on your flow with symbolic notation. We suggest that you use arrows. This relational notation will help you with rebuttal summaries: "We said X, to which they said Y and Z, but Y and Z don't really answer X, and here's why..."

Suggested Exercises

1. Have teammates or group members make speeches. Practice flowing these speeches.

2. Practice flowing the nightly television newscast or news programs with guests who debate each other or the host—in the United States, you might flow "Face the Nation" or a similar program. Work to get down as much of the delivered information as possible by developing a series of issue-specific abbreviations.

Chapter 4

Topics and Topic Interpretation

An Introduction to Topic Interpretation

In competitive parliamentary debating, each debate has a different **topic**. The topic is also known as a **motion**. The topic is a statement or phrase, on occasion a single word. Topics are used to focus or direct the discussion of a debate.

The use of a topic to open argument in a debate is no different than the use of topics in daily communication. People use a topic statement to trigger a discussion or debate with friends and families, in class, and at work. "Baseball players should go on strike." "Let's watch a movie." "In history class today, we will discuss the causes of the Civil War." "That videogame is mine." "You don't know me." In each of these cases, the person supporting the topic must **interpret** it, that is, give the topic meaning.

In the example, "Let's watch a movie," the person interpreting the statement should be prepared to say who should watch the movie, whether the movie would be watched at home or in a theater, and which movie should be viewed. This clarifies or interprets the meaning of the topic statement. It makes the topic understandable for listeners. After an interpretation of the topic statement, any listener might then realize that "Let's watch a movie," means inviting several others, traveling to a theater, and watching "Pokemon XII: Jason's Return." On hearing this information, a consideration or analysis of this topic might begin, with potential arguments for and against each of these issues. (You might think: "I'll go but I don't want to go with Tiffany." "I'd rather just stay at home and watch the same film on a DVD player." "Good idea. I'm bored and it would be nice to do something." "I don't want to see that movie. Even my younger brother wasn't interested. Isn't another movie available?")

In parliamentary debating, the topic is announced before the debate. Parliamentary debates may have set topics, known many hours or days in advance of a debate. In the United States, set topics are used primarily for public, non-competitive debates, so that the topic can be publicized to attract an audience. They may be used for select competitions, although this does not occur frequently. Set topics for tournament and other competitions allow debaters additional time for topic analysis, research, and practice debates. In debates with set topics, however, few notes are used and no prepared manuscripts or argument briefs are read.

At parliamentary tournaments, debating is generally **extemporaneous**. That means that debaters have limited preparation time before they must deliver their speeches and that the speeches are neither written out nor memorized. The method of announcing debate topics limits advanced preparation. There is little time from the announcement of the topic to the opening speech of a debate and the topic is different for each debate. The tournament host will assign teams to debate on the proposition and opposition side and make the sides known to all the participants. Then the host will announce the topic. The topic is usually announced approximately fifteen or twenty minutes before each round of debate. (In debate competitions, teams generally debate an equal number of times on the proposition and opposition sides.) When the proposition and opposition teams receive the topic, they know on which side they will debate. They begin their preparation.

How do debate teams prepare to argue a topic? As noted previously, a topic for debate is a cue, prompt, or idea, which the proposition team will interpret and eventually make its case. In other words, the proposition team interprets the topic in a way that makes a **case**, which is a logical claim, a carefully thought out opinion, supported with reasoning and examples. At the same time that the proposition team learns the topic, the opposition team does as well. The opposition team then tries to anticipate the arguments that the proposition team will make in the debate and prepare answers to that case. During preparation time, the participants analyze the topic. They ask themselves: What does this topic mean? What important issues are raised by it? How could a case be made to support it? How would it be opposed? What contemporary and historical examples are relevant to it? The answers to these and other questions will serve as the basis for the proposition team's case. If the opposition team successfully anticipates the case, the answers to these questions will also help prepare the opposition's refutation.

Toward the end of preparation time, the teams outline the major arguments from their analysis of the topic. Debaters will create and adapt their own ideas for many of the arguments they will later use in the debate. Other ideas may come from notes and reference materials. It is possible, in many circumstances, to examine reference materials to assist in topic analysis. Some tournaments and competitive leagues permit the use of dictionaries, atlases, prepared notes and argument briefs, and other materials during preparation time. Other debate tournaments and leagues have policies to limit or even prohibit the use of prepared materials or any coaching or consultations, with the exception of communication with a debate partner, prior to the debates. Even in cases when materials and coaching are available during the preparation time period, use of the materials is only available during preparation time. No published materials or notes made before preparation time may be used in the actual debate.

What topics are used in parliamentary debates? Topics may be based on current events—the political, social, economic, and cultural issues of the day that are argued by leaders of nations, legislatures, and citizens (e.g., The United States Federal Government should significantly improve environmental protection, The United States should participate in the International Criminal Court, or The United Nations should take action to depose Saddam Hussein.) Some motions address historical issues (e.g., The atomic bombing of Hiroshima was unjustified, This House believes that the United States has been more sinned against than sinning, or America would be better off without its Revolution.) Some topics compare important personal or social values (e.g., When in conflict, the rights of the victim should be favored to the rights of a criminal defendant, or This House believes that the local is preferable to the global.)

Other topics are ambiguous. In these cases, it is less clear or predictable as to how the proposition team might interpret the debate topic. Ambiguous topics might be just a single word specifying a political or geographical region (e.g., Africa.) They might call for an action, without identifying who should take the action or what specific action ought to be taken in a particular circumstance (Bury it or Televise it.) In these debates, the proposition team must still interpret the motion by making a case related to the topic. For the topics listed here, the proposition team might argue on Africa: that the United Nations should relieve starvation in Africa; on Bury it: that the Russian Government should bury Lenin's body rather than continuing to have it lie in state in the Kremlin, or on Televise it: that states should televise the executions of criminals. Quite obviously, it is more difficult to predict the proposition team's case if the topic is vague. There are still effective strategies to help prepare the opposition team for debates on vague topics, which we include in this book.

Some topics begin with the phrase "This House..." Academic parliamentary debate is modeled after argumentation in the British Parliament. "This House" is a reference to the British legislature, primarily the House of Commons, and its debate on motions and bills. In that context, for "The House" to support a motion, (e.g., "This House would join the World Trade Organization") it means that the members of the British legislature would vote for it to become law. In tournament debating, unless the first proposition speaker says otherwise, the phrase, "This House," now refers to the judge(s) and audience attending the debate, as these are the people called on to "vote" for or against the debate motion.

In other circumstances, the first proposition speaker may define or interpret "This House" for the purpose of advancing her arguments in the debate, providing an altogether different understanding of the phrase. For example, on the motion "This House would improve health," the opening speaker for the proposition might say, "For the purpose of this debate, the proposition team will interpret 'This House' to mean 'the United States Federal Government.' Our case will focus on the ways the federal government might improve access to quality medical care through national health insurance..."

Categories of Motions for Debate: Closed and Open Motions

Topics are categorized in different ways. This is a convenience for debaters and judges in competitions. Categorization of a topic allows participants to make a quick assessment of the arguments and examples likely to prove it or disprove it. In an event with little formal preparation time and virtually no preparation time during the course of the debate, the ability to quickly identify and evaluate issues can be a key to competitive success.

There are two basic categories for motions for debate. Topics are identified as **closed** or **open**. A closed motion is sometimes called a **straight** resolution. An open motion is also known as a **linkable** resolution. The terms **closed** and **open** refer to the degree of flexibility that a proposition team has in interpreting a motion. A closed motion limits the possibilities for interpretation (that is the reason it is "closed"—there are few possibilities for creative interpretation of the terms of the topic.) In other words, closed or straight topics are taken literally. For example, on the motion, "This House would send peacekeeping troops to the Middle East," it is expected that the proposition team would offer a relatively conservative and easily anticipated interpretation of the motion, namely, a justification for military intervention in the nations bordering the eastern Mediterranean Sea—Israel, Lebanon, Syria, Egypt, and Jordan.

An open or linkable motion is more vague, ambiguous, or abstract. Examples include "There should be a new song for America," and "Don't fear the reaper." The proposition team may interpret the terms of these open or linkable motions in a creative way (although it must still be a reasonable one for debate), generally *linking* the vague wording of the motion to a current or historical public policy controversy.

A defense of the topic "Bury it," for example, might have the proposition team call for an end to national missile defense plans in the USA, "burying" the plan for the defense program for reasons of technical and political unfeasibility. For some proposition teams, as well as representatives of the United States Department of Energy, "bury it," means the disposal of nuclear waste from unstable, temporary sites to the newly licensed central waste repository at Yucca Mountain, Nevada. According to Benjamin Grove, "Waste piling up at nuclear power pants and defense sites nationwide could be shipped to Nevada for permanent burial as early as 2010."[1] For others, the topic might mean hiding sensitive or confidential information, for good or malicious reasons. In a Los Angeles Times news article regarding ongoing lawsuits against American tobacco companies, reporter Henry Weinstein noted, "One memo written in November 1977 by a Philip Morris scientist to the company's director of research said that if studies on nicotine's addictive properties turned out unfavorably, "we will want to bury it."[2] For those individuals appreciative of historical literary gossip, there is the story of the prominent English author, Thomas Hardy. Hardy, as a final request, asked to be buried with his first wife,

Emma. But "his wishes were only partly regarded; his body was interred in Poet's Corner, Westminster Abbey, and only his heart was buried in Emma's grave at Stinsford."[3] One might argue that the motion, "Bury it," calls for the protection of personal privacy and demands reburial of Hardy's remains in his family grave, according to his wishes. These interpretations of "Bury it" are creative and varied, addressing issues of national defense, environmental protection, and corporate and personal privacy.

Who decides if a motion is closed or open? It may be done in a formal way, meaning that the tournament host or the sponsor of a debate will identify that a motion is either closed or open. This announcement will be made before a tournament or before a round of debate. If the sponsor of a debate tells the participants that the motion is closed, the debaters should argue the motion that way. In other circumstances, the categorization of a debate motion as closed or open is in the eye of the beholder. It is up to the debaters to decide if the motion is closed or open. Some will conclude that the topic, "The United States Federal Government should increase gun control," is a closed motion. They will understand the topic to mean that the federal government ought to pass laws and regulations to restrict the private ownership of handguns. Others, however, will have a different understanding of this topic. They might believe it is open, and think that a more flexible interpretation of the topic is acceptable. The motion might be interpreted to mean that the federal government should stop its sales of military equipment to other governments. This difference of opinion about what the topic means can makes debates interesting. It may even be necessary for the existence of debate. After all, people understand the world differently, based on their identity, knowledge, culture, values, etc. It is those differences that create the basis for debates (it is unlikely that you would have much of a debate with people always in agreement with your opinions). Debaters disagree about many things, including the way to interpret a topic. It is not surprising that debaters will disagree about whether a motion is closed or open.

The term *closed* usually refers to topics that focus discussion on a single or limited set of major ideas. A **literal interpretation** suggests that there is a single interpretation of a topic. A **defined set interpretation** suggests that there are several, limited possibilities for interpretation of a motion.

A literal interpretation A literal interpretation is an obvious, conventional, or popular understanding of a motion. If the topic were, "This House would establish a system of national health insurance in the USA," a literal interpretation would presume that there is one, and only one, way to understand the topic and that it is evident to all those reading the topic. A debater might introduce the interpretation in the debate by saying the following:

"We are here to debate the motion, 'This House would establish a system of national health insurance in the USA.' It is obvious that this topic is designed for us to discuss whether the federal government should pay for health insurance for all citizens and residents in the United States. We accept the challenge of the topic and will prove that it is a good idea for the federal government to insure health care. That is the basis for today's debate."

A defined set or parametric interpretation Words have more than one meaning. A quick look in any dictionary will confirm that. "Cool" for example, means a moderate degree of cold, pleasing, calm, and aloof. You know that words mean more than one thing from slang, which often creates new meanings for words.

Topics are made of words. Some topics are but a single word—"Africa." Other motions use a lot of words—"The United States Federal Government should alter its sentencing guidelines to decriminalize the medicinal use of marijuana." Because they consist of words and words have multiple meanings, topics often have multiple meanings.

Any single motion may, therefore, have a "set" of meanings, a group or collection of logical ways that the motion is understood. It is not quite a literal interpretation of the topic (there isn't just one, and only one, interpretation of the motion) but it is not an open interpretation either. There are some limits on the interpretation, namely parameters, brackets, or boundaries on the set of possible interpretations. The set consists only of topic interpretations that may be said to be "reasonable" and "evident," although the interpretations may differ substantially from each other.

An example is the motion, "This House opposes the death penalty." This has more than one possible interpretation. This is because the phrase "death penalty" is used in public policy debates in more than one reasonable way with some frequency. If the topic called for opposition to "capital punishment," this would be a different matter, as capital punishment, unlike death penalty, typically is used to refer to one and only one thing—the execution of felons for special circumstances crimes.

The death penalty is used more generally to refer to matters from NCAA penalties limiting university football scholarships to the use of animals in cosmetic and scientific testing. Included in her article on spaying and neutering programs, for example, Carolyn Mitchell calls on the public to renounce the death penalty—that is, the "killing of homeless animals" that have been impounded by animal shelters.[4] Activists interested in reducing white-collar crime have a different understanding of the death penalty. For them, a death penalty means revocation of a business license: "What does it mean to talk about the 'death penalty" for corporations? Simply this: Commit an egregious wrong, and have your charter revoked. In other words, lose the state's permission to exist."[5]

On the topic, "This House opposes the death penalty," the proposition team might interpret the topic in any of the following ways:

- The proposition team might call for an end to the administration of capital punishment, interpreting the death penalty to mean capital punishment, that is, execution for certain crimes.

- The proposition team might interpret the topic to call for the abolition of factory farms, arguing that modern farming techniques are certainly a death sentence for any animal unfortunate enough to be bred for slaughter.

- The team interpreting the motion might abolish the estate tax, a federally imposed tax on the property and assets of a deceased person. This tax is often described as a "death penalty."

Open Motions

An open motion, on the other hand, gives the proposition team a considerable amount of interpretive freedom. This may be intimidating for new debaters. Proposition debaters are sometimes paralyzed by an open motion's possibilities. Opposition debaters have concerns about debating a case for which they will surely have limited preparation time, as it is difficult, sometimes seemingly impossible, to anticipate a proposition team's strategy successfully.

Open motions, however, are important for parliamentary debating. For the proposition team, they inspire creativity and dynamic thinking. Open motions are opportunities for self-expression and student voice. They encourage interdisciplinary and impromptu connections for effective opposition replies. Because closed motions and open motions have their strengths, most tournament hosts use a mix of closed and open motions during the course of a competition.

To interpret an open motion for a debate, the proposition team may use an extended analogy.

Interpretation by extended analogy   An analogy is the point-by-point comparison of two things or the development of a relationship between two things. In a topic interpretation, the proposition team develops a 'relationship' between the actual wording of the topic and a corresponding target statement. The target statement is developed by the proposition team. It is the team's interpretation of the motion and should follow the semantic structure, grammar, and syntax of the original statement.

On the motion, "This House would fight the power," a first speaker for the proposition might identify the key terms of the topic (fight and power) and prepare an analogy, a target word or phrase, for each of the terms. She might, for example, offer a case to stop or resist (fight) the imposition of economic sanctions against Iraq by the United Nations (the power).

On the motion "Don't fear the reaper," a proposition team might argue the topic is a metaphor for life (one should not fear death, as the "Grim Reaper" is a symbol of death), subsequently interpreting the topic to call for expanded infant health care services. Another debater might argue that the topic is a metaphor for farming (the reaper is an agricultural tool) and advocate agricultural price supports to assist small farmers. A third debater could argue that the topic stands for acceptance of the principles of nuclear deterrence. Nuclear deterrence, or mutually assured destruction, is the idea that countries with nuclear weapons are unlikely to wage war against each other because they would each be destroyed. In this third interpretation, a debater could argue that the United States should not fear the specter of death (nuclear annihilation) but ought to embrace it because a defense policy based on deterrence would better protect national security.

Disagreements About Interpretation: Topicality Arguments

The differences in categorizing and interpreting a motion are also the basis for debate arguments. Debaters can argue about the interpretation of a topic. Is it reasonable to define the terms the way the proposition team did? Does the interpretation create the possibility for a good debate? The arguments in a debate about the topic are known as **topicality** arguments. A topicality argument is introduced in the debate by the opposition team, usually in the opening opposition constructive speech. To present a topicality argument, the first opposition speaker would argue that the proposition's interpretation of the topic is an unreasonable one, that it undermines the purpose of sound debating because it strays too far from the obvious meaning of the topic. An opposition speaker concludes that the case offered by the proposition is **non-topical**, meaning that it is off the topic or out of bounds for the debate.

Topicality arguments are an examination of the issue of relevance. The teams are given a topic for debate. If the proposition's interpretation of the topic seems to support a generally unrelated or opposite idea, the opposition team should rightly point out that the proposition is no longer supporting the motion and ought to lose the debate. This is because the proposition has a responsibility to support the motion. (If the proposition could argue *anything* it wanted, it could even argue against the topic. In this case, the opposition would also have prepared for a debate in which it argued against the topic. Both teams might, therefore, agree that the topic is a bad idea but there certainly would not be much of a debate.)

An opposition team may argue that a proposition team has presented a case that does not fairly support the motion for debate. For example, on the motion, "This House would significantly change the jury system," an opposition team could object to a proposition team's interpretation that called for an expansion of the Endangered Species Act to protect plant and animal life. They would be right to do so. The protection of wildlife has little, if anything, to do with changing the jury system in courts. Debate topics are meant to allow for predictable and fair debating. Unless debate teams are given an open motion or an ambiguously worded topic, there is a general expectation of opposition teams, judges, and audiences that a good number of substantive issues will be generally known before the debate begins.

If the opposition proves that the proposition team does not support the motion, the opposition wins the debate. The topic is the focal point of a debate, and only arguments related to the topic are relevant to the discussion and may be considered by the judge. In addition, debates are brief, with a total of 38 minutes of speaking time. It is important to avoid distractions and focus the discussion on the most important issues. A case that does not support the topic interpretation is irrelevant to the discussion. It cannot make a logical case for the motion. If the case is off the topic, the opposition wins.

If the opposition team has an honest dispute with the interpretation of the topic, then a topicality argument is appropriate. If the opposition team simply wants to debate an issue other than the one presented by the proposition team, then a topicality argument is not appropriate. Fair debate permits the proposition team to select the more meaningful and defensible interpretations from among the potential ones. (Remember, the proposition team will often have a choice of possible interpretations of the motion because words have more than one meaning. Just look in a dictionary.) There will always be an "other" interpretation of the topic that might be easier to challenge (that is, there will always be a reason that the opposition side would prefer to debate a case other than the one with which it is faced—there is always a weaker version of the proposition's argument.) Topicality argumentation is not part of debate theory and practice simply to give the opposition side a chance to propose a different interpretation of a motion, to begin a debate again on a second issue. Reasonable topicality argumentation requires that the opposition prove that the proposition team's interpretation is illegitimate—the proposition's interpretation is at odds with a sensible understanding of the topic. The opposition might then suggest another possible interpretation as proof that meaningful debate could have been available on the motion, if not for the poor interpretation of the motion by the proposition team. The standard of proof for an opposition's topicality argument is high—they must demonstrate that the debate, on the basis of the proposition interpretation, is entirely illegitimate and *should never have occurred.* This requires convincing argumentation.

There are, to be sure, different possible interpretations of any topic statement. For every meaningful interpretation of a motion, there are a lot of bad ones. For good debate, the proposition team must be able to select a legitimate interpretation of the topic from a pool of worthwhile, insignificant, odd, dysfunctional, or counterproductive possibilities. For example, on the motion, "The United States Federal Government should end capital punishment," there are sound, sensible interpretations. A debater could argue that the federal government should pass legislation to eliminate the execution of felons. Or, a proposition debater could argue that the United States Supreme Court should issue a ruling that the death penalty violates the Eighth Amendment's prohibition on cruel and unusual punishment. This would effectively abolish capital punishment.

In addition to sensible interpretations, however, a proposition team could also introduce foolish interpretations, even dangerous ones. They could argue that the federal government should use magic to eliminate the death penalty. Or, they could argue that the federal government should kill all those in favor of the death penalty, leaving only those who would never use it. In debates, the proposition team ought to select the best possible argument for its side. If they are called on to defend all possible versions of a topic, or the interpretation most favored by their opponent, we might never have a debate on a legitimate interpretation. This is the reason that, in the majority of debates, the judge lets the proposition team determine the interpretation of the topic—the team responsible for proving the topic chooses the way to do it.

Opposition interpretation of the motion may be a way for the opposition team to simply duck the challenge of debating the proposition team on its interpretation of the topic. This is never a good way for either side to approach the debate. Just as the proposition team should not attempt to avoid the substantive and serious matter of the motion, so too should the opposition team try to confront the proposition team's case head-on.

The proposition team may answer a topicality argument according to the following guidelines:

- They may argue that the opposition has failed to advance a sound position in the debate. Why should the opposition select the basis for debate? What is the authority for an opposition interpretation of the motion? The opposition team does not have to defend the motion during the debate. The proposition team has that duty. The proposition team has legitimate authority to define the motion because it has the burden of proof for it. The opposition team does not. The proposition team, therefore, rightly interprets the motion.

- The proposition team might argue against the topicality argument itself. The proposition speakers would carefully analyze the elements of the argument, as well as the examples offered to support the argument. In other words, the proposition team would debate the issue in the same way they would consider any other argument in the debate.

In addition, the opposition has an enormous conflict of interest when it interprets the debate motion. The opposition team opposes the motion in the debate and has every reason to provide a bankrupt or easily defeated interpretation. This tactic simply makes the debate easier for them. The debate then becomes a rigged game. The opposition side sets the agenda for the proposition team and, at the same time, gets to argue against that agenda. This situation would be similar to a state district attorney exclusively setting the rules of procedure and evidence for a criminal trial, limiting the choices and rules for the defense, and then getting to argue the case. Not fair.

If all this were not enough, the underlying assumption of many topicality arguments is that the opposition side in the debate needs full preparation time to engage the proposition team's case effectively. To the opposition, this usually means they must have an idea about the direction or substance of the proposition case during the fifteen-minute preparation time period prior to the debate. Opposition teams seem to suggest that they are treated unfairly if the proposition presents a case they have not adequately anticipated during the preparation time. This is a popular myth in parliamentary debating. Preparation time is not necessarily for equal use for both teams in a debate. Although it may be used, and quite effectively, by the opposition, preparation time exists for the proposition team to select a topic interpretation and write a case.

Preparation time is primarily for the proposition and it is not necessarily for the opposition team. The proposition team must make a convincing case for debate. This is a challenging enterprise. It is more difficult to build than to destroy. The proposition must provide consistent, unifying principles for its case. It is more likely than not that the proposition team will have to use several different arguments to make its logical proof of the case. The opposition team, however, will not need to endorse unifying or even consistent positions to win a debate. In fact, many opposition teams win debates because they are able to identify and support a single powerful argument against their opponents.

The proposition team quite clearly, maybe desperately, needs preparation time before the debate begins. They need to brainstorm the motion, select an appropriate case, identify the substantive issues that support the case, anticipate the likely opposition replies, and write an outline for the case. Fifteen minutes is just enough time to complete these tasks efficiently.

The first speaker for the opposition, like the second speakers for the proposition and opposition, can make do without much preparation time. The opposition should be able to successfully debate with much more limited preparation time than that given to the proposition team. That is, in fact, what parliamentary debate training teaches.

Does this mean that there are no occasions for the opposition side to challenge the interpretation of the motion by the proposition team? Of course not. It is possible to argue that the proposition team has provided an illegitimate interpretation of the motion. To accomplish this, the opposition should first identify the statements or arguments in the opening speech that describe proposition's interpretation of the motion. The opposition speaker should then explain why the interpretation is unsatisfactory ("The proposition does not follow the grammar of the topic sentence." "They use a different method of action than the one in the topic." "They are calling for action by the United States, but the topic clearly states United Nations.") The opposition speaker should then explain that this is an illegitimate interpretation and that the opposition should win the debate because the proposition's case does not support the motion for debate.

On the motion "This House would starve a cold and feed a fever," the proposition might introduce a case that would increase the ability of victims to testify during criminal sentencing decisions in the USA. The opening speaker would argue that the criminal justice system should "starve a cold," that is, reduce due process protections for criminal defendants, and "feed a fever," increase consideration for crime victims.

In this circumstance, however, imagine a case presentation that accidentally supported both due process protections for criminals and victims' rights. What if the proposition team *fed* a cold and *fed* a fever? What if the first proposition speaker said, "It is a good idea to promote constitutional protections for criminals and victims?" This claim might be the opposite of the section of the topic calling for the proposition to "starve a cold." The proposition should have to argue that something should be reduced at the same time that another is increased. By arguing that it is acceptable to increase two things at the same time, the proposition speaker would be arguing *against* the topic.

The opposition team might then legitimately argue that the first proposition speaker has every right to interpret the motion but once an interpretation is offered, the proposition team must show some loyalty to it. In this case, the proposition speaker has failed to offer a case consistent with their interpretation. The argument might be presented as follows:

> "The proposition team has presented a case that contradicts its interpretation of the motion. The first proposition speaker said that the criminal justice system was out of balance and that more attention ought to be paid to victims and less to criminals. This is their interpretation of the phrase 'starve a cold' in the motion. To prove the motion, they must reduce due process protections: they must 'starve the cold.'"

> "*But* the proposition speaker supports constitutional due process protections later in her speech. They are arguing that they should feed the cold and the fever. This is at odds with their interpretation. The case does not support the topic. The proposition team must lose the debate, as they have presented a case that does not support the motion."

Although topics are called closed and open, the distinction is more art than science. Closed motions are never as "closed" as they might first appear—there is often some "wiggle room" for clever interpretation of a motion, unpopular or unconventional opinions, alterior perspectives, intellectual innovations, and minority and radical voices in the interpretation of a topic statement. And open topics do not permit any conceivable idea to enter the debate. Judges and audiences are reluctant to accept interpretations that are not logically extended analogies of ambiguously worded topics.

Some motions are also categorized as fact, value, or policy topics. These categories refer to a closed interpretation of the language of the topic. If the topic language appears to suggest that a factual dispute is central to the motion, it is often called a "topic of fact" by debaters and judges. A topic of fact presents a supposed factual claim that is subject to debate: This House believes that the economy of the USA is recovering from recession. In this debate, the teams would likely prepare to debate the "fact" that the US economy was rebounding from slow growth. A motion of value is one that expresses or compares values (a value is nothing more than expression of a "good"). The comparison of the values is the subject of the debate in the following topic: It is appropriate to sacrifice personal freedom to promote security. A policy motion calls for an action to be taken: The United States Federal Government should ban the three strikes law. These kinds of categories help debaters to identify the core elements of a case and relevant examples that ought to be included in the opening proposition speech to establish a proof of the motion. Debating fact, value, and policy topics is discussed in detail in the case construction chapter.

Suggested Exercise

> Take a list of topics and categorize them as closed or open motions. Explain why you think each motion is "closed" or "open." If the motion is "closed," what terms in the topic limit its interpretation to a single issue or limited set of issues? If the motion is "open," how does the language of the topic support different, perhaps even contradictory, interpretations?

Additional Disagreements on Interpretation: Specific Knowledge, Truism, Tautology

Specific Knowledge

If it were not obvious, the point of scheduling debates is to have *debate*. In other words, strategies and tactics that undermine the possibility for good debate, reasoned and conflicting discourse, are not permitted. This does not mean that one side cannot take advantage of the other side. In fact, that must happen for a team to be declared the winner. But it should be a fair contest, rather than a rigged or biased game.

There are three issues, each involving the interpretation of the topic, that have been said to interfere with the fairness of debates. They are specific knowledge, truism, and tautology.

Specific knowledge refers to an issue that allegedly violates the principles of fair debating. By definition, specific knowledge is the claim that the first proposition speaker has made an interpretation of a topic with "specific," or private, information. In other words, the information used to support the interpretation of the motion is not publicly available and is held only by the proposition speaker. This is claimed to be unfair, because the information is not available to the opposition team and the subject is, therefore, difficult to debate. If private information forms the basis of a proposition case, it will undermine the chance for fair and meaningful debate. For example, on the motion, "Bury it," it would be difficult to debate against an opening proposition speaker's claim that her maternal grandfather ought to be buried rather than cremated, according to the wishes of her family. In this circumstance, the charge of "specific knowledge" from the opposition team would be appropriate. If the proposition team presented sophisticated or complex information or used abbreviations for organizations or ideas that could confuse the opposition team (e.g., econometric information, ideas associated with mathematical biology, or ASEAN) and they refused to define technical terms or fully describe the organization or concept, this would also be an example of specific knowledge. These things happen in parliamentary debates but not very frequently. In too many cases, the claim of "specific knowledge" is not a legitimate argument.

Specific knowledge presumes that the best debates are based on shared information, that is, factual material, opinions, and other data available in the public sphere or generally understood by informed students. There are, however, problems with the claims supporting the theory of specific knowledge.

The charge that an opponent is using specific knowledge is almost always suspect. It usually involves a claim that a debater does not have the same information as her opponent. Debaters making the charge of specific knowledge seem to believe that if other students have facts they do not possess, the opponent's information must be private, specific, illegitimate knowledge. Debaters, however, are usually unable to determine if knowledge used in the debate is public or private (the important distinction here). In the majority of cases, we suspect that it is "public," in that the material substance of the majority of debates involves current events, and issues of historical, philosophical, and literary merit. These issues are not developed independently of outside influence (this is not private knowledge). Rather, they have been gained from schooling, reading, and research.

In addition, debaters do not have "common understandings" of the issues introduced in debate topics. Students have very different personal knowledge, nationalities, cultural practices, identities, and histories. They concentrate their studies in different academic disciplines. (Is it specific knowledge for a student who has studied economics to exploit her knowledge against a student who has not taken an economics class? How would it be possible to police the knowledge that students have?) These differences actually serve as points of conflict and tension that ultimately *produce* debate. In addition, the information that students use in debates is not generated internally or privately. Students read textbooks, newspapers, academic journals, novels, websites, electronic newsletters, and magazines. They speak with faculty and friends. They develop life experience in their communities, at work, and during travel. The information they possess is externally generated. In other words, it is public information and should be considered in debates.

Specific knowledge claims are often appeals to ignorance. They suggest that debaters could satisfy themselves by *not knowing* important information, ultimately censoring challenging, intriguing, paradoxical, innovative, and complex ideas and excluding them from debates. It seems odd, indeed, that debaters might be penalized for having sophisticated knowledge or critical insight that goes beyond obvious, conventional wisdom. If debate is to accomplish anything, it ought to inform its participants and provide serious critical training. In other circumstances, we call this "education" and encourage its development.

Specific knowledge produces a race to the bottom. In other words, specific knowledge claims suggest that the student with the least information may be better positioned for success in debate competitions. For that student, any argument claims of the opposing side with which they are unfamiliar or which they are ill-equipped to answer could be examples of specific knowledge that ought to be challenged and excluded from debates. Specific knowledge, in this case, guarantees a win for the side that loses the most arguments the fastest: "Brilliant opening speech! I have never heard any such ideas before. Really. What a knowledge base! What an impressive command of the facts! Alas, all of it is new to me. Never heard of any of it or anything like it. Your information must be specific knowledge. It is, therefore, not possible for me to debate. So, the matter of this debate is now settled. I win! Thanks, everyone, for attending. On to my next challenging round of debate!"

Specific knowledge turns the debate world on its head, providing a theoretical defense for anti-intellectualism. It suggests that debaters prepare for their event by "dumbing down" sophisticated ideas or creative perspectives. This only puts a modern spin on surrender, trying to turn it into a winning strategy.

When confronted with the presentation of facts that seem to be specific knowledge, debaters should work with what they are given rather than react by simply crying "specific knowledge." Provided that the proposition team gives all of the relevant information to support a particular case, the opposition can still win the debate by using that information. It is inevitable that the proposition team, in making its argument, will provide reasoning and examples that can be challenged and analogized by the opposition. Debate teaches argumentative skills. These skills can help you to analyze and refute an issue, even on the occasions when you are unfamiliar with the ideas.

Truism

The truism, another example of a fairness violation in parliamentary debating, is also suspect. The **truism** is an opposition argument explaining that the proposition team has offered an interpretation of the motion that is an objective TRUTH. In other words, the proposition's case is an incontrovertible fact. Because the proposition case is *true*, it cannot be argued with or satisfactorily disputed. It cannot be debated. The opposition team asks the judge to conclude that the proposition team has not presented a fair case for debate and, therefore, should lose the debate.

There are few motions that can literally be considered truisms, and few ever appear in debate rounds. This does not mean that the truism argument has no place in parliamentary debate. It does indicate that the genuine number of "true" cases—for example, "Gravity exists"—is quite small. Debaters will not be asked, for example, to debate whether or not the earth revolves around the sun or if two plus two equals four. Other topics that are considered to be truisms are extraordinarily difficult to debate: "Child pornography is bad"; "Women should be excluded from the workplace"; "The poor should be forced to undergo involuntary sterilization." Tournament hosts generally avoid topics that have a one-sided bias.

In actual debate practice, the opposition's claim that the proposition's interpretation is a truism is unlikely to get them anywhere. The proposition team's interpretation of the motion is typically an argument that may be effectively refuted. In the overwhelming majority of debates, the proposition team presents a case that makes for a fair debate. The proposition's arguments may be challenging but they typically also permit the opposition team to fully participate in the debate.

Most opposition claims of truism are nothing other than an error. When introducing a truism argument, the opposition debater argues against the proposition team's case, claiming that the case is true. She is not just arguing that she alone is incapable of arguing against the case. If she did that, she would only prove that she is incapable of making a valid argument in the debate. That is not a good position for a debater. To prove that the case is a truism, she must prove the extraordinary claim that there is no one—not one person— who could argue against the case. Put another way, she must suggest that she has scanned infinite thought and reached the conclusion that no one could answer the proposition team's arguments. Quite a claim!

In debates, you may have the occasion to debate proposition cases that seem to be truistic or otherwise unable to be debated. This does not mean that you should throw up your hands and surrender. Often these cases can be refuted by creative opposition strategies. For ideas, we suggest you learn more about the practice of criticism by reading the several argument chapters in this book. Remember that there are many ways to negate a case. One excellent strategy is to debate against the underlying assumptions of the case rather than the claims of the case itself.

Here is an example. On the topic "This House regrets the injustice," a proposition team might argue that the Holocaust should be condemned. How should opposition debaters argue this case? It appears to be a truism. Shouldn't society condemn the Holocaust? But there are actually have many possible lines of argument available. A debater might argue that the Holocaust shouldn't be removed from the historical list of genocidal atrocities and condemned in an individual way. You could say that this creates a special status for the Holocaust, and that the Holocaust shouldn't necessarily have a special status, even in the confines of World War II (during which at least 75 million died), nor among other genocides in history in which millions were killed, such as the ten million or more who perished in the conquest of the "New World," the Middle Passage, or the Belgian colonization of the Congo. The danger here is the marginalization of other genocides in order to focus on the Holocaust. One could argue that this exclusion might lead us to ignore the genocides in our midst—we therefore do nothing about Rwanda or Bosnia-Herzegovina, or we don't do anything in circumstances in which aboriginal people are assimilated into cultures or lose their land. Paradoxically, society may actually produce genocide victims by condemning the Holocaust or otherwise giving it a special status.

Further, a debater could say that when governments move to condemn the Holocaust, they do not identify their own moral responsibility in acts of violence. The implication of this argument might be that one shouldn't externalize blame for the problem. The United States refused to increase immigration quotas for Jews in the 1930's and did little to stop the Holocaust when it was underway. The US government continues to trade with—and to provide military and financial support to—countries that engage in serious human rights violations. Condemnation of the Holocaust might make us feel better about ourselves but may serve as a distraction from the serious questions that need to be asked about governmental and personal blame in past and present genocidal behavior. If you think these arguments are long shots or irrelevant, you should think again. These are all serious academic arguments—for example, these issues are raised in Ward Churchill's book, *A Little Matter of Genocide.*

Although specific knowledge and truism arguments can be valuable tools for the opposition, there are few occasions to introduce them in a legitimate way. Most topics interpretations are based on public information and produce cases that can be well argued by both teams in a debate. There is one additional theoretical matter regarding topic interpretation. This argument has a more standing than specific knowledge and truism claims—it genuinely directs itself to a logical inconsistency in a proposition team's case. Like specific knowledge and truism, it is unlikely that a debater will encounter many cases with the following flaw.

Tautology

Tautology is the final theoretical issue regarding the interpretation of a motion. A tautology, also known as circular logic, is an argument fallacy in which a speaker fails to engage the issues of the topic in a reasoned way. The complaint from the opposition team is that a proposition speaker, instead of providing a reasonable understanding or analysis of a motion, has merely repeated the motion again and again, typically confusing repetition of an idea with analysis or reasoning. Do not do this. Instead, offer reasoning to support your interpretation. Tautology is a rare affliction. It is possible to debate or judge for years and never cross one of these creatures.

Here is an example. On the motion, "This House prefers liberty to equality," a proposition speaker might offer the following tautological claims. "In this debate, we support the idea of liberty. Liberty is valuable—it is precious to all of us. That is because we all cherish our independence. Nothing is more important than our personal freedom." None of this explains the topic; it only needlessly repeats it. Debaters must offer a *proof* of the motion. Reasoning will provide a proof—repetition will not.

Repetition of claims may not be apparent to participants in the debate. Opposition debaters must be careful to pay attention to the full presentation of ideas in the opening proposition speech as well as the development of ideas in the second proposition constructive speech. Some tautologies develop during the debate. For example, an opening speaker might suggest that an important value for consideration is "equality—treating different people in the same way." When the value claim is challenged by the first opposition speaker, the second speaker for the proposition might reply to her by suggesting that equality matters because of its effect—it has the ability to eliminate disparities. The language of the second proposition speaker repeats the claim of the first proposition speaker. This may be difficult to identify, since the arguments are separated in time and delivered by different speakers.

The proposition team interprets a motion and subsequently provides a case that provides reasoning and examples to prove the motion. A tautology does not provide the required reasoning to prove the topic. This is the reason that an opposition team's successful claim that the proposition team has introduced a tautology is considered a sufficiently strong argument to win the debate for the opposition.

Suggested Exercises

1. Practice interpreting topics. Select a motion for interpretation. (There are more than 1,000 sample motions listed in Appendix 1.) Then take two minutes to imagine and outline an interpretation of the motion. Finally, take one minute to make a verbal presentation of the motion. Speak to an audience of your peers, who then have to answer the following questions:

Would the interpretation be convincing to a debate judge and why?

Has the speaker interpreted the motion in a way that successfully restricts the possibilities for opposing arguments?

What foundation is there for replies to opposition arguments about truism and specific knowledge?

2. Practice brainstorming interpretations. Have your teacher or coach present you with a motion for debate. By yourself or in a small group, take five minutes to list as many reasonable and different cases for the motion as possible.

Experimental Forms of Debate Motions

Debate tournaments will experiment with the language and number of motions for a debate. In each of these experiments, the proposed motion may be written as closed or open, although some of these experimental forms are designed to encourage more of one type of motion, either closed or open. In some cases, the proposition team is presented with a topic that may be logically affirmed or denied (e.g., *The United States should/should not end economic sanctions on Cuba.*) In some competitions using this form, the proposition team must announce the specific motion it will support (either end or do not end economic sanctions) before preparation time begins. In other events, the proposition team is not required to reveal its choice of interpretation until the debate is underway.

Some tournaments use conventional motions but provide 3 topics for each debate. In this case, the proposition team is able to strike or eliminate one of the topics from consideration and the opposition team is able to eliminate another from the pool of topics for the debate. The proposition team must use the remaining motion. This provides some topic choice, although a limited one, for the participants of a debate.

There are other, somewhat novel or experimental, forms of motions. There are motions that propose a general area of investigation, for example, "Africa" or "Olympic Games." Any reasonable idea related to the topic area could serve as a proper interpretation of the motion and a foundation for debate. This topic form provides the proposition team with considerable liberty. The opposition might not be able to anticipate, with any degree of success, either the issues for the debate or the direction of any suggested reform. (Will the proposition advocate more engagement with one or more African nations? Or will they suggest that nations withdraw support for national and sub-national groups engaging in human rights violations?) This motion type might be used in those circumstances in which a tournament director has determined that there is a decided bias for the opposition in the outcomes of debates about more specifically worded resolutions. The director might then use a focused but more ambiguous motion to provide equal opportunity for the proposition side to participate in a fair contest.

Another motion is the scenario. This motion offers an extended, detailed explanation of a crisis, condition, or bargaining position. Rather than a motion as a traditional single, simple, declarative sentence, the scenario may use one or several paragraphs to describe, through a series of chronological events, logical claims, or personal narratives, events that might constitute the subject for debate. Scenario construction necessarily limits substantive debating to the specifics designed by the tournament host. This may be appropriate as an academic exercise, a public event, or conference project, particularly for presentations to a specialized audience interested in the finely detailed descriptions of a case study. One example of a case study proposition is this one, used at a parliamentary tournament in the USA:

> Case Scenario: A doctor has just learned that the patient she is treating will probably not live beyond the next day. The patient knows he is terminal, but thinks he has at least another few weeks to live and has hope that there is a slim chance to pull through. Family members are already near by. The doctor's dilemma is whether to reveal the truth about patient's anticipated time of death. The proposition team must support the statement "the physician must make a full and complete disclosure to the patient and his family."

This kind of case study or scenario for debate may be an interesting and relevant exercise for conference debates or other kinds of public events; however, its use in intervarsity tournament competition can be problematic. Longer topics can inadvertently advantage the opposition team by providing more grist for opposition arguments, while binding the proposition team to a relatively narrower area to defend. In the example above, the opposition team could persuasively contest the phrase "and his family," arguing that the doctor only has a responsibility to the patient, and that the patient (rather than the physician) should decide whether and how to inform the family.

Experimental motions are valuable teaching tools and may provide challenging practice opportunities for students. A tournament host should consider testing any novel motion in practice debates and provide fair notice in tournament invitations and other announcements before "experimenting" on guests.

Notes

[1]Grove, Benjamin, "Anti-Yucca message spreads to Oregon, Utah: Donations to fund growing." *Las Vegas Sun*, May 10, 2002, www.lasvegassun.com.

[2]Weinstein, Henry, "Phillip Morris tried to 'bury' damaging nicotine research," South Coast Today.com (An Edition of the *Standard Times*), www.s-t.com/daily/09-96/09-18-96/b03lo073.htm.

[3]David Ross and Britain Express, http://www.britainexpress.com.

[4]Mitchell, Carolyn, "Renouncing the Death Penalty!" July 2000, www.bestfriends.org/nmhp/communities/renounce-ut.htm.

[5]Russel Mokhiber, "Business Ethics," November/December 1998, www.lightparty.com/Misc/CorporateDeath.html.

Chapter 5

Case Construction

Introduction to Case Construction

In parliamentary debate, the team that defends the proposition must persuade the judge to vote for the proposition. Basically, when you are on the side of the proposition, you are trying to convince the judge that the proposition is a good idea, so he or she should vote for it. In order to get the judge to vote for the proposition, you will have to make a *case* for voting for the topic. *If you are on the side of the proposition, your case is your proof of the motion for debate.* The proposition team must present a case in their first constructive speech. The opposition team tries to refute the case, or otherwise show why the case does not prove that the topic should be endorsed. The proposition team then tries to defend their case against the objections of the opposition team.

When you are confronted with a topic for debate, the first thing you need to figure out is how to prove the topic by making a case. This term "case" comes to us from law, where prosecutors will make a case against the defendant. How is this accomplished in the courtroom? Attorneys usually present different kinds of evidence and testimony to prove that the defendant is guilty. When you make a case for the topic, you will have to present evidence to prove the motion. You will also have to find a persuasive way to structure your evidence. It will not be good enough simply to present a bunch of arguments that are related to the topic in some way. You will need to organize your evidence to create a logical proof of the topic at hand.

Because the proposition team's case for the motion is so important if they are to win the debate, they must invest time and care when planning and constructing their case. In the four-person format, the proposition team seems to have some advantages because it has the first and last speeches in the debate. Because they get to interpret the motion, this team determines, to some extent, the subject matter for the debate. The proposition team establishes the decision-making framework for the debate.

Despite these obvious format advantages, there are also substantial advantages for the opposition. At the conclusion of the second proposition speech, the opposition has two consecutive speeches with a total of twelve minutes of speaking time (a seven-minute second opposition constructive speech followed immediately by a five-minute opposition rebuttal speech). As you have learned, these consecutive speeches are known as the opposition block.

The opposition team has more than enough time to manage the arguments made by the second proposition speaker. With a twelve-minute block of time, they can create some trouble for the final proposition speaker, who has only five minutes to answer their arguments. This imbalance has traditionally contributed to a small but significant bias for the opposition side in parliamentary debating in the USA. This bias may also occur in parliamentary debating with the four-person format outside the USA.

It is easier to tear down than to build a case. Opposition arguments might only need to target a single part of a case for victory in a debate. The proposition team must usually defend every element of its case to prove its side of the motion. Because of some important format advantages for the opposition, the proposition team must take great care in the selection, organization, and execution of its case.

In debates, you may be called upon to make a persuasive case for a policy motion, a fact motion, or a value motion. We will examine how to make a case in each of these circumstances.

Proving Policy Propositions

A policy proposition suggests or endorses a course of action or a range of courses of action. To prove a proposition of policy, you need to make a persuasive case for a course of action. For a few lessons on how to make this kind of case, we should turn to the experts: advertisers. All advertising is a type of persuasion. Advertisers try to persuade you to buy products, to change your lifestyle, or to take other actions. There are three basic components to any persuasive case for a course of action.

First: You must establish a need for change. You do this by showing an existing harm. Advertisers might try to convince you that you are thirsty, or unattractive, or that your existing phone service is bad and unreliable. Let's say the topic is "The government should provide comprehensive national health insurance." A proposition team should try to establish a need by arguing that existing health insurance provisions are inadequate. How would you prove this?

You might argue that millions go without health insurance now. In order to prove that this is a problem, you would have to demonstrate why this lack of insurance is bad. You need to describe the importance of your arguments in order to convince or persuade the judge to vote for your position. So after you argue that in the present system, millions are without health insurance, you should argue that this lack is bad because of health and economic harms. In debate, we call this establishing a *harm*, or a *need*.

Second: Once you have shown that there's a problem with the present system, you should move to present a solution or proposal. In advertising, they will show you the product. In debate, you may present a proposal, or plan. A **plan** is your proposal to solve the problem. Each specific proposal has its own advantages and disadvantages.

Third: Demonstrate that your proposal is, in fact, a solution to the harm you have outlined. If the proposition team presents a problem, then they must logically prove that their plan *solves* the problem. Why is this? Well, consider a scenario where the proposition team has persuasively argued that global warming is a serious problem. Once they have proven this harm, the proposition team advances a proposal to regulate lawnmowers (which use unleaded gasoline). Will this small proposal solve the larger problem? Unlikely, since the real cause of excessive worldwide greenhouse gas emission is *not* lawnmowers in the United States. This plan is an example of a proposal that does not solve the given harm.

In order to win the debate for their side, the proposition team must make a persuasive case for change of the type specified in the resolution. This means they must *at least* prove that a problem exists, propose a solution, and show that the plan will solve the problem. These are the basic burdens shouldered by the proposition team.

Suggested Exercise

> Practice making cases for propositions of policy. To start, make a simple case for "Students should be required to wear uniforms."

Proving Propositions of Fact

It is hard to debate propositions of fact. We usually do not even think about facts as things that are debatable. Instead, we are likely to think that something is either a fact or it is not. However, the idea that facts are not debatable is mistaken. At one time, everyone agreed that it was a *fact* that the sun revolved around the earth. It was also, for many thousands of years, a *fact* that the earth was flat. These ideas are, of course, not longer considered to be facts. Can you think of some other ideas that were once considered to be facts? What is it that makes something a *fact*? How is a fact said to be different from an *opinion*?

In debate, when you are called on to debate a proposition of fact, you will not have to try to prove or disprove the theory of gravity or other widely accepted scientific laws. It is more likely that you will have to debate about facts that are widely in dispute. How do you prove a scientific hypothesis? You have to test it, and produce a compelling body of evidence that the hypothesis is valid. When dealing with any proposition of fact, you first need to answer this question: *Under what circumstances could we call this statement a valid fact?* You will have to figure out the answer to this question yourself, but this endeavor is not as difficult as it might sound. Let's look at an example.

You might have to debate about whether or not the current welfare system works to keep people out of poverty: "The welfare system does not work." This is a proposition of fact. Clearly, to defend this proposition you must present a proof that the welfare system does not work. The best way to prove a proposition of fact is to establish several independent lines of proof. First, you will have to define your terms, so that everyone understands what it would mean to agree that the system does not work. Everyone can probably agree on what it means to say that a toaster does not work: it does not perform the function it is supposed to perform. What is a toaster supposed to do? It is supposed to heat bread to a designated temperature. Perhaps the toaster does not heat the bread at all. Perhaps it only burns the bread you put into it. Either of these possibilities means the toaster does not work.

So, to establish that the welfare system does not work, you will have to show that it does not perform the function it is supposed to perform. At this point in your analysis, you have found out the answer to the earlier question, *Under what circumstances could we call this statement a valid fact?* If we can show that the welfare system does not perform the function it is supposed to perform, then we have proven that the proposition is true.

So, now that you've discovered *how* to prove the proposition, you can proceed to the business of actually proving the proposition. The second step in analyzing a proposition of fact is to brainstorm arguments about the topic. What expectations do we have about our welfare systems? We expect a social safety net to keep people out of poverty. We expect that welfare will, in particular, help the most fragile elements of society—for example, children and the physically or mentally disabled. Finally, we might expect that our welfare system should help unemployed people get back into the workforce. These three expectations could all be part of your case. You might use each expectation as a segment of your case, structuring each as a separate line of argument or independent proof of the motion. A simple preliminary outline of your case for the motion might look like this:

> **1.** The welfare system does not work because it does not keep people out of poverty.
>
> **2.** The welfare system does not work because it does not protect the most fragile elements of society, such as children and the mentally or physically disabled.
>
> **3.** The welfare system does not work because it does not help unemployed people get back into the workforce.

Here, we have simply transferred the expectations we brainstormed previously into the form of arguments. We've taken the assertion of the topic, "The welfare system does not work," and offered three different reasons to prove that assertion. But following the A-R-E model of argument construction presented in chapter 1, this is incomplete, isn't it? The next step of constructing this simple case is to add evidence for each of these lines of reasoning.

Suggested Exercise

> As a research assignment, find some evidence for each of the lines of reasoning listed above in the sample 3-part case on the welfare system. You might work with a partner or a small group to accomplish this assignment. Once you have found some statistics or examples to prove each of these arguments, plug them into the case outline to complete the proof of the topic. Compare your findings with what other people in your class found. Which of the three claims, in your opinion, is the strongest? Which of the three claims, in your opinion, is the weakest? In your research, what other arguments did you find that might support this topic? What arguments and evidence did you find that might support the opposition side of this topic?

Generally, when you construct a case on a proposition of fact, you should advance at least three different lines of argument, or *reasons*, as your proof of the motion. It is important to emphasize that each of these reasons can be considered independently. In other words, you should argue that if you establish any one of these proofs of the topic, you should win the debate because you will have proven that, at least in this instance, the welfare system does not work. You want to make more than one argument for the motion because you want to maximize your options for later in the debate. It is usually foolish to make only one argument for the topic in the first proposition speech, because if the opposition team is able to answer that argument, or worse, is able to *turn* it and make it into an argument for their side, you will be in a bad position. It is better to make several good arguments at the beginning of the debate. You can always narrow your position down as the debate progresses.

The process we have used to build a case for welfare reform can be used to build a case for any proposition of fact. There are four major steps:

Step One: Figure out *how* to prove the topic. When you encounter a proposition of fact, define the terms in the topic so you can answer the question: Under what circumstances could we agree that this proposition is a fact?

Step Two: Brainstorm arguments for the topic. Come up with as many arguments as you can to prove the motion. Try adding "because" to the end of the topic to help you come up with reasons that it might be true.

Step Three: Organize those arguments, picking two to four arguments to serve as major points in your speech. Take the arguments you have brainstormed, then put similar arguments together. Pick your strongest arguments—usually the arguments for which you have the best evidence.

Step Four: Fill in your case by adding evidence to prove each point. Using your research as well as knowledge from your own life, add examples to prove each of your major points.

Once you have these parts of your case completed, and you have written an outline for your argument for the motion, you should make sure that you add an introduction, a conclusion, and appropriate transitions between your major points. We will discuss these aspects of making a case later in this chapter.

Suggested Exercise

Using what you have learned in this section, construct a case to prove the following proposition of fact: "The educational system prepares students for the world of work."

Proving Propositions of Value

Some topics, as you have learned, can be classified as *value topics*. This usually means that the topic compares two values or that the topic makes another argument about a value. Making a case on a value topic can be very similar to making a case on a proposition of fact. In many ways, thinking about values is the same as thinking about facts. A value case provides a proof for the motion by supporting a particular value. On the topic, "Give me liberty or give me death," the first speaker for the proposition team would identify reasons and evidence to support the value of liberty, in direct contrast with the value of life. On a proposition of fact, you have to prove that something is a valid fact. On a proposition of value, you have to prove that some value is good, or better than another value to which it is opposed.

We have just discussed the business of proving that something is a fact. How do you suppose that we might prove that something is good? This can be difficult. How do you explain, for example, that liberty is good, or is something that we should value? How about safety? Why do we believe that safety is good? Now, what if the two are in conflict? If you think this sounds complicated, you are right. Issues of value have been debated for many thousands of years, and in spite of this history we are still having significant debates today about these same values. Part of the problem is that it is hard to agree on what is meant by different kinds of values.

For example, many people these days talk a lot about family values, but it is not at all clear that there is general agreement on what they mean by the term "family values." Do all families look the same? Do they all behave in the same way? Do they all have the same values? Of course not. This diversity of perspectives guarantees that there are many different interpretations of what the values called "family values" actually are. When people talk about "family values," they may take that term to mean, "respect for others." Others might interpret the term to mean "supporting households led by a married male and female." Finally, others might use that term to support or reject same-sex marriages and adoptions. There is a substantial debate over the meaning of the term. Interpretation is important in this, as in any debate.

Values are abstract ideas that mean different things to different people in different circumstances. Values may also contain contradictory meanings. For example, we all experience liberty when independent. We also experience liberty in dependence. You experience freedom when you are able to do something. You also experience freedom when someone else protects you. Consider that nobody wants the government to control their lives, since that would restrict their freedom. However, most people want to win the lottery, even though that would mean substantial government control over their life. Having the government provide your income for the rest of your life is a pretty serious dependence on the government. Yet we can all agree that it would be liberating to win the lottery, because you would be pretty much free to do or buy whatever you wanted.

All this means that *we have to look at a specific circumstance* to determine whether or not we are going to endorse a particular value. Just agreeing that you support liberty in the abstract does not really mean anything because that support needs to be given context by looking at a specific example. Instead of saying, "I support liberty," you might say, "I support your liberty *to...*" Liberty is not just good on its own. As another example, consider the value of equality. All of us want equality. We want to be treated the same as other people, and do not like it when we feel we are being treated unequally. However, we *also* want a kind of special treatment in that we want be acknowledged for our unique talents. If you have a competitive debate with another team and you feel as if you have won the debate, you want to be recognized as the winner.

Consider that very few people, if any, would say that they are opposed to liberty. In fact, most people say that they are in favor of liberty. But, as it turns out, these people are seldom *always* in favor of liberty all the time and in every circumstance. Most people would not argue that other people were free to kill them. If you are in favor of freedom, but not the freedom of someone else to kill or injure you, then you are in favor of a kind of liberty that does you no harm.

You can't just prove that a value is good in the abstract. To make a case for a value in a debate, you need to pick a specific scenario or policy and then use that scenario to prove the topic. You should pick an application of the idea expressed in the topic that has to do with personal, corporate, or governmental decision-making. When interpreting a value topic, you should work to *come up with a central example to serve as a proof of the larger motion.* In other words, do not try and debate the statement generally. Instead, use an example to provide your proof. It is difficult to talk about security and personal freedom in the abstract. As an experiment, try to explain what freedom is without using any concrete examples.

Most (but not all) value topics compare two values and ask the proposition team to show why we should endorse one value rather than the other. Let's say that you are asked to make a case for the topic: "This House would value security over personal freedoms." How would you go about proving this proposition? As you already know, you first need to interpret the topic and define your terms so you know *how* to prove the topic. This will usually mean that you need to interpret the topic so that it is narrow. It is difficult to talk about security and personal freedom in the abstract. As an experiment, try to explain what freedom is without using any concrete examples.

You will need to explain what you mean by security and personal freedom, so that you know how to prove the proposition. The statement is too vague to be proven in the abstract: Personal freedom to do what? Whose security? Who provides the security? The topic statement is given to you to interpret. Your case should prove your interpretation of the topic, because once you have given an interpretation, your interpretation *is* the topic.

When you brainstorm, you should think of examples that prove your interpretation of the motion. For this topic, you would need to come up with some specific situations in which security is more important than personal freedom. Using specific examples or scenarios will help you to build a persuasive case for the proposition. What are some situations in which you could argue that security is more important than personal freedom? Most societies have legal limits on who can own a gun and on what kind of guns those people can own. This is a situation in which society has agreed that security is more important than personal freedom—it would be very dangerous, for example, to have convicted murderers wandering around with automatic weapons.

So you now have the kernel of your case. To prove the topic, you will need to make a case for gun control. What arguments can you make for gun control? People who advocate gun control argue that gun control would reduce violent crime, because people are likely to use their guns in disputes. Gun control might also save children's lives. Every year in the US alone, thousands of children die from gun-related accidents. Finally, you need to argue these risks to personal security are more important than the potential harm to personal freedoms. All three of these arguments for gun control might become major points in your case for the topic.

Think of this case for the topic using the A-R-E model. The *assertion* is the topic: "This House would value security over personal freedoms." The *reasoning* can be found in your basic case statement: "Safety from guns is more important than the personal freedom to own guns." Finally, the *evidence* for the overall proof of the motion is found in your other arguments, which show that the costs of gun violence are high and the potential impact on personal liberties is relatively low.

Once you have come up with your examples, use the four-part model to build a case for the topic:

Step One: Discover *how* to prove the topic. You need to define the terms of the topic and interpret the topic so that you will know *how* to go about making a case for the topic.

Step Two: Brainstorm examples and arguments. Come up with a core example that you feel proves your side of the topic.

Step Three: Organize your examples and arguments. Sort the results of step two into two to four major points that will form the bulk of your case for the proposition. Choose your best examples and arguments during this process.

Step Four: Draw conclusions from your examples to show that they prove the topic. In this last step, you will need to link your examples back to the proposition. In the gun control example we gave above, you would have to show that that example *proves* that security should be valued above personal freedom.

Suggested Exercise ═══════════════════════════════

Using the four-step model, practice making different cases on value topics. Make a case for the topic: "This House would endorse the right to privacy." After you have accomplished this, make a case for the topic "Free speech should be restricted."

Preparation Time Prior to the Debate

Now that you know some of the basics of case construction, you will have to learn to apply this knowledge in debates. In debates, you use your preparation time to construct cases. Sometimes you will have a long time to prepare a case. You may have assignments in class where you have a week or more to prepare for a debate. In competitive tournament debating, however, there are limits to the time you will have to prepare. There is only one preparation time ("prep time") period in parliamentary debating, the period between the announcement of the topic and the first speech by the first proposition speaker. Usually, this period will be 15 to 20 minutes long, and will be the only preparation time available to the debaters. This short preparation time is one of the most unique and challenging parts of parliamentary debate. Topics for debate come from a variety of areas, and you will have to be ready to make and dispute cases on all kinds of subject matter. This may seem intimidating, but with the right preparation and knowledge you will be able to succeed and thrive in this format.

Usually, you will be familiar enough with the topic to begin preparation in earnest after the motion is announced. How should you prepare? There is no one way to do this effectively. The language of the topic will influence how you prepare. Also, you will probably prepare differently depending on how much you know about the topic.

Proper prep time management involves individual work and teamwork. Since 15–20 minutes is not a very long period of time, you and your partner will need to develop a plan, lest you waste this time on unnecessary tasks and end up starting the debate unprepared and flustered. Part of this plan should be an arrangement with your partner for how you will use your prep time. This will allow the two of you to maximize the available time and start the debate with your best foot forward. Once you have participated in several debates, it will be easier for you to know how to best use your prep time.

Debaters sometimes work together for the full duration of preparation time. This is a common mistake. If you work with your partner the whole time, you will limit your prep time (more on debate mathematics in a moment). You might also end up engaging in *groupthink*. Also known as tunnel vision, groupthink occurs when the two partners on a debate team share an agenda set by only one person. This means that you will produce fewer arguments during prep time. Debaters with tunnel vision are more likely to have unseen errors in the design of their cases. These errors are often unseen until the opposing side gets a chance to listen to the first proposition speaker.

What should the proposition team do during preparation time? Our recommendation is for the two debaters to work individually for a minute or so. During this time, each debater should carefully analyze the topic. Both should think of several ideas for the case that they must construct. Then, the debaters should work together for a minute or two. During this time, the debaters should share their ideas on:

- How they should interpret the topic.
- What kind of case they should make for the topic.
- What examples and other evidence they can use to flesh out the case and subsequent speeches.

After the debaters reach agreement on these issues, they should resume individual work. The first speaker for the proposition should immediately start preparing the opening speech. She should generate lines of argument and organize them for a coherent and entertaining address. At the same time, the second speaker for the proposition should begin preparing her speech.

How should the second proposition speaker prepare her stand on the floor? Is it possible for her to prepare before she has heard the opposition's first speech? The proposition team's second speaker should anticipate the opposing side's likely strategy for the debate and prepare her arguments accordingly. This speaker should begin to analyze the debate from the opposition team's perspective. She should ask herself:

- What are the potential weaknesses in our case?
- What kinds of arguments would I make if I were facing this case on the opposition?
- What are the general opposition arguments one might expect on this topic?
- Finally, how will I answer these arguments when they come up?

This process of anticipation accomplishes the following:

- **Preparation for the second speech**. The second speaker in the debate has little free time to craft an organized and clever speech once the proceedings are underway. It is better to begin preparation in a less stressful environment.

- **Argument anticipation**. The second speaker can identify potential flaws or inconsistencies in the opening speaker's argument by identifying arguments the other team may make and finding answers to those arguments.

Instead of collaborating with her partner, this debater should critically evaluate the logic of her partner's case and expose those problems before the debate begins. Also, anticipating the opposition's arguments allows the second speaker to advise her partner to make changes or additions to the first proposition speech.

After the individual preparation, the speakers need to join together and review ideas for several minutes. Sharing information at this point is particularly valuable, as the opportunity for individual work has spurred creativity, and there are plenty of new ideas on the table. The debaters should use the final few minutes of prep time to complete the case outline or the second speaker's replies to opposition points. The second speaker may have also found one or more clever ways to amplify the arguments in the opening speech.

Debaters should have an inexpensive digital timer as an aid for debate. The timer will help debaters track speech time during the debate, and also help with prep time management. It is too easy for debaters to become distracted during preparation time. A digital clock will keep you on task.

A sample 15-minute preparation period might look like the one below:

Individual assessment of the motion	1 minute
Shared discussion of the motion	3 minutes
Individual preparation of speeches	5 minutes
Shared discussion of speech preparation	3 minutes
Final speech preparation	3 minutes

Debate teams should experiment with their prep time to find the time allocations that work for them. Times should be adjusted for different partners, topics, or other circumstances. If you use your prep time this way, you will find that you have more than 15 minutes of actual preparation time, with some time devoted exclusively to the second speaker's preparation.

When preparing for debate, you should carefully consider all of the different issues on a topic. You should try to devote some prep time to all of the following:

- Anticipate several of the major lines of argument from the opposing side.
- Preparing the introductions and conclusions for your speeches.
- Interpreting the motion.
- Speech structure and humor.

In other words, your preparation should be comprehensive. Before a competition, you should prepare notes on many of these issues. As you will learn later, it is a good idea to prepare cases and other notes for debate before every competition. If you organize materials and information before the competition, you will not have to "reinvent the wheel" before each debate.

Suggested Exercise ══════════════════════════════

Practice timed preparation. Have your coach, trainer, or another teammate announce a motion, or pick one from the list at the end of this book. With a partner, take 15 minutes to prepare to debate that motion. After the 15 minutes has expired, review the materials you have produced. Would you feel comfortable debating with these materials? How could you have improved your use of prep time? What research materials or other prepared notes could have made preparation easier?

This exercise should be repeated periodically. Practicing timed preparation is critical to learning to work with your partner. It also keeps your skills sharp between competitive debates.

Structuring the Proposition Case

Debates can be quite complicated. Topics usually deal with fairly sophisticated social, political and cultural issues. Debaters can introduce as many as a dozen major lines of argument in each debate, with accompanying examples. The best way to keep a debate manageable and winnable is to start with a simple and elegant case design. Whether you are making a case for a fact, value, or policy motion, you should pay careful attention to the basics of speech organization.

A basic proposition case should be based on a basic narrative form—that is, your case should have an introduction, a body and a conclusion. The opening speech for the proposition should include the following:

- A speech introduction.
- An interpretation of the motion.
- A case that supports the motion.
- A speech conclusion.

Introducing the Speech

Although it may be tempting to just begin discussing the substance of your case, you need to use a speech introduction to establish your credibility and offer a powerful introduction on the subject matter of the case. For example, on the topic, "This House would right the wrongs," a proposition team might argue for checks on the presentation of eyewitness testimony in courts. Although eyewitness testimony is very persuasive to jurors and therefore affects many criminal trials, it is extremely unreliable. Thousands of individuals are wrongly convicted each year because of the prosecution's decision to present eyewitness testimony.

A first proposition speaker might offer the following introduction for the case:

"There is no greater wrong, no greater injustice than the wrongful conviction of an innocent person. When you hear about someone who was wrongfully committed, you may think that perhaps there was a serious mistake by the defense. But the fact is that the leading cause of wrongful conviction is testimony that jurors hear from eyewitnesses.

Ladies and gentlemen of the audience, the proposition team has an opportunity to address a disgraceful problem that victimizes thousands of people every year. We do so with our support of the motion, 'This House would right the wrongs.'"

The introduction should be brief. It should provide striking information to get the attention of the judge and audience. An effective introduction provides a preview of the case without giving away the most critical issues in the first 30 seconds of the debate. If the introduction offers too much information, the opposing side will immediately begin preparing refutation for their speeches. This will allow the opposition more time for preparation during the debate, something you should try to avoid if you are on the proposition side. In a typical debate, ideas unfold throughout the proposition team's opening speech. This delays (if only by a little) the opposition's preparation of effective refutation strategies.

All speakers in a debate should have introductions to their speeches. As a speaker, you will need to establish yourself as an effective participant in the debate before you can engage an audience. You may also want to gain favor with an audience by using humor to introduce your speech. There is nothing quite as powerful as being able to entertain an audience. If the audience believes that you can entertain them as well as inform them, they are more likely to be persuaded by your speeches.

Don't introduce your presentation as a *reaction* to an opposing side's preceding speech. This technique subtly shifts the focus of the debate to your opponent's issues. The ideas that you want to present in the debate might be lost along the way. It is better to establish *your* foundation for argument before you begin to react to arguments made by your opponents.

Interpreting the Motion

The first speaker for the proposition team should interpret the topic. This means that she should give meaning to the topic to focus the debate. The topic really has no meaning until the opening proposition speaker interprets it for debate. Without this part of the opening speech, the debate topic may have different meanings for different teams in the debate. The meaning of words is not fixed and changes with the context of their use.

As you learned in Chapter 3, there are many potential interpretations of any given topic. Some of the possibilities are reasonable and might serve as a foundation for a powerful case. Other potential interpretations make little sense. The proposition team is responsible for selecting a *meaningful interpretation for debate*. There are several options here for the proposition team but many are unsavory or fail to focus the discussion in a coherent way. The proposition side will not able to sustain a case without solid and comprehensive lines of argument offering a proof for the motion.

The opposing side is not concerned, in the same manner as the proposition team, about the successful interpretation of the motion. If the motion is absurd or otherwise incoherent, it should be easy for the opposition to win the debate. This is a primary reason that the interpretation of the motion ought to remain mostly within the control of the proposition side.

Constructing the Case Proper

A **case** is a set of arguments that provide a proof for the motion. Debaters sometimes use the term **"case proper"** to refer to the elements of their case that provide the substance of the debate. The "case proper" is usually that part of the first proposition speaker's presentation that directly provides support for the topic.

Most parliamentary cases could generally be described as policy cases. A **policy case**, as you have already learned, endorses a specific public policy reform. The opening speaker for the proposition does this using a process that identifies a problem and proposes a solution to the problem. In other words, the proposition team offers a case that attempts to correct a serious economic, social or political problem.

With this case form, the proposition team constructs a comparison between the present system and a hypothetical future. The opening speaker for the proposition identifies problems in the present system. The present system is also sometimes known as the **status quo** in some forms of debate. *Status quo* is a Latin phrase that basically means "the existing state of affairs at this time."

The speaker has certain obligations in order to prove the legitimacy of her case. The speaker must first identify a **problem**. Debaters are aware of many of the world's problems, social crises, and other calamities. But what are the constituent elements of a problem? You'll need to know these to offer a proof that an intractable problem does indeed exist. A condition is said to be a problem if it is (1) **ongoing** with (2) **serious negative repercussions**.

If an issue is no longer a contemporary economic, social or political matter, it is not a problem. Few people today are worried about the potential of forced conscription to participate in the Crusades. But many individuals are concerned with increasing cycles of violence and intolerance in the Middle East. Considering the ongoing nature of the matter, the former is not a problem but the latter most definitely is.

Negative repercussions are often identified as matters of **significance**. The significance of an issue has to do with its qualitative and quantitative dimension. For example, how seriously does the issue profoundly affect the life of an individual and how many individuals are troubled by this matter? A problem grows greater as it bothers people more and as more lives are touched.

In a debate, you should include an explanation of the ongoing nature of a problem and the degree of its significance. It is not necessary to include formal debate jargon while undertaking these tasks in a speech, but it is important that you (and by extension, your audience) understand the elements of a problem. This knowledge is the only way to ensure that you will have a comprehensive and logical presentation of a proof. In addition, the logic of the construction provides some basic structure to a speech. It assists the speaker to organize her comments for easy understanding by a judge or audience.

After establishing the foundation of a problem, the speaker proposes a **solution**. The name of this kind of argument is a **solvency claim**. A debater claims solvency when she claims that her proposal will solve a harm. Once again, it is not necessary to use debate jargon in an actual debate to discuss arguments involving solutions. Jargon and technical speech are not elegant forms of communication and can also confuse an audience unused to the terminology. It is, however, helpful to be familiar with technical debate speech, if only to understand an opponent who might use such language.

The solution to a problem should be well defined and technically feasible. A comprehensive solution to a problem should include a plan of action and sufficient argumentation and information to sustain the claim that the plan adequately fixes the problem.

The **plan** is the formal expression of a solution to a problem. It should be brief but sufficient to provide a meaningful solution to the identified problem. The plan might be a summary of model legislation, agency or executive action, a sample court decree, etc. that would successfully address the problem.

A plan might answer the following questions regarding agency, scope of regulatory authority and implementation:

- Who will do it?
- What are they required to do?
- How will they accomplish their goals?

Answers to these questions will satisfactorily address the issues regarding a solution to a problem, at least for the purposes of initiating debate on the matter. The proposition team should identify one or more of the parties responsible for an action, describe the scope of their authority, and discuss the manner of policy implementation. If you are suggesting that a particular policy should be enacted, you might want to look for models in other, similar policies that have been tried elsewhere or in the past.

There may be other advantages to a plan of action. The opening proposition speaker may discuss the scope of a problem, its proposed solution, and additional benefits. For example, a proposition team might argue for a single-payer system of national health insurance in the USA. The reason for the proposal might be to offer a proof for the motion that "This House would bring them in." A proposition team might interpret this motion to be a reference to those individuals currently without health insurance or underinsured. The case may be based on principles of equality but might have the additional benefit of spurring health and medical research. The proposition team might argue that if there are more people involved in the public health care system, it would be easier for investors to commit funds to health research and development, because the addition of tens of millions of new health and medical consumers is likely to add to the payoffs of future research and development.

Suggested Exercise

Debaters should take a motion and construct a model opening speech for the proposition side of the motion, including introduction, interpretation of the motion, case proper, and conclusion. This exercise should be repeated using any of the sample topics from the selection in the back of this book.

The Speech Conclusion

The conclusion of a speech is as important as the introduction. Debaters should deliver powerful final comments in support of their side of the motion. A concluding remark of no more than 10 or 15 seconds ought to summarize the relative positions of the teams in the debate, identify a consistent and powerful theme associated with the presentation of the case, or remind the judge and audience of the serious matters under consideration. This technique will leave the judge with a final persuasive appeal for the case.

Final Notes on Case Construction

Framing the Debate

Every discussion or debate has a frame, or context, that determines the course of the conversation. To understand the concept of framing, think about how a frame affects a picture. The frame acts to direct the eye, to emphasize that you (the viewer) are supposed to pay attention to what is inside the frame and disregard what is outside the frame. In school, class discussions are framed by the content of the course. For example, in a math class, you probably never hear extended discussions about literature. This is because the title of the course ("Math") and expectations about that title ("I think we're going to learn about math in this class") guide the course of conversations in that class.

Usually, conversations are framed by factors other than course title. Your standing in an interaction with another person can determine the course of that interaction. Your title, age, or other social role can determine where you stand in a conversation and what kind of credibility you will have in that conversation. For example, what kind of credibility do children normally have when arguing with their parents? How about the credibility drivers have with police officers that have stopped them for speeding? The roles of the participants frame the discussion, and to some extent will determine the outcome of these discussions.

Debates, like any conversation, are also subject to framing. Because debaters compete to win debates, both sides in a contest will try to frame the debate so that they are more likely to win. Debaters should think forward, always anticipating their final speech. They should plan accordingly. It is not enough to know how to begin a debate. We know, for example, that all ideas are subject to disagreement. We know that debaters will present opposing viewpoints on the motion. But debate is about more than disagreement. Clash between arguments is necessary for debate, but simple clash does not make a debate. The art of debate is about the effective *resolution* of arguments in dispute.

Debaters should frame issues for comparison so that the debate will conclude in their favor. As experienced competitors know, what matters is not how debates begin but how they end. Judges are often persuaded largely by the last few speeches of the debate, when issues are summarized and compared. During the debate, you need to anticipate the "end game." This means that you should introduce arguments that you hope will ultimately resolve the debate in your favor. For example, if you were arguing for gun control, you might try to frame the debate by saying that the judge should endorse the proposal that saves the most lives rather than trying to preserve rights, because life is a more important value than freedom.

This framing process will ideally begin in the first proposition speech and continue throughout the debate as both sides try to frame the debate to their advantage. This sometimes results in two debates happening in the same debate—often, you will find yourself debating a debate and also debating about the debate as you try to frame the arguments to your advantage.

In some parliamentary formats and leagues, debaters present formal decision-making **criteria** to direct the judge's decision. The decision-making criterion may involve general guidelines for a judge's consideration of the debate's arguments. Debaters often call for judges to decide debates on "the preponderance of the evidence" or "a cost-benefit calculus." These proof standards are like the standards used in criminal or civil trials, or the standards used in government agencies. The judge is instructed to use the offered criterion to decide the debate. For example, if both teams agree that the debate should be decided using a cost-benefit analysis, then the judge should assess the costs and benefits of proposed action. The judge should then, according to this standard, choose the course of action that has the most benefits and the fewest costs.

The problem for proposition teams using criteria to frame a debate is usually the exclusive use of a single criterion for decision making. Decision making is complex. Many factors are involved in reaching a decision. Even a simple decision involves a series of important decisions. For example, consider the act of getting a meal in a restaurant. When you order something off the menu, you do not only use price to make your decision. ("The quality and taste of the food do not matter, just bring me the cheapest item.") Nor would you decide exclusively because of a food's taste, presentation, or nutritional content. It is the combination of these decision-making elements that lead to an action.

Debate decisions are much more complicated than ordering off a menu. The issues of a debate may involve sophisticated discussions of public policy reform. They might involve multiple actors and stakeholders. They might deal with national or international issues. A single, exclusive criterion will probably be too simplistic to deal with all of the complicated issues in any given debate.

The Diversity of Topics

In parliamentary debate, most cases can loosely be called policy cases. Debaters identify a problem and then propose a solution. This is consistent with the parliamentary roots of parliamentary debating. Parliamentary governing bodies do not get together to debate about issues of fact or value for the sake of doing so. They are serious about the business of governing. Parliamentary bodies convene to plan and re-shape public policies. This means that even if a parliamentary body is discussing whether or not, for example, the welfare system works, they are having that discussion in order to shape public policy; they are not having the discussion for its own sake. For this reason, debaters should not be shy about proposing solutions or arguing policy cases on propositions that seem to be exclusively about facts or values. Remember that it is more or less impossible to argue about facts and values without talking about specific policies in any case. So why not use those issues of fact and value as jumping-off points to talk about potential solutions to the problems you are describing?

Suggested Exercise

Imagine that you are given the topic for debate: "Protecting individual liberty is more important than promoting security." Use the articles that follow to construct a case for the topic. Read the articles carefully, underlining or highlighting relevant arguments and evidence. Then use your research to build a case and an outline for your case for the topic.

Civil Liberties and War; How Bright The Beacon?

By Mary L. Dudziak. Mary L. Dudziak is a professor of law at the University of Southern California and author of "Cold War Civil Rights: Race and the Image of American Democracy;"

Civil liberties are domestic matters. Foreign affairs are international matters. The two issues would not seem to intersect, and yet they did last week in the Senate Judiciary Committee. Attorney General John Ashcroft testified before the committee, defending the Bush administration's executive order providing for military tribunals to prosecute non-citizens charged with terrorism and the wielding of other broad new powers. Some senators and others fear that these measures could violate civil liberties, but Ashcroft's concern was that this debate itself could weaken the war on terrorism. "To those who pit Americans against immigrants and citizens against non-citizens, to those who scare peace-loving people with phantoms of lost liberty, my message is this: Your tactics only aid terrorists, for they erode our national unity and diminish our resolve. They give ammunition to America's enemies, and pause to America's friends."

The attorney general emphasized that these powers would be applied only against immigrants. He defended secret detention of persons that the government cannot link to terrorist activity and the legitimacy of death sentences by a military tribunal decided on just a majority vote, insisting that all of these measures are "designed to protect the interests of the United States."

But just what are the "interests of the United States" at a time like this? Is the United States best served by expanding prosecutorial powers to their outermost limits, or by tempering law enforcement with a respect for individual liberties? It's an especially important question at this moment, because the ability of the United States to hold together its thinly glued multinational coalition against terror could hang in the balance.

Is anyone in the administration giving thought to what message these measures communicate to the rest of the world? The lessons of history suggest that they should be. Domestic social and cultural matters can impact U.S. prestige and influence around the world.

Nearly 40 years ago, the Senate also took up the issue of domestic individual rights and foreign affairs. In 1963, it was Secretary of State Dean Rusk who told senators that the country's record on civil rights "had a profound impact on the world's view of the United States and, therefore, on our foreign relations." In his view, the interests of the United States required greater civil rights protection and passage of a bill that would eventually become the Civil Rights Act of 1964.

At the height of the Cold War, U.S. leaders presented the nation as a beacon of light and as a model for others struggling to overcome oppression. Yet domestic injustice undercut the moral power of the nation's message and in fact damaged relations with many countries.

Said Rusk: "The United States is widely regarded as the home of democracy and the leader of the struggle for freedom, for human rights, for human dignity. We are expected to be the model....So our failure to live up to our proclaimed ideals are noted—and magnified and distorted."

Normally, we do not think of the secretary of state as engaged in domestic issues, yet Rusk would write in his memoirs that "racism and discrimination...had a major impact on my life as secretary of state....Stories of racial discrimination in the United States and discriminatory treatment accorded diplomats from the many newly independent countries of the old colonial empires began to undermine our relations with these countries." And, Rusk wrote, "In their efforts to enhance their influence among the nonwhite peoples and to alienate them from us, the Communists clearly regard racial discrimination in the United States as one of their most valuable assets."

Race discrimination was widely thought to be America's Achilles heel—by the nation's friends as well as its critics. According to a 1950 report, "Our segregation, mob violence and our Dixiecrats contribute grist to European mills of anti-Americanism. To preach democratic equality while making distinctions of color and race strikes Europeans as bizarre, if not perverse." Secretary of State Dean Acheson said in 1952 that in many countries "the view is expressed more and more vocally that the United States is hypocritical in claiming to be the champion of democracy while permitting practices of racial discrimination here in this country."

When the Kennedy administration sent troops to Oxford, Miss., to enable James Meredith, an African-American student, to register at the university there, the U.S. ambassador to India, Chester Bowles, believed the action could be "a turning point not only in our struggle against segregation in this country, but in our efforts to make the people of Asia, Africa and Latin America understand what we are trying to do."

The Bush administration has recognized the importance of overseas perceptions of the United States and recently even turned to Hollywood in the hope that the movie industry will produce films that will help polish the nation's image overseas. But history shows that during the Cold War, films, books and pamphlets pointing out the benefits of American democracy went only so far if the news from America told a different story. For example, the U.S. Information Agency prepared a positive film about the 1963 March on Washington and hoped that African leaders would view it. But in the aftermath of a church bombing in Birmingham that killed four African-American girls, one African leader replied to an invitation to view the film by saying, "Don't you have a film of the church dynamiting, too?"

Today, as we try to maintain an international coalition against terrorism, our allies have objected to threats to civil liberties in the United States. Spanish officials are balking about extraditing eight men charged in the Sept. 11 attacks unless the men are tried in a civilian court, and the 15 European Union countries, all of which have banned the death penalty, are said to have similar reservations. It is a good time to recall the words of President Harry S Truman, spoken before Congress in 1948: "If we wish to inspire the people of the world whose freedom is in jeopardy, if we wish to restore hope to those who have already lost their civil liberties, if we wish to fulfill the promise that is ours, we must correct the remaining imperfections in our practice of democracy." Protecting rather than restricting liberties is vital to maintaining our influence in the world.

On gag rules, spy tools and freedom of speech

John Ashcroft wants to know what you're reading.

That's but one chilling implication of the USA Patriot Act, which was rushed into law following the Sept. 11 tragedy, ostensibly to expand the tools authorities use to catch spies and terrorists. Combine it with new Bush administration policies obscuring the public's view of government and limiting access to public records and presidential papers, and what emerges is a pattern of assaults on the First Amendment, cloaked in swagger about national security and patriotism. America will be neither safer nor stronger if its elected leaders hide their activities, and if free-thinking citizens cannot assess the merits and foundations of their decisions. Yet Mr. Ashcroft has made it easier for federal agencies to deny citizens' Freedom of Information requests for documents paving a paper trail of government action. And repositories of federal reports have been ordered to shred dozens of documents to prevent public inspection.

America will not be made secure by allowing the Justice Department to pry into library patron records, which many states have declared confidential, or by requiring bookshops to reveal the titles that customers are buying. Yet the Patriot Act allows the FBI to act on suspicion and secretly study a person's reading habits in terrorism or espionage investigations. There's a gag order prohibiting librarians and booksellers from telling anyone—even the customer himself—that borrowing records have been seized.

The chilling effect is far-reaching.

A decade ago, the American Library Association (ALA) believed it had successfully ended snooping in the stacks by exposing and protesting the FBI's monitoring of Eastern European patrons with the hope of catching Soviet spies. Now the Patriot Act reissues Big Brother's library pass, according to ALA spokesmen.

American Booksellers Association members, especially small independent stores, also are alarmed. Should they maintain or purge customer records, which could build the business but now also can be used to breach the customers' trust?

To be sure, the anxiety existed before Sept. 11, but booksellers were able to rely on the First Amendment to challenge and, where possible, quash search warrants. This month, for example, the Colorado Supreme Court upheld a Denver bookstore's right to protect its sales record from police review. According to the ALA, searches initiated under the Patriot Act cannot be challenged.

Librarians and booksellers are joining forces with civil liberties groups to protest these incursions on the freedom to read, which is a cornerstone of free speech. But they need readers as well to join in asserting that intellectual curiosity is not a luxury but a patriotic and democratic duty.

The worthy goal of protecting America from assault does not justify the dismantling of freedoms protected by the Constitution. And if the heinous acts of Sept. 11 prompt us to abandon the very liberties essential to our democracy, what are we fighting for?

The Progressive Magazine, *December 2001.*

Why should we care? It's only the Constitution
by Nat Henthoff

Two nights after the September 11 attack, the Senate swiftly, by voice vote after thirty minutes of debate, attached to a previously written appropriations bill an amendment making it much easier for the government to wiretap computers of terrorism suspects without having to go to various courts to get multiple search warrants. The bipartisan bill was introduced by Senator Orrin Hatch, Republican of Utah, and Dianne Feinstein, Democrat of California. "Terrorism" was not defined.

That was the beginning of the steamroll. Now Attorney General John Ashcroft has gotten his way with his originally titled Anti-Terrorism Act of 2001, which coolly contradicted the earnest assertions of the President and the Secretary of Defense that necessary security measures would not violate our fundamental liberties because our freedom is what we are fighting for. The final legislation passed the Senate on October 25 by a vote of 98 to 1, with only Russ Feingold, Democrat of Wisconsin, dissenting. In the House, the bill passed 356 to 66.

The new law will permit government agents to search a suspect's home without immediately notifying the object of the search. In J. Edgar Hoover's day, this was known as a "black bag job." The FBI then never bothered to get a search warrant for such operations. Now, a warrant would be required, but very few judges would turn a government investigator down in this time of fear. Ashcroft's "secret searches" provision can now extend to all criminal cases and can include taking photographs, the contents of your hard drive, and other property. This is now a permanent part of the law, not subject to any sunset review by Congress.

Ashcroft also asked for roving wiretaps-a single warrant for a suspect's telephone must include any and all types of phones he or she uses in any and all locations, including pay phones. If a suspect uses a relative's phone or your phone, that owner becomes part of the investigative database. So does anyone using the same pay phone or any pay phone in the area.

Ashcroft neglected to tell us, however, that roving wiretaps already became law under the Clinton Administration in 1998. At that time, only Congressman Bob Barr, Republican of Georgia, spoke against it in Congress, while the media paid little attention to this brazen attack on the Fourth Amendment.

But Ashcroft demanded and received a radical extension of these roving wiretaps: a one-stop national warrant for wiretapping these peripatetic phones. Until now, a wiretap warrant was valid only in the jurisdiction in which it was issued. But now, the government won't have to waste time by having to keep going to court to provide a basis for each warrant in each locale.

The expansion of wiretapping to computers, and thereby the Internet, makes a mockery of Internet champion John Perry Barlow's 1996 "Declaration of the Independence of Cyberspace":

"Governments of the industrial world, on behalf of the future, I ask you of the past to leave us alone....You have no sovereignty where we gather...nor do you possess any methods of enforcement we have true reason to fear. Cyberspace does not lie within your borders."

This government invasion of cyberspace fulfills the prophecy of Justice Louis Brandeis, who warned, in his dissent in the first wiretapping case before the Supreme Court, Olmstead v United States (1928), "Ways may some day be developed by which the Government, without removing papers from secret drawers, can reproduce them in court, and by which it will be enabled to

expose to a jury the most intimate occurrences of the home."

This has come to pass. The government now has access to bank records, credit card purchases, what has been searched for on the Internet, and a great deal more for those who have "supported," or are suspected of terrorism.

Moreover, as Brandan Koerner, a fellow at the New America Foundation, has pointed out in the Village Voice, the bill that Congress passed so hastily on the night of September 13-and is now part of the law- "lowers the legal standards necessary for the FBI to deploy its infamous Carnivore surveillance system." Without showing-as the Fourth Amendment requires-probable cause that a crime has been committed or is about to be committed, the government invades what's left of your privacy.

The fearful name "Carnivore" disturbed some folks, and so it has been renamed DCS 1000. Carnivore, Koerner notes, is "a computer that the Feds attach to an Internet service provider. Once in place, it scans email traffic for 'suspicious' subjects which, in the current climate, could be something as innocent as a message with the word 'Allah' in the header." Or maybe: "SAVE THE FOURTH AMENDMENT FROM TYRANTS!" Carnivore also records other electronic communications.

There was resistance to the assault on the Bill of Rights. In Congress, such previously unlikely alliances between Maxine Waters and Bob Barr, Barney Frank and Dick Armey, helped hold back Ashcroft's rush to enact his anti-terrorism weapons within a week, as he had demanded. In the Senate, Patrick Leahy, chairman of the Judiciary Committee, also tried to allow some deliberation, but Majority Leader Tom Daschle usurped and undermined Leahy's authority. Leahy ultimately caved and declared the law signed by Bush on October 26 "a good bill that protects our liberties."

The House Judiciary Committee did pass by a 36-to-0 vote a bipartisan bill that restored some mention of the Bill of Rights to Ashcroft's proposals. But, late at night, that bill was scuttled behind closed doors by Speaker of the House Dennis Hastert and other Republican leaders, along with emissaries from the White House.

As a result, on October 12, the House, 337 to 39, approved a harsh 175-page bill that most of its members had not had time even to read. David Dreier, chairman of the Committee on Rules, often seen being smoothly disingenuous on television, said casually that it was hardly the first time bills had been passed that House members had not read.

Democrat David Obey of Wisconsin accurately described the maneuver as "a back-room quick fix," adding mordantly: "Why should we care? It's only the Constitution."

And Barney Frank made the grim point that this subversion of representative government was "the least democratic process for debating questions fundamental to democracy I have ever seen. A bill drafted by a handful of people in secret, subject to no committee process, comes before us immune from amendment."

Among those voting against the final bill were: Barney Frank, John Conyers, David Bonior, Barbara Lee, Cynthia McKinney, John Dingell, Jesse Jackson Jr., Jerrold Nadler, Melvin Watt, and Maxine Waters. Unaccountably, Bob Barr voted for the bill.

But House Judiciary Committee Chairman James Sensenbrenner, as reported on National Public Radio, assured us all that this steamrollered bill did not diminish the freedom of "innocent citizens."

Providing, of course, that the presumption of innocence holds.

Also late at night, on October 11, the Senate, in a closed-door session, attended only by Senate leaders and members of the Administration, crafted a similar, expansive anti-terrorism bill that the Senate went on to pass by a vote of 96 to 1. Only Russ Feingold, a Wisconsin Democrat, had the truly patriotic courage to vote against this attack on the Bill of Rights that the President and the Secretaries of State and defense have said we are fighting for.

As Feingold had said while the Senate was allegedly deliberating the bill, "It is crucial that civil liberties in this country be preserved. Otherwise I'm afraid terror will win this battle without firing a shot."

In essence, the new law will, as The Wall Street Journal noted, "make it easier for government agents to track e-mail sent and web sites visited by someone involved in an investigation; to collect call records for phones such a person might use; and to share information between the Federal Bureau of Investigation and the Central Intelligence Agency."

Until now, the CIA was not legally allowed to spy on Americans. Also, previously secret grand jury proceedings will now be shared among law enforcement and intelligence agencies.

In addition, the new law subverts the Fourth Amendment's standards of reasonable searches and seizures by allowing anti-terrorism investigations to obtain a warrant not on the basis of "probable cause," as has been required in domestic criminal probes, but on the much looser basis that the information is "relevant to an ongoing criminal investigation"-not just terrorism.

The new law has a "sunset clause," requiring it to be reviewed after four years to determine if these stringent measures are still needed. But before this collusion in reducing our liberties was effected, George W. Bush had assured us that the war on worldwide terrorism will be of indeterminate length. A Congress that so overwhelmingly passed this anti-terrorism bill is hardly likely to expunge parts of it in four-or more-years. And even if it did, evidence gathered in the first four years could be used in prosecutions after that.

In self-defense, all of us should be interested in how terrorism is defined in this historic legislation. As summarized by the ACLU, the language in the final bill said: A person "commits the crime of domestic terrorism if within the U.S., activity is engaged in that involves acts dangerous to human life that violate the laws of the United States or any State, and appear to be intended to: 1) intimidate or coerce a civilian population; 2) influence the policy of a government by intimidation or coercion; or 3) affect the conduct of the government by mass destruction, assassination, or kidnapping." (Note the words: "appear to be intended to" and "intimidate. ")

Considering the loose language of the first two provisions, the ACLU points out that "this over-broad terrorism definition would sweep in people who engage in acts of political protest if those acts were dangerous to human life. People associated with organizations such as Operation Rescue and the Environmental Liberation Front, and the World Trade Organization protesters have engaged in activities that should subject them to prosecution as terrorists."

Furthermore, "once the government decides that conduct is 'domestic terrorism,' law enforcement agents have the authority to charge anyone who provides assistance to that person, even if the assistance is an act as minor as providing lodging. They would have the authority to wiretap the home of anyone who is providing assistance."

"Assistance" includes "support." So, contributions to any group later charged with domestic terrorism—even if the donor was unaware of its range of activities—could lead to an investigation or those giving support.

The Bush Administration and its allies in Congress are confident of continued public backing of these anti-terrorism measures, and other incursions into what is left of the Bill of Rights. As James Madison prophesied: "Wherever the real power in a Government lies, there is the danger of oppression. In our democracy, the real power lies in the majority of the Community."

After the terrorist attacks on September 11, poll after poll has shown that 70 or more percent of Americans are willing to give up some of their freedoms in order to stay free.

In all the news and commentary so far, little attention has been paid to the fact that before September 11, the majority of Americans had little knowledge of their own rights and liberties, to begin with. So what do they have to fear now, losing what is guaranteed to them under the Bill of Rights and the rest of the Constitution, let alone care about what happens to the rights of others?

In a survey conducted by the Freedom Forum's First Amendment Center, Americans were asked: "To the best of your recollection, have you ever taken classes in either school or college that dealt with the First Amendment?"

Forty-seven percent of the respondents answered "No." As I can attest from many years of visiting schools, including graduate schools, such classes, when they exist, are quick and superficial. As for the rest of the Bill of Rights, in classes at Columbia and NYU graduate schools of journalism, eyes have glazed when I ask what's in the Fourth Amendment or, for that matter, the Fifth, Sixth, and Eighth Amendments.

As for the First Amendment-and the right to criticize the government is never more fundamental than in a period of justified national fear of a nearly invisible enemy-consider these results of the First Amendment Center's "State of the First Amendment" 2001 survey released on July 4 of this year.

Seventy-one percent believe "it is important for the government to hold the media in check." Only 24 percent strongly agree that "people should be allowed to display in a public place art that has content that may be offensive to others."

How about art that severely condemns the President's war on terrorism? There's more. Only 53 percent strongly agree that "newspapers should be allowed to publish freely without government approval of a story."

Again, this survey was taken months before the killings at the World Trade Center and the Pentagon.

And, only 57 percent agree strongly that "newspapers should be allowed to criticize public officials."

As Judge Learned Hand once said, "Liberty lies in the hearts of men and women; when it dies there, no constitution, no law, no court can even do much to help it. While it lies there, it needs no constitution, no law, no court to save it."

We and the Constitution have survived the contempt for the Bill of Rights in the Alien and Sedition Acts of 1798; Abraham Lincoln's suspension of habeas corpus, and the jailing of editors and other dissenters during the Civil War; Woodrow Wilson's near annihilation of the First Amendment in the First World War; and the "Red Scares" of 1919 and the early 1920s when Attorney General A. Mitchell Palmer and his enthusiastic aide, J. Edgar Hoover, rounded up hundreds of "radicals," "subversives," and "Bolsheviks" in thirty-three cities and summarily

deported many of them. And we also survived Joe McCarthy.

This will be one of our severest tests yet to rescue the Constitution from our government. Benjamin Franklin has been quoted a lot lately: "They that can give up essential liberty to obtain a little temporary safety deserve neither liberty nor safety."

There are teach-ins taking place on whether reciprocal killing in this war will make us secure. Teach-ins were a key factor in generating opposition to the Vietnam War. But an even more fundamental subject for teach-ins, on and off campuses, is essential now. And that subject, of course, is how all of us on all sides can remain free—now that we finally know how much John Ashcroft has won in his evisceration of the Bill of Rights.

Across the land, with flags flying, what George W. Bush has called "Operation Enduring Freedom" is being trumpeted. But in a little noted publication of the Worcester County, Massachusetts, Bar Association, James Van Buren, president of the association, said, without flourishes: "Preserving our freedoms is the only sure way to thwart the terrorists' goal."

He is among the minority that James Madison hoped would secure the Constitution in times of danger. Mr. Van Buren needs support.

Nat Hentoff is a columnist for the Village Voice, NEA Newspapers Syndicate, Legal Times, and Editor & Publisher. His most recent books are "Living the Bill of Rights" (University of California, 1999) and "The Nat Hentoff Reader" (Da Capo Press, 2001).

National Review Online September 18, 2001 8:45 a.m.

Freedom's Value Paramount in the war against terrorism

By Clint Bolick, *vice-president of the Washington-based Institute for Justice. Bolick heads its new office in Phoenix.*

Soviet dictator Nikita Khrushchev is said to have quipped that American capitalists would sell Communists the rope by which to hang them.

I've thought about that quote repeatedly when hearing about the ease by which Middle Eastern terrorists navigated American freedom for their diabolical ends: enrolling in American flight schools, using Internet access at public libraries, traveling freely from place to place.

One immediate and logical response is to curtail the freedom. At least temporarily, or for certain people.

Such calls in times of crisis are inevitable. Senate Minority Leader Trent Lott laid the groundwork by commenting, "When you are at war, civil liberties are treated differently."

Indeed, our history is replete with examples of just that; and not always even in times of war. John Adams signed the Alien and Sedition Acts designed to punish activity considered adverse to American interests. Andrew Jackson gave orders to intercept mail carrying inflammatory anti-slavery rhetoric. Abraham Lincoln suspended the writ of *habeas corpus* during the Civil War. Franklin D. Roosevelt attempted to nationalize American industries in World War II. Most shameful was the internment of Japanese citizens during that same period. And of course, the Cold War gave rise to unparalleled surveillance of American citizens. Sordid examples all.

America never has effectively protected its interests by suspending individual liberties. Such efforts typically deprive us of our most potent weapon, which is freedom. That is what sets us apart, first and foremost, from our adversaries.

We are always at our strongest when we fight not just with bombs and bullets, but with a real effort to win the hearts and minds of the world's people. And we do that by steadfastly adhering to our principles. A potent example: In our war against Hitler, America set aside its racist policies and began to vindicate our own ideals of equality. It not only established clear moral superiority but made us a stronger foe.

If we are not mindful of our true objectives, we could go badly astray in our noble quest to rid the world of terrorism. Already there is talk that security officials are employing ethnicity in antiterrorist profiling, stopping people not because they are foreign nationals of governments known to harbor terrorists, but because their skin is dark or they wear beards. An efficient antiterrorism device? Perhaps. A violation of our core belief that the state must treat people as individuals, not as members of racial groups? Definitely. Once that absolute principle is compromised, it is only a matter of degree before we return to the nightmare of Japanese incarceration.

Likewise, we hear calls to allow government to step up electronic surveillance, and to require national ID cards so that government can monitor our travels. Even before last week's bombings, the Supreme Court struck down by a slender 5-4 vote the use of thermal imaging in law enforcement. The requirement of warrants is an essential protection of civil liberty—in times of peace as well as war. So too is the right to travel.

Do these rights impair the fight against terrorism? In a certain sense, yes. It would be easier if government could monitor our conversations and activities, or could stop or segregate those whose skin color or religious beliefs resemble the terrorists' It is tempting to trade freedom for security. But to do so sacrifices both. For the freedoms we have not only make America a moral exemplar but provide us with the wealth and means to effectively combat terrorism.

To be sure, Americans will have to surrender convenience in this war. But not their freedoms. Whenever a politician or pundit argues for a suspension in civil liberties, we should ask: Isn't that what this battle is all about? If we surrender our freedom, haven't the terrorists won?

So as we wage this war, we need to keep our priorities straight. If freedom is the objective, it ought not constitute the first casualty. Our most potent weapon is the system that rests upon the sanctity of our Constitution and Bill of Rights.

Senator Lott is correct. We have treated civil liberties differently in wartime. Let us remember those horrible mistakes so we do not repeat them again.

And Khrushchev was right, too. Funny thing though: Communism in the Soviet Union is dead, but we're still selling rope.

Chapter 6

Arguing Against the Proposition Case

Debaters must be prepared to speak on either side of any given topic. One of the most challenging aspects of debate participation is that you will have to both propose and oppose—you must practice building cases and tearing them down. This chapter is about how to oppose the proposition team's case. Normally, to win a debate, the opposition must refute the proposition team's case. The opposition's job is to *oppose* the proposition team's case. The opposition does not have to offer a case of their own, because their job is to oppose the case made by the other team. Sometimes opposition teams may choose to present proposals of their own, but that is their choice and is not a requirement.

Basic Opposition to the Case

The initial opposition speech can be the most important speech of the debate for the opposition team. In this speech, the opposition lays out the foundation for their attack against the case. The arguments in the first opposition speech are refined and advanced through the rest of the debate. The first opposition speaker must make a thorough attack on the proposition team's case.

This can be done in a number of ways. The best opposition teams engage in both direct and indirect refutation. This chapter discusses how to engage in direct case refutation. (We will discuss indirect refutation in later chapters on disadvantages, counterplans, and critiques.) Direct refutation involves *specific challenges to the arguments in the opening proposition speech*. The opposition arguments that specifically address the major lines of proof of the first proposition speaker are called **case arguments** or **"on-case" arguments**. They fundamentally challenge the original case position.

There are usually many issues in a debate that might be relevant to the discussion but are not included in the proposition team's opening remarks. After all, the proposition team tries to put on its best face in the opening speech. The proposition case includes the outstanding arguments for a proof of the motion and little else. The proposition team does not usually present information that might hurt its position. There are, inevitably, many issues excluded by the proposition team. The opposing side may wish to introduce one or more of these otherwise excluded ideas into the debate, thereby using *indirect refutation.* In addition, the opposition might choose to present major arguments—disadvantages, counterplans, and critiques—that are based on the proposition case but move well beyond the case text. These ideas are sometimes known as **"off-case" arguments**, because they are not found within the text of the proposition team's case arguments.

When you debate on the opposition side, you should answer the substance of the proposition team's case. While it may be tempting to disagree with everything the other team says, this is not a particularly wise course of action. You should learn to choose your battles wisely. The tactic of *strategic agreement* is a friend to opposition teams. When using this tactic, the opposing side concedes one or more of the proposition side's arguments in order to advance their own interests in the debate.

This kind of agreement might bring a needed focus to the debate. For example, a speaker might agree to relatively modest claims that serve as a distraction for the debaters and the judge. If a case supports restrictions on immigration, the proposition side might argue that closing national borders would be good because such an action would (1)Improve security against terrorists who would potentially use weapons of mass destruction, and (2) Save some administrative costs for government processing of immigrants.
The advantages of this case might fairly be described as a battleship pulling a dinghy. The first advantage could affect the lives of tens of thousands or millions of people. The second advantage is small and might save some money, which would probably be redirected to some other government project. It is perhaps a better approach for the opposition team to simply ignore or concede the relatively small advantage of unspectacular savings. This allows them to concentrate their arguments on the more significant issues related to terrorism and weapons of mass destruction.

As we have mentioned, the majority of cases in parliamentary debate are policy cases. When you debate these cases, you may want to challenge any of the case elements describing the problem and the proposed solution. We will discuss some basic ways to answer all of these lines of argument for the case.

Proposition teams may make inherency arguments. An *inherency* argument is a proof that a problem is ongoing. To answer this line of argument, an opposition team should explain why the proposition team's proposal has not been implemented. One reason might be that authorities are worried that the plan, and their policy, might fail. The opposition might also argue that more study is required before one should attempt policy action.

Of course, the opposition might also identify other causes of the stated problem. The suggestion of another reason for the problem is called an *alternate causality*. If you can show alternate causalities, you can undermine the claim that a particular flaw is responsible for the problem. Most problems have multiple causes. For example, there are many causes of obesity: genetics, diet, and lack of exercise. If you deal with only one of the potential causes, you may not solve the problem. This explains why many people who diet do not lose weight— they have failed to account for the alternate causes of their weight problem.

Identifying alternate causalities can be an important line of argument for the opposition. A proposition team might claim there is an ongoing crime problem and propose a guaranteed annual income to alleviate the putative cause of crime—that is, poverty. If the opposition is able to identify other major causes of crime (family violence, prejudice, drug abuse), then they will be able to show that the primary cause of the problem is not the one identified by the proposition team. The purpose of this line of argument is to show that the problem will not be resolved by the proposed plan.

The opposition team may choose to refute the significance or harms of the case. This text includes some additional tactics for arguing impact assessments and issues of significance in the chapter on debate skills. Basically, there are three primary strategies for refuting claims of significance:

- The opposition team may attempt to minimize an argument.
- The opposition team may *turn* or capture an argument.
- The opposition team may choose to answer an argument.

Arguments have different kinds of significance. Some issues matter a great deal to an individual. We say that these issues have *qualitative* significance.

For example, the wrongful incarceration of a person is a very serious matter. The loss of one job due to race discrimination is a compelling violation of individual liberty. As serious as these conditions may be for any single person, however, the arbitrary loss of liberty for a single individual may not be a sufficient reason to reform the entire criminal justice system. Some arguments are very significant but do not have wide effects. They are serious matters, indeed, but may fail to justify major reform of a public policy field.

Other expressions of significance might apply to a large number of people but have relatively little consequence. We say that issues that have a sweeping scope have *quantitative* significance. For example, a small increase in the price of a postage stamp or a longer wait for the bus may affect the lives of tens of millions of individuals. However, in these examples the degree of disruption in people's lives is so small that it could not be said to be a serious problem. A debater might minimize an argument describing harms or benefits by showing how that argument does not have both qualitative and quantitative scope.

It is possible to compare the measure of an argument with the measure of another argument. Debaters should evaluate the outcomes of their different lines of argument. What if a proposition team suggests a public policy reform that would save 1,000 lives and the opposition team is able to show that the same policy will cost 10,000 lives? In this situation, the opposition team should contrast the advantage of the policy and disadvantage of the policy in like terms: that is, in the number of lives saved.

The opposition team may also *turn* or capture an opponent's argument. An argumentative **turn** is a technique with which a debater takes an argument from a team arguing one side of a motion and makes the claim that the argument actually supports the other side of the motion instead—that is, her own side. This is a highly effective argumentative strategy because it does not necessarily resist or refute the material substance of an opponent's argument. In its most effective form, this tactic "spins" the opposing side's issue. *When you turn an opponent's argument, you take one of their arguments and use it for your own purposes, usually by showing that it better supports your side of the motion.*

There are two types of turns: link turns and impact turns. A **link turn** is a claim that a causal connection (or "link") for an argument better supports the opposing side of the topic. For example, a proposition team might argue for a motion to increase the war on drugs, with the expressed purpose to reduce criminal drug use. The opposing side might respond that the war on drugs paradoxically increases criminal drug use, as it forces drug users, particularly novice users, to associate with criminal drug dealers to purchase recreational drugs. These new associations would increase the possibility of new users being recruited as drug sellers or couriers. It also initiates drug users to a world of lawbreakers who might lead them into other criminal activity. In this case, the opposition team agrees with the proposition team's premise. Both teams are interested in reducing criminal drug use. The fundamental *difference* in the teams' position is that the opposition team makes the claim that the war on drugs is responsible for increasing criminal drug use. The increase in the war on drugs, therefore, is likely to *increase* criminal drug use, rather than *reduce* it. By agreeing with the proposition case, the opposition team has turned the argument to their advantage.

An **impact turn** is an argument that reverses the claims associated with an argument's impact or outcome. In other words, you turn the impact of an argument when you show that what was claimed to be good is in fact bad, or vice versa. Here's an example: many parents encourage their children to wash their hands dozens of times a day on the grounds that such a practice will help their health. However, new research shows that this practice may actually hurt health because it decreases routine exposure to helpful bacteria.

A proposition team might argue about the risks associated with the spread of nuclear weapons, or "proliferation." They might suggest that proliferation is destabilizing and leads to the possibility of nuclear conflict. The opposition team might reply that proliferation is actually a valued public policy rather than a reason for fear. The opposition speaker would claim that the history of effective nuclear deterrence among major nuclear powers for the 50 years of the Cold War proves that nuclear proliferation will increase stability and reduce the potential for nuclear conflict. In addition, the team might argue that nuclear proliferation would also deter the use of chemical, biological, and conventional weapons, making conflict dramatically less likely with new nuclear regimes. In this case, the opposition team is able to reverse the standing of the issue of significance in the debate. That which was "bad" is now determined to be "good." There is additional information on link turns and impact turns in Chapter 9, which focuses on disadvantages.

If your opponent introduces an argument that is very significant and cannot be turned, it is then necessary to answer the argument. Many effective debate arguments are supported by examples. The most effective counter is to refute the examples initiated by your opponent directly. We will now discuss some ways you can answer examples brought up by the other team.

Examples may be answered with counterexamples. These counters should match the original example in scope. In other words, the opposition team should provide appropriate counterexamples that consider the scale of the proposition team's examples and try either to (1) Directly match or exceed the significance of the original example in the same area (e.g., the opposition could use an example of a favorable military intervention to counter a claim of an unfavorable military adventure); or (2) Make analogies to counterexamples in other fields (e.g., the opposition might argue about failures of regulation in environmental policies to counter a proposition team advocating new regulations in consumer product safety).

There are other ways you can challenge examples:

- They ought to be *representative* or *typical* of the claims made by the proposition team. Remember that exceptions do not prove rules.
- They should express significance.
- They ought to show that problems can be resolved and are not intractable.
- There should be enough examples to prove the core elements of a motion.

It is also possible for the opposition team to answer the solvency claims of the proposition team. Will the proposed solution resolve the problem? Alternate causality arguments may effectively undermine a proposition team's claim that they have proposed the correct solution to a problem. The opposition team should carefully examine the elements of the plan. Are there difficulties that might occur during program implementation? Will the plan be supported in the long term? Would any social groups opposing the plan or any other party engage in a backlash against new policy initiatives? These questions might produce a significant number of objections to the implementation and ultimate success of a policy proposal.

The best position for the opposition is to argue that the proposition case is "bad." By that, we mean that the proposition makes a case that is an expression of a "good." *It is not an effective counter to say that the case may not be good enough.* If the proposition team lowers their original expectations (that is, they are not "good enough") but they are still superior to the opposition team, who would logically prevail in a debate? The proposition team. The opposition team should show that the proposition is counterproductive or dangerous.

Suggested Exercise ══════════════════════════════════

> In Appendix 6, you will find a transcript of the opening speeches for the proposition and the opposition sides of the motion: "This House should return the goods." Debaters should work as individuals or in small groups on the full text of a speech or a speech section, analyzing it for (1) the elements of a narrative construction of a proposition case, including introduction, interpretation, case proper, and conclusion; (2) effective opposition argumentation, identifying types of arguments; (3) speech structure and argument organization; and (4) argument clash.

Structuring Opposition Arguments to the Case

Just as it is important to make good arguments against the proposition team's case, it is also important to structure your opposition arguments appropriately to maximize their effectiveness. Appropriate structure is particularly important for the arguments made in the constructive speech of the first opposition speaker, because these arguments frame the rest of the debate on the proposition team's case. There are at least two faulty and very different strategies employed by the first opposition speaker:

- **The undifferentiated mass.** Sometimes the lead opposition speaker will advance her arguments against the proposition team's case without structure. This kind of presentation may be pleasing from an oratorical perspective, but its lack of structure can be ultimately crippling to the opposition team and annoying to the judge. ("This plan is a bad idea, and it's not inherent, and it has little significance, and here's an example of why it wouldn't solve the problem, and the plan makes no sense, and...")

- **The hyper-structure.** Sometimes the lead opposition speaker will advance her arguments using too much structure, rather than not enough. This presentation strategy is, in effect, the opposite of the undifferentiated mass strategy. It meets the organizational needs of the judge and the other team and then goes too far, cluttering the debate with needless detail, much to the annoyance of all the participants. ("Off of their first observation, in their A subpoint, on their small two point, sub 'b...'")

Neither strategy is optimal. Instead, the first opposition speaker should seek to differentiate and explain her arguments using a simple structure to facilitate note-taking, refutation, and consolidation in the later parts of the debate.

The problem for the first opposition speaker is how to respond to specific components of the proposition team's case without devoting too much confusing time and energy referencing the specific (and often highly detailed) structure of that case. Let's consider an example to see how this might work in practice. Perhaps the proposition team has presented a case that contends that the USA should get rid of its nuclear weapons arsenal. The basic outline of the case might look something like the example that follows. We do not include the full articulation of the arguments that might be made by a first proposition speaker defending disarmament; rather, we want to show a potential outline for refutation.

I. Observation: There is a pressing need for nuclear disarmament by the USA.

A. Accidents are likely and dangerous

1. False alarms. Empirically, nuclear powers' early warning systems receive false alarms that could cause an automatic launch of nuclear weapons. This has almost happened many times in the past, and reliable sources assure us that it is only a matter of time before an accidental nuclear war breaks out for real. (Examples follow.)

2. This situation is particularly true in Russia, where deteriorating command and control systems, as well as an under-funded military and reliance on hair-trigger alert status mean that accidental launches could happen at any time.

3. Even one accidental detonation would kill tens of thousands of people—every additional warhead detonation would of course add to this death toll. There is a serious risk that an accidental nuclear war might break out, killing millions.

B. Proliferation

1. By refusing to commit to nuclear disarmament, the USA is essentially in the process of spitting in the eye of

the international nonproliferation regime, as codified in the Non Proliferation Treaty (NPT). In that treaty, the USA and other nuclear powers agreed to a goal of disarmament; they just have not yet put that plan into practice.

2. This policy poisons the well of nonproliferation. The USA's hypocrisy on this issue communicates the message that what the NPT is *really* about is dividing the world into two classes: the nuclear "haves" and "have nots." This state of affairs is perceived as colonialist, unfair, and unacceptable by the majority of the world. Thus the NPT, the linchpin of the global nonproliferation regime, has largely been rendered obsolete by the obstinance of the USA.

3. Proliferation is risky business. As more states acquire nuclear weapons, their use becomes more likely. Because nuclear deterrence is largely a fictive construct with no empirical evidence, it is really only a matter of time before all kinds of conflicts begin to escalate to the nuclear level, killing millions.

II. The Plan: The USA should formally commit to nuclear disarmament, pursued in an expedient manner, while assuring that all relevant safety and security steps are made in the interim.

III. Solvency

A. Antiproliferation credibility. The plan will bolster the nonproliferation regime, assuring that international nuclear proliferation can be effectively checked.

B. Norms. The plan will establish an international norm that clearly communicates that nuclear weapons are not an acceptable currency or lever in politics and thus will not be tolerated.

C. Other nations will follow. The international community has repeatedly communicated that if the USA were to pursue meaningful nuclear disarmament, others would follow its lead.

D. Moral imperative. It is in all nations' best interests to work towards nuclear disarmament. The weapons themselves are so immensely destructive, both physically and psychologically, that we must commit ourselves to ridding the world of them. The plan is a giant step in this direction.

The first opposition speaker and her partner should generate arguments against this case as it is being presented. As a general rule, the first opposition speaker should use only the *most general structure* of the proposition team's case to signpost her arguments. All debaters must *signpost* their arguments in the refutation and extension process. By this we mean that you should provide a signpost for the judge that clearly states which argument or group of arguments you are refuting or extending. Signposting fulfills the "they say" step of the four-step refutation process discussed in Chapter 1. Many first opposition speakers will carry this signposting process too far, resulting in the "hyper-structure" problem discussed above. Let's say that you wanted to make some arguments against the "accidental launch" claims of the proposition case above. You would phrase your arguments in this way:

> "I'll begin by answering their first observation, which is their statement of harms. They give two specific scenarios, which I will answer in order. On their accidental launch scenario— scenario A, I have a few answers:

> "First, the false-alarm risk is low. This is empirically proven by decades of nuclear possession by many countries. There has never been a single accidental nuclear launch, much less an all-out nuclear exchange, which is what their impact claims assume. This scenario is nothing but reckless fear-mongering on the part of the proposition team.

> "Second, safety is high. We have hotlines, diplomacy, constructive engagement, and other weapons mitigation procedures *because* of the risk of accidental launch. The accidental launch possibility is *why* we have all of the existing safety procedures.

> "Third, a turn: This scenario encourages the nonproliferation regime and additional safety procedures. The possibility of an accidental launch encourages other countries to think twice about weapons buildups. By disarming, the proposition case makes it seem that the threat is ending, paradoxically increasing the risk of accidental launch by decreasing overall vigilance."

This is excellent technique for structuring and presenting the initial opposition arguments against the proposition case. Notice that the opposition speaker numbers her arguments consecutively, rather than trying to signpost them off of specific components of the presentation of Scenario 1. Also notice that the speaker *tags*, or assigns a concise label to, her arguments before relating the substance of the argument: "First, the false-alarm risk is low"; "Second, safety is high." This is a good debate habit because it enables the judge to get a concise summary of each argument onto her flow. The average judge will only get the first three to five words of each argument in her notes, so debaters must make sure that those first three to five words are the most important.

Notice also that the speaker answers the first scenario as a whole, without attempting to refute all of its constituent parts. This shows good technique. You can easily refute a specific scenario, or a whole contention, without directly referring to each of its constituent parts. You should try to *group* arguments, whenever possible, to simplify the record of arguments. *Grouping* arguments is just what it sounds like—a tactic that answers a few similar arguments as a group, rather than individually. In the example above, the speaker has grouped together all the arguments in the first scenario to answer them more effectively.

After making the above arguments, this speaker should continue on to answer the second scenario and the solvency contention. She should group each of those sections rather than answering the substructure of the case specifically. This does not mean that the speaker should not *answer* the specific components of a proposition case contention. She can easily answer specific proposition arguments using the grouping method. Consider the following potential answers to the proposition team's solvency contention:

> "First, norm establishment won't solve the problem. This has been proven again and again with international treaties—the Chemical Weapons Convention has been ratified, but countries still pursue chemical weapons. Likewise, the United Nations Declaration of Human Rights establishes norms, and those aren't followed, either. There's no reason to believe the plan would induce others to disarm.

> "Second, nuclear weapons deter conflict. This means that after the plan is implemented, more wars will occur as deterrence evaporates.

> "Third, the nonproliferation regime is doomed anyway. The plan can't revitalize the nonproliferation regime because it relies on outdated supply-side controls that have never worked. Countries like India, Pakistan, and Israel have acquired nuclear weapons

in the existing system. They also got nuclear weapons for reasons of their own, not because of any of the USA's policies."

These arguments answer parts of the proposition team's solvency contention specifically, but without using confusing signposting to refer to overly specific parts of the proposition team's case. The speaker does *not* say:

"They say in their B subpoint of their solvency that the plan
will encourage other countries to give up nuclear weapons and
that this will create some kind of norm, but..."

The speaker here has not yet made an argument, despite having spoken for about fifteen seconds. This preface to an argument commits several common errors. First, obviously, it is too long. Second, it gives too much credit to the proposition team's argument by repeating it at length. Third, the speaker is trying to respond to each sub-point of solvency individually rather than responding to the observation as a whole. Finally, the speaker damages her own credibility by failing to state her argument clearly and concisely at the beginning. The speaker could improve her presentation a bit by saying something like the following:

"They say that their plan will create a norm against nuclear
weapons, but this won't work because..."

This is still a less than ideal framing of a response. Although it fulfills the "they say" component of the refutation process, it can still be improved. The speaker is still beginning her argument by reiterating the proposition team's argument rather than by declaring one of her own:

"First, norm establishment won't solve the problem. This has
been proven again and again with international treaties..."

You should practice this technique of phrasing your arguments offensively and concisely rather than defensively and with too many words.

A few final notes about opposition arguments against the proposition team's case. First, while you should definitely make arguments about the weaknesses of the plan (e.g., its inadequacy, its poor wording, its foolish and naïve assumptions about the world), you should make those arguments where they will have an impact on the substantive claims of the case. For example, if the plan has no possibility or provisions for enforcement, it is unlikely to solve the designated problem. Make this argument on the solvency contention. Do not confuse the matter by signposting your argument on the plan. Perhaps the plan does not account for alternate causalities discussed in the harms contentions. Make this argument on the relevant harms contentions, rather than on the plan. This technique points to a more general rule about placing opposition arguments—*make your arguments against the part of the case where they will have the most impact.*

Second, you should always design your opposition strategies with an eye toward crystallization in the opposition's final stand on the floor. This means you should try to ensure that your arguments are relatively consistent with each other and appropriately diversified. Do not put all of your oppositional eggs in one basket in the first opposition speech. Make several different kinds of arguments, both on the case and off the case, to ensure that you will have a broad spectrum of arguments to choose from when your subsequent speeches come around.

On That Point!

Panel Discussions

The information provided by one person's speech or the give and take of clashing arguments in a debate may shine considerable light on a subject. In other circumstances, a single speech, even a debate, may conceal more than it reveals. For some issues, it is appropriate to engage in open, moderated discussion. Panel discussions can be lively and informative. They can include opinions from a number of different perspectives. Participants speak when and how they want, making the event a bit easier for beginning and anxious public speakers, although the format is also appropriate for experienced and confident speakers. The dynamic nature of a panel discussion makes it fun for participants and entertaining for an audience.

A discussion typically involves a panel of speakers and a moderator. The moderator introduces the members of the panel and offers a brief, four or five-sentence topic summary, such as: "Good evening, ladies and gentlemen. After recent incidents in our state, many parents and community leaders are concerned about school safety. This panel has gathered to discuss potential solutions to violence in our schools. We will discuss different proposed solutions and see whether they truly address the causes of school violence." *The moderator is also a panelist, not just a questioner or facilitator of the discussion.* After opening the discussion with an initial question for the panel, the moderator acts as one of its members. Although she participates in the discussion, the moderator should be mindful to limit her comments in order to encourage the involvement of other panelists.

If you moderate a discussion, you should prepare questions on a wide range of relevant subjects. The panelists will be encouraged to expand the discussion and ask questions of each other but you will have the responsibility of avoiding "dead air," an awkward, silent pause during which each person waits for a comment from other panelists. It is your responsibility as moderator to keep the discussion going.

On That Point!

There should be 4–5 panelists. The members of the panel ought to represent differing opinions on the topic. The discussion should last for at least 15 minutes and should not exceed 25 minutes. The moderator should keep time of the discussion or a member of the audience should be assigned as a timekeeper. The introduction and conclusion should each last approximately 2–3 minutes, with the remaining time being used for general discussion. The event is 'open,' i.e., panelists may speak at any time and for any duration, as long as their behavior satisfies the other panelists and the moderator. As in any conversation, respectful interruption is appropriate and no individual ought to dominate the discussion. A panel discussion is an outstanding opportunity for civil discourse. The discussion may involve serious disagreement about issues, but should be carried out with dignified behavior and respect for the other panelists.

Panelists may present new ideas and/or refute the claims of other participants. Members of the discussion panel are expected to express their own opinions and may also quote expert authorities and statistics to support ideas. The moderator, or any member of the panel, may introduce new material, shift the discussion, ask a question, or interrupt a speaker to advance an investigation of the issues or prevent any monopoly of opinions by one or two panelists. If this happens, the new information should not interrupt a meaningful segment of the discussion and it should relate to the topic. Consider the following example on a "gun control" topic.

> Panelist 1: "Gun control just does not work. Even the states with serious gun control laws have significant gun crime and deaths from handguns. Passing new gun control laws has not made those places safer."

> Panelist 2: "But that is because people bring guns from states that have weak gun control laws into the states with strong gun control laws. If we had national gun controls..."

> Panelist 3: "Excuse me, but I have information about the number of nonviolent crimes in Montana last year and..."

> Panelist 2: "Maybe we can get to that in a minute. I think we should finish discussing whether gun control laws work. Can we agree to talk about that briefly and then get to your argument about nonviolent crime?"

> Panelist 3: "OK."

On That Point!

Panelists should make their points briefly (there are, after all, a number of speakers on the panel who will want time to express their own opinions on the topic) but effectively. You will want to use sophisticated analytical techniques, refutation tactics, and the power of persuasive speaking to influence other panelists and the audience.

After a discussion of the topic and with approximately 2 minutes remaining in the scheduled time for the discussion, the moderator will ask each of the panelists for a final comment. Your comment should not last more than fifteen seconds. It is not supposed to be a summary of all the things you said during the discussion nor is it an opportunity for the presentation of a new idea. If the audience could take with them only the most important point from your participation in the discussion, what would it be? A final comment is an opportunity to let the audience know one thing that might influence or change their opinion on the topic.

The moderator may encourage audience questions or comments during or after the panel discussion. This period should be limited to 5–15 minutes. Members of the audience may direct a statement or question to the panel for up to 1 minute, with a member of the panel given 30 seconds for a reply. This is an opportunity for observers to participate in the discussion. The moderator should keep the time for this session and call on members of the audience to ask questions or make comments.

Exercise

Have a panel discussion on the topic of "national service." Begin with the selection of panelists and a moderator. The participants should brainstorm and research the topic. The attached article from the San Francisco Chronicle is an example of the material available on this topic. It presents many of the issues involved in an examination of national service: should it be encouraged and paid for by the government? Should it be compulsory, that is, should you be required to participate in national service or the military by law or as a requirement for high school or college graduation? Which service programs should be developed—AmeriCorps, Teach for America, Senior Corps, the US military? Is mandatory national service a patriotic duty or a threat to personal freedom? Is it effective? Is it too costly? The panel should be an open discussion on these and other relevant questions.

On That Point!

Panelists should anticipate these issues and prepare information on them. They should make notes of important and relevant evidence (statistical information, expert opinion, personal experience). They should prepare to answer the questions and ideas that would challenge or refute their opinions. They should also prepare questions to ask the other panelists.

The assigned moderator should have many prepared questions to make sure that the discussion will remain interesting and will not fade.

PUBLIC SERVICE;
Making Americans;
New push for national service;
Sept. 11 revives interest in citizenship duty for youth

Edward Epstein

Maybe it's just a burst of post-Sept. 11 patriotism, but leading members of Congress and some intellectuals who say young Americans need a common experience are calling for **vastly expanded national service.**

It is quite a change from the early 1990s, when Republicans in Congress derided President Bill Clinton's effort to establish AmeriCorps, a program that allows 18- to 24-year-olds to spend a year or two in community service, doing everything from teaching kids to read to shoveling snow for seniors in blizzard-blocked Buffalo, N.Y.

Now some leading Republicans are behind the effort to widen the scope of national service.

They are riding a wave of increased interest from the public. AmeriCorps says inquiries about joining have risen 30 percent since the Sept. 11 attacks. In California, the increase has been 48 percent. "Young Americans, particularly since 9/11, are looking for ways to give back, to fulfill their roles as citizens,"

said Chuck Supple, director of Gov. Gray Davis' Office on Service and Volunteerism, which oversees 9,600 AmeriCorps workers in the state.

Effort to Expand AmeriCorps

Sen. John McCain, R-Ariz., a former AmeriCorps critic, is co-sponsoring a bill with Democratic Sen. Evan Bayh of Indiana that over seven years would expand AmeriCorps' numbers from 50,000 young people in the ranks each year to 250,000.

Half the program's slots would go for homeland defense, a widely defined term that includes disaster preparation and relief, public health work and helping police by relieving them of some administrative tasks.

The plan, which would make more education grants available to participants, would also increase options for serving in the military, which now takes in about 200,000 volunteers annually.

McCain said the proposal "harnesses the patriotic spirit by providing more

On That Point!

opportunities for people to volunteer or serve in the military."

President Bush, who even before Sept. 11 made increased volunteerism a theme of his administration, has already mobilized 20,000 AmeriCorps workers and volunteers in the country's Senior Corps to help with homeland defense.

In his State of the Union address Jan. 29, Bush is expected to outline plans for more community service programs as part of a request for additional billions of dollars for domestic security against terrorist attacks.

"We have to reach out and engage the American people and take advantage of this moment," said Leslie Lenkowsky, Bush's appointee to head the Corporation for National and Community Service. The agency administers AmeriCorps and its 50,000 young workers, who earn about $9,300 a year and qualify for an education benefit of as much as $9,500.

Calls for Mandatory Service

Outside Congress, proposals are being floated for a vastly larger approach. Some want the military draft reinstated. Others would require a year of mandatory community service for 18-year-old high school graduates, who would serve either in the military or in AmeriCorps-type programs.

For instance, Robert Litan of the Brookings Institution in Washington, D.C., wants all 18-year-old high school graduates, about 2.5 million people a year, to be inducted into a year of compulsory national service, either in the military or in community programs. He puts the price tag at $25 billion a year.

Litan views such service as a way of bringing together young people in an increasingly diverse nation in which people from various groups rarely mix.

"For many people, their year in compulsory service may be the only time in their lives where they mix for an extended time and on an equal footing

with others from very different backgrounds," Litan wrote recently.

Skeptics say neither Congress nor Bush would go for such huge programs.

"It's a nice hope that we could get everyone more engaged, but it's not realistic," said Mike Meneer, a former reading tutor for AmeriCorps in Columbus, Ohio, who is now executive director of the 25,000-member AmeriCorps Alums Inc.

Meneer said the Bayh-McCain bill raises a lot of interesting ideas for expanding community service. Mandatory service, however, raises questions about basic American ideas of personal freedom, he said.

"Is it fair or right to require people to give one or two years of their lives when they wouldn't do it on their own?" he asked.

To a longtime AmeriCorps critic, Doug Bandow of the libertarian Cato Institute, required universal service poses a nightmare scenario.

'Frightening Concept'

"It's a frightening concept in a country based on individual liberty and limited government," he said.

Bandow said traditional charities provide the best venue for volunteerism, while AmeriCorps is little more than a government jobs program that takes money away from more pressing needs.

"It's a job, but we shouldn't confuse the notion of jobs with traditional volunteerism," Bandow said. Creating more government-backed service jobs, he said, would deprive people of the true meaning of donating to charities.

"Part of our civic duty is sacrificing and giving and working for charities," Bandow said.

No one has been drafted into the military in the United States since 1973. Universal community or military service is too much to expect now, Lenkowsky said.

On That Point!

"I'm not sure we are ready to say to 18-year-old people that they can't go to college unless they do two years of service," he said.

But the AmeriCorps boss said quick action is vital, to seize the post-Sept. 11 spike in interest.

"It won't persist unless we do things now," Lenkowsky said. "We need to convey this expectation, that everyone should expect to give something back to their country."

National Service
Several countries already have compulsory national service programs other than a military draft:

Nigeria—One year in the National Youth Service Corps is required for all university graduates under age 30. Most people serve in schools.

Mexico—All university students must participate in a national service program to receive their degrees, and medical students must work in disadvantaged communities for a year before being licensed.

Egypt—Young female graduates of secondary schools, exempt from the military draft, must spend six months in a service program. Most take part in literacy campaigns.

Costa Rica—Medical professionals must serve a year treating disadvantaged communities. There are also mandatory community service programs for high school students.

Chapter 7

Argument Analysis

In debate, we don't just make arguments; we also *analyze* them. When we analyze arguments, we ask questions of arguments to determine their viability as well as their potential weak points. Debaters need to learn to think critically about arguments: there is little place for uncritical acceptance in debate, particularly if you want to have the best arguments or rejoinders. When we encounter an argument, we should ask ourselves a series of questions about it. The A-R-E model gives us a few pointers about questions we can ask. For example, you might analyze a particular argument by answering the following questions about it:

- What's the assertion being made? What is it that the speaker ultimately wants you to believe or agree with?
- Does the assertion have reasoning? What reasons does the speaker give to support her assertion?
- Is the reasoning supported by evidence? What kind of evidence? What is the source of the evidence?

These questions provide information that you need to know about an argument. You need to know how an argument works in order to be able to criticize it effectively. You should also ask further critical questions, such as:

- Are there exceptions that could be made to the stated assertion? What are they? How do those exceptions affect the overall validity of the assertion?
- Is the reasoning sound? What assumptions are made in the reasoning?
- Is the evidence credible? Does it come from a credible source? What kinds of circumstances might the data not take into account?

In this section, you will learn how to analyze specific kinds of arguments with versions of these and other questions. There are as many types of arguments as there are debaters who do not want to have to memorize all the different types of arguments. We will discuss the strengths and potential pitfalls of a few basic types of reasoning.

One of the most common arguments is the **argument from example**. When we use examples to reason, we may proceed from a specific case to a general theory or conclusion. This is called *inductive reasoning*. We may *also* use a general theory to predict how specific examples might play out. This is called *deductive* reasoning. The most relevant issue for debaters when thinking about reasoning by example is always simply this: *What is the relationship between the specific cases and the general theories being presented?*

Reasoning by example is a powerful way to prove any point. Proposition teams usually try to prove that there is a need for their proposed solution by providing examples of people or things that are harmed in the present system. They may show that their plan solves the problem by providing an example of a situation it would help. Advertisers may sell a product using similar tactics. They may try to show that the average toilet bowl is filthy by showing the toilet bowl of the Jones family, thus creating a need. Then they may show that their product works by showing that same toilet, cleaned to a blinding white, presumably by means of their product. As a debater, you can use a variety of examples to prove your arguments. You might provide factual examples, drawn from research or personal experience. You might also use hypothetical examples to draw the listener into your story.

Many people use faulty forms of reasoning by example that an alert debater might catch and use to her advantage. Thus it is important to carefully analyze these arguments Ask yourself:

- Are there enough examples to prove the claim? Too often, debaters will reason using only one example.

- Are there examples that might directly counter the given examples?

- Are the examples typical of the category the speaker wants to generalize about? It is important to have a representative sample if you wish to reason from example.

Finally, reasoning from example often falls prey to the logical fallacies known as the *fallacy of composition* and the *fallacy of division*. These are discussed in Appendix 3.

Another kind of reasoning is **reasoning from analogy**. When we argue from analogy, we are trying to show that what was true in one situation will be true in an analogous situation. An analogy is a comparison of people, places, things, events, or even abstract concepts. Debaters reason from analogy all the time. In making a case for non-violent resistance to a political policy, you might argue that since such resistance worked in the American civil rights movement, it could work in another case as well. Advertisers also reason by analogy. In the case of the Jones's toilet, referenced above, the advertiser clearly wants viewers to draw an analogy between the Jones's toilet and their own toilet: "Well, if it worked for their toilet, it's *bound* to work in mine!" When analyzing these arguments, you should ask the following questions:

- How strong is the analogy? Are there differences between the two situations, people, events, etc. that are being compared? What are those differences?
- What are the similarities between the two things being compared?
- Do the similarities outweigh the differences? Do the differences outweigh the similarities?

Beware the fallacy of the *false analogy*. Keep your analogies precise and sparing to make your arguments more effective.

Debaters often try to establish causal relationships, either to prove their case or to refute the case of the other side. This technique is called **reasoning by cause**, and it can either be from cause to effect or from effect to cause. When you reason from cause to effect, you begin with a cause and attempt to show what its effects might be. You might argue, for example, that if we act to ban human cloning, the effect would be to drive that research underground into an unregulated "black market." In debate, one of the most common forms of causal reasoning is the *disadvantage*, when the opposition team argues that the proposition's proposed policy will cause negative consequences.

When reasoning by cause, you can also look at existing effects and try to determine their cause(s). Proposition teams use this tactic all the time when they make their case for change. If you were arguing for gun control, for example, you might start by showing how many deaths guns inflict every day. You might then argue that these deaths are the result of (that is, they are *caused by*) the existing, permissive gun laws. This process would be an example of reasoning from effect to cause and is the same tactic doctors often use to make a diagnosis: they will note that you have a cough and a fever, and will reason, based on these symptoms, that you have the flu. As you might imagine, though, reasoning by cause is a tricky business. A few questions to keep in mind when analyzing causal arguments:

- Are there other causes that could have prompted the discussed effect?
- What other effects does the cause produce? How do these weigh against the already specified effects?

Causal reasoning is also prone to many logical fallacies, such as the *post hoc* fallacy and the fallacy of *common cause*, which are defined in Appendix 3.

It is worth noting here that there is another type of reasoning, closely related to causal reasoning, known as **argument by sign**. A sign, of course, is something that stands for something else. When you see a sign, you often assume that certain conditions are true based on your knowledge of what that sign usually represents. For example, when you see a "For Rent" sign on an apartment building, you might believe that you could rent an apartment in that building if you wanted to. Often we mistake signs for causes. It does not follow, for example, that the apartment is for rent *because* the sign is there. *Correlation of events does not imply causality.* Just because the sun rises every morning after you get out of bed, it does not therefore follow that you make the sun rise by getting out of bed.

A final kind of argument is called **argument from authority**, or **reasoning from testimony**. Sometimes when we make arguments, we rely on the opinions or statements of others to help make our point. Most often, arguments from authority or testimony are found in the data component of an argument. Debaters routinely cite various studies or expert opinions to provide the proofs for their claims. The practice of evidence analysis and comparison is a critical part of successful debating, and the evaluation of arguments from authority or testimony is a good place to start in your quest to figure out what constitutes good evidence and what constitutes bad evidence. Here are some preliminary questions to ask of reasoning from authority:

- What are the qualifications of the person(s) cited as a source? Are they qualified to speak about the subject they are cited in?
- Is the source relatively more or less biased about the topic at hand?

Argument from authority is a good way to establish your credibility as a speaker. Audiences are more likely to believe speakers who appear to have credible, relevant facts and testimony to support their conclusions than those who appear to use localized examples or hearsay.

Suggested Exercises

1. Find advertisements that represent each of the categories of reasoning listed above (from authority, from cause, from example, from analogy, from sign). Break down the argument made in each ad using the components of the A-R-E model. In other words, identify the assertion, reasoning, and evidence for each major argument.

2. Examine the editorial page of your local newspaper. Take each editorial and analyze the argument using the techniques listed above. What is the primary argument made by the author? What reasoning does she use? What kind of evidence does she offer as support? Which of the major kinds of reasoning are used in the editorial?

3. Everyone in your group or class should write out an argument in the A-R-E form. Put all of these arguments in a hat and pass the hat around. Pick an argument out of the hat and analyze that argument. Present the argument and your analysis to the rest of the group. Make sure that you identify the potential weaknesses of the argument.

4. Play another game of "I disagree." Make a complete argument on any topic, following the A-R-E model. Then have a partner or classmate refute your argument. Switch roles and repeat the exercise.

When we analyze arguments in debate, we're not just trying to figure out what kinds of arguments they are. We are also trying to figure out which arguments are important and why. In every debate, some arguments are more important than others. If you can identify which arguments are the most important, you will have learned an important skill. Part of debate is convincing the judge that your arguments are the most important. In the section that follows, we explain how to debate the importance of your arguments in a persuasive manner.

Debating Impacts

One thing that differentiates successful debaters from their less accomplished colleagues is their ability to assess and explain impacts. In this section, we will discuss some common criteria for assessing impacts and then proceed to offer some advice about explaining impacts in a way that makes them seem tangible and realistic.

To debate effectively, you will need to learn how to weigh and measure impacts using an array of criteria by which you can assess their relative importance and significance. One of the interesting things about debate is that the criteria for what is to count as significant are always up for debate. Do not assume that you, the judge, and the other debaters agree on what is important for the purpose of evaluating the debate. Even in a non-confrontational situation, you could most likely not agree on a flavor of ice cream. Far better to stake out the battle for what is to count as significant early and often in the debate. Contrary to some popular coaching advice, weighing arguments is not and should not be confined to the last rebuttal (though it is certainly essential to that speech). What follows is a list of some common criteria you can use to compare and contrast impacts (and also, not coincidentally, all kinds of other arguments, argument components, food choices, television programs, vacation options, and elective surgeries).

Number of People Affected

This is one of the simplest impact yardsticks you can employ. It seems too basic to say that some things affect more people than others, yet debaters routinely forget to use this basic calculus. If your case for the proposition claims to save millions of lives by preventing war, pestilence, famine, or plague, then you should probably mention at some point that your plan will save a lot of lives. This tactic becomes particularly important when the opposition argues a disadvantage with a substantially smaller impact than that of your truly massive advantage.

Degree of Harm Inflicted

The number of people affected is rarely, however, an adequate yardstick by itself. You also have to ask yourself what *happens* to those people. Otherwise, you would have to say that it would be worth it to summarily execute ten people if it meant that 50 would not have to wait in line for the bus. You also need to assess the degree of harm inflicted on the potentially hapless victims of the present system and the disadvantage (for example). The aggregate "size" of an impact is usually evaluated with reference to *both* the number of people affected and the degree of harm they must endure.

Probability/Risk

Of course, it is not enough simply to assess the "size" of an impact: All too often, debaters ignore this basic dictate and fetishize impacts of great size and magnitude. Probability *must* figure into any even remotely sophisticated impact calculus. It is an integral part of our everyday decision making, after all. We decide, for example, to cross the street on a daily basis despite the low-probability, high-impact possibility that we might be run over by a bus. We make this decision because we think the probability of such a collision is a *low risk.* Risk is a very important concept in assessing impact debates. As a debater, a judge, or both, you will routinely have to assign *risk* to particular arguments in debates. A convenient formula that some people use to determine the real risk of something is "**Risk = Probability x Impact**." While we are adverse to the mad proliferation of quasi-mathematical formulas that claim to describe everything in our society these days ("War = Peace," "Social Value = Income x Good Looks"), we do find a particular charm in this equation.

In the case of your potential surprise meeting with a wayward bus, we could assess the risk using this kind of formula: the probability is very low, so we see the risk as small even though the impact is high. We could tinker with this formula as it suited us. For example, if the street you needed to cross was routinely full of runaway traffic, the probability of getting hit would go up and you might have to think seriously about how much you *really* need to cross that street. You can also change perceived risk by boosting the impact. Let's say that we could somehow convince you that there was a very small, but real chance that if you walked across the street you would set into motion a chain of events that would lead to human extinction. Here we've got an almost incalculably large impact combined with a small risk. What do you do? Do you decide that you'll just skip that street altogether? Or do you take the risk anyway?

It is important to think about questions like this because you need to think about how average judges and audience members see and evaluate risks in their own lives.

Systemic vs. One-Time

Impacts, like gelatin desserts and other taste treats from the critical "hooves" group, come in a vast range of types. One useful way to categorize impacts is as either *systemic* or *one-time.* A one-time impact is just that: an impact that will only happen once. If you argue that the proposition team's case to regulate genetically modified organisms (GMOs) will cause a trade war or a shooting war, that is a one-time impact that may or may not outweigh the case advantages depending on their relative established magnitude.

Systemic impacts, on the other hand, occur continuously, either through-out time or space or some Star Trek-ish combination of both. Many environmental impacts are systemic, e.g., the presence of PCBs and dioxins in water can cause cancer, deformities, and death for many generations. So we can say, for example, that in a particular region one hundred incidents of cancer per year are due to contaminated air or water. *Over time*, this impact adds up to be a tremendous amount of disease and death. It is critical that when you argue systemic impacts, you impress upon the judge or audience that the *cumulative effect* is quite staggering. It's not as if, for example, the Great Lakes will spontaneously clean themselves.

In the final rebuttals, debates about impact often come down to a comparison of systemic consequences to one-time consequences. You need to compare these risks explicitly for the judge:

> **"The opposition team says that our pesticide regulations will cause a trade war and that this *may* lead to a shooting war. Even if they're right about this dubious claim, we still win this debate because our case advantages are bigger over time. The continued effects of dangerous pesticides will cause tens of thousands of deaths over time. This is certainly a larger consequence than a minor fistfight over sneaker imports."**

The debate over continuing sanctions on Iraq is a good example of how this kind of impact comparison works in public policy forums. The argument for continuing sanctions is, basically, that the probability and impact of Iraq developing weapons of mass destruction is very large. This (more or less) one-time impact is thought by some to trump the systemic impacts of sanctions, which include mass starvation and the death of tens of thousands of children every year. Whether or not you agree with this conclusion is another thing entirely.

Prior Consideration

In some debates, impact comparison and assessment will involve a debate about competing ethical or moral frameworks. One team may argue that their impacts must be considered before evaluating the opposing team's impacts. One classic example of this phenomenon is the "life vs. rights" debate. Let's say that the proposition team defends a case that puts a stop to racial profiling in the USA. They argue that this profiling by race or ethnicity is a violation of human and constitutional rights and should be rejected because of its latent racism. The opposition team argues, in response, that a ban on racial profiling will greatly hamper the ability of law enforcement agencies to fight crime and terrorism, leading to loss of life and property. How should we compare these impacts?

A smart proposition team will argue, in essence, that the ends of a policy do not justify its means of implementation. That is, they will say that the government's obligation to protect rights is a *prior consideration.* In order to win the debate on their terrorism disadvantage, the opposition team will have to show that the debate should be resolved using a *consequentialist* calculus. Consequentialism is a doctrine that the moral rightness of an act or policy depends entirely on its outcome or consequences.

We do not intend here to rehash the last several thousand years' worth of thinking about political and moral philosophy in order to clarify the difference between consequentialist and non-consequentialist perspectives on policy making. It will, however, greatly behoove you to read up on these perspectives so that you can defend both sides of this debate. Consider preparing a critique of consequentialist reasoning, which can be very useful, particularly on the proposition side, if many of your prepared cases have small advantages or impacts.

Independent vs. Dependent

Some impacts are said to be dependent on others to achieve their full force. How would you compare, for example, the relative importance of equality and liberty? One way would be to explain that equality is dependent on liberty. Consider that equality is (generally speaking) the equitable distribution of freedoms, resources, opportunities, or happiness. In order to ensure equality, you could say, we must first have liberty, resources, opportunity, or happiness. Others say (in a very simplistic manner, to be sure), when weighing loss of life against loss of rights, that rights are useless if you are dead.

"Most Grievous Error"

Some impacts are said to be so unbelievably catastrophic (usually nuclear war or global climate change) that even a negligible risk warrants action to prevent them. If you look again at the risk equation above, you'll see how this works. If the impact is infinite, then any non-zero probability multiplied by infinity still adds up to be an infinite risk. See, math class isn't so tough. If this calculus seems a little odd to you, though, you're not alone. Even though the consequences of nuclear war or global climate change are potentially inconceivably horrible, it does not therefore follow that they are literally infinite. Further, this example clearly demonstrates the ultimate fallibility of the risk equation. Useful though math formulas are in debate (which is to say not very much), they are no substitute for good, well-reasoned argument. If we could just calculate our way through the dilemmas of human affairs, we would have no need for debate (or perhaps language) at all.

"Try or die"

A cousin to the "most grievous error" argument, the "try or die" argument has become immensely popular in debate in recent years. The phrase "try or die" is a kind of slogan that appears with alarming frequency in proposition team rebuttals as an attempt to justify implementation of the plan. Here's how this argument works: the proposition team tries to show that there is a gigantic problem in the status quo. This is the "die" part of the equation. The proposition team is trying to establish that we're all going to die (not literally *all* of us, nor will it necessarily involve our *deaths*, per se—perhaps just a light maiming; the idea is to show that a catastrophic impact is inevitable in the status quo). The "try" part of the equation is the part where the judge decides to endorse the plan, even if she is unsure whether it can actually solve the harm. Thus the rhetorical device "try or die": The proposition team tries to convince the judge that they might as well *try* the plan since the consequences of not solving the problem would be so unbelievably huge. This rebuttal technique, while startlingly effective, is generally recognized to be the last resort of proposition teams with poor solvency arguments and dubious plans.

Suggested Exercise

Below find several pairs of competing impacts. Using the techniques above, compare them. You could, for example, argue that one is bigger than the other in scope or magnitude. Perhaps one is systemic while the other is one-time. Pick one of the pair and show why it is worse than its companion impact. Then switch to the other term, and show how it could be argued that it is actually worse.

- economic growth vs. environmental degradation
- warfare vs. poverty
- individual rights vs. social welfare
- earthquakes vs. flooding
- nuclear proliferation vs. biological weapons proliferation

Explaining Impacts

You should explain your impacts. Do not assume that the judge or other debaters involved will see them as the tragic, grievous circumstances that you perceive them to be. To win debates about impacts consistently and successfully, you must appeal to both the reason and the emotions of your judges. All too often, debaters simply fail to explain their impacts in a way that makes them tangible to the judge. It is *not enough*, for example, to say that your plan is a good idea because it ameliorates poverty, or stops inflation, or cleans up the air, or bans bad toupees, or even because nine out of ten dentists endorse it. To make an impact persuasive, you must flesh it out. Personalize it. Help the judge visualize the potential consequences of not voting for your side. Judges like to vote for plans that seem realistic and beneficial. In this way, they are just like average consumers, who want to purchase products that they are reasonably certain will solve an immediate need. Understanding this aspect of judge psychology will enable you to adapt your arguments accordingly.

Most debates are, in fact, won or lost on good impact assessment and explanation. We've already given you some tools to use in comparing your impacts against those of the other team. But comparison is no good without a concomitant explanation of exactly what the judge "gets" when she votes for your side. For example, you *could* just say:

> **"The plan is good because it brings people out of poverty. This outweighs the opposition team's economy disadvantage."**

Or, you could say:

> "Hundreds of thousands of people, many of them children, are starving or malnourished in our country right now because of endemic poverty, and few of these have any hope of surviving to make a meaningful life for themselves. Imagine what it's like to live like this—no food, no shelter, no clothing, constantly wracked by disease. Then, imagine what a tremendous boon the plan would be. Income redistribution would give these families a real chance at life and would, over time, save millions and millions of lives by lifting a whole segment of society out of poverty. The opposition team would have you believe that economic considerations come first, but this is the same economic system that is built on the backs of the same people the plan is trying to help. So corporations lose some

money? So what? That's a small price to pay to lift up the most indigent among us."

The speaker is making the same basic argument as "The plan is good and outweighs their economy disadvantage," but she uses a variety of verbal and persuasive techniques to make the argument more tangible by building on it.

If you have trouble with this process, try thinking in terms of "because." Begin with an impact claim like this one: "Ozone depletion is bad." Then expand on it by using a series of "because" statements:

"Ozone depletion is bad.... *Because*.... More UV radiation will reach the surface of the earth, and that's bad.... *Because*.... Many people will get skin cancer as a result, and that's bad.... *Because*.... Skin cancer is often fatal, and will become more fatal as UV intensity increases."

Try this process using the suggested exercise below to learn how to explain impacts. Remember—judges like to vote for some tangible risk or result. If you can convince them that your risks or results are more tangible, then you will win more debates.

Suggested Exercise

Explain why each of the following impacts is bad. If you have trouble generating explanations, use the "because" method.

- floods
- global warming
- breast cancer
- sexism
- drought
- slavery
- cheese in a can
- famine
- forest fires
- opera
- imperialism
- inflation
- weapons proliferation
- imprisonment
- resource wars
- inequality

Chapter 8

Research and Evidence

Basic Research Issues

In a debate, as in any discussion, it is better to know what you are talking about. The more information, the better. The better the information, the better. Research improves preparation, argument anticipation, refutation, and the general quality of debates. More important for debaters, research may improve debate success; it can provide an edge in debates. The informed are able to draw on a greater range of issues. Additional information assists debaters who want to have more analytical depth on issues. Good debates require extensive preparation. It is a terrible experience for audiences and judges to listen to speakers try to debate a subject about which they are not knowledgeable. You should not even think of debating if you are not committed to reading and researching current issues.

Parliamentary debate requires research on a broad range of issues, as topics may be drawn from many subject areas. This means that parliamentary debaters must be prepared to debate a wide range of current events. Research for parliamentary debate requires substantial advance preparation.

Debaters must prepare on specific issues. This includes knowledge of current events and notes from previous debates, each of which helps prepare students for upcoming contests and debate events. Core value claims—such as life, liberty, equality, justice, privacy, and aesthetics—form the foundation of many debate motions. Students prepared to debate about these concepts will have an edge.

But what does it mean to research a debate subject? What does it mean to research "liberty"? This issue has been investigated for thousands of years. There are millions of pages of texts on the subject. Liberty interests are relevant to virtually every public policy issue. There are thousands of Web pages exploring issues of personal freedom. How is it possible for debaters to investigate this issue carefully? It would take much longer than a lifetime to examine all these materials prior to a debate. This means that research must be targeted and practical. The reality of debating is that you are unlikely to devote more than two or three minutes to even a major line of argument. Debaters, therefore, do not need to master an academic discipline to gain knowledge sufficient to make and refute arguments. You won't need to know everything about the issue of liberty. You need only that information that will produce an edge compared to the knowledge of your opponent.

On an issue like liberty, you will need to have sufficient information to discuss different ideas about liberty. You should be able to compare the value of liberty to other values (e.g., why liberty interests ought to trump equality or privacy rights). You will want to know examples of the benefits and the costs of liberty. You should test your knowledge on several topics that call for debate on liberty issues. For example, do you have enough information to participate in a debate about censorship on the internet? How about sacrificing personal freedom to promote security? Your information should be sufficient to anticipate and counter your opponent's arguments.

Debaters should read at least one newspaper every day. There is no substitute for the diversity of information available in a daily newspaper. Because of the nature of parliamentary debate, debaters must have a variety of information on a wide range of topics. If you read a newspaper every day, you will at least be up to date on current events and topics of general importance. When you read the newspaper, read it with an eye towards debate. Try to identify articles that might contain the information necessary to make good cases for future debates. Take notes. We suggest that you keep a notebook where you store notes from articles and publications that you read so that you will be able to access this information when you are writing cases or putting together information to oppose the cases argued by other teams.

Different debate motions frequently raise similar issues. In other words, the topics might not repeat themselves but the arguments might. Consider, for example, these motions: "This House would televise it"; "The United State Federal Government should increase support for human rights." You might support the first topic with a case that advocated more news and public affairs programs on television. You might argue that this would give more information to citizens for responsible, democratic decision-making. In supporting the second topic, you might construct a case that called for more government support for Voice of America, Radio Free Europe, Radio Free Asia and other public radio and television broadcasts. This would provide information to people throughout the world to resist tyranny and build democracies. Although the topics are clearly different, the debates about them would focus on issues that are quite similar— you would discuss news broadcasts and their influence on promoting democratic behavior and individual decision-making.

On multiple topics, there is substantial repetition of issues. Imagine receiving a third topic—"This House would substantially reform educational practice." Your opponents might argue in favor of the topic. They might do so by arguing that educational reform will improve schools, producing more responsible students and better citizens. You will, of course, note that this issue is similar to general support for democracy, an issue that you have already debated on the two other topics, on television and government support for human rights.

Argument similarity makes parliamentary debate research more manageable. Immigration reform, the use of peacekeeping forces, tax reform, gun control, educational policy, free speech, affirmative action, terrorism, drug legalization, and other popular issues are often debated on more than one topic or as a subset of different topics. A file of topics and issues—that is, a history of debates—will help to direct research and preparation for competitors.

On a competitive parliamentary debate squad, it is also possible to assign different policy and value issues to different debaters. Each student then prepares a "fact and argument sheet" on the subject, noting recent statistical information and arguments for and against the value or policy issue. This sheet may then be shared with other debaters. Even a modest parliamentary debate squad will be able to produce enough notes to provide "background" information on dozens of issues, without overburdening any single debater or team.

Suggested Exercises:

1. Identify a diverse set of issues for research—equality, cloning, paying college athletes, gun control, US military intervention, school uniforms, etc. Debaters should be placed in small groups (3–5 students per group) to brainstorm each issue. The group

should gather fact and credible opinion on the issue, as well as several major arguments for and against. Each group should prepare a fact and argument background sheet for presentation to debaters.

2. Individuals or debate teams should take a daily newspaper and read news articles for promising cases. The issues should be controversial, with substantial consequences for people or institutions. They should identify the proposed case, explain why it is important, and note the relevant supporting information from the newspaper article.

Debate squads should compile notes for each researched topic, building up the base of research over time. We suggest that each squad, or group of colleagues on a debate team, divide up responsibilities for examining different periodicals and publications throughout the year for maximum efficiency in obtaining information. Come up with a list of uniquely useful weekly, monthly, or quarterly publications and assign everyone on the squad to one or more of these resources. That person should be responsible for reading her assignments and reporting to the rest of the group whatever content she found interesting.

Ethics and Evidence

Parliamentary debate is unique among debating formats in that it accepts the voice of the debater as an authority on the subject being debated. This feature of parliamentary debate places a tremendous responsibility on the debater, who takes on the ethical responsibility to represent her sources and information fairly and honestly. At times, some debaters have disregarded or ignored this responsibility and invented facts, figures, and case studies to bolster their arguments in debates. These tactics are to be deplored. *It is not acceptable to make up information in debates.* We repeat: *It is not acceptable to make up information in debates.* This is not ethical behavior. It is also impolite—your opponents deserve your respect and the opportunity to engage in a fair debate. Consider, for a moment, that you ought to treat others as you yourself would want to be treated. When you enter a debate, you expect that your opponents will behave in an ethical and respectful manner. They will expect the same of you. We urge you to act accordingly.

On occasion, you may encounter a debater who, you believe, has her facts wrong. What should you do in this situation? We advise you not to assume that the opposition is cheating or deliberately distorting the truth in order to trick you. They may have made a simple factual error. People do—it is quite common. Even students with a 4.0 grade point average get some of the answers wrong. You need to be tolerant of your opponent's errors. We encourage you to give your opponents the benefit of the doubt; you would want to be given the same treatment in a similar situation. You yourself may be wrong about the facts. Many people are convinced that they know "the facts," but are later proven to be gravely mistaken (e.g., the critics of Galileo, flat earth theorists, phrenologists, particle physicists—all people allegedly operating under the high evidentiary standards of physical science). Of course, when you believe that someone is wrong about an issue, you should debate them on that point. This is the whole purpose of debate.

Preparing Cases

In addition to general preparation, it is wise to prepare specific proposition and opposition argument positions. Here is an example of case development. It includes the following steps:

Step One. Identify a public policy issue. These issues are easily found in the news section of a daily newspaper. In just one issue of the New York Times, for example, there were stories on lifting economic sanctions on terrorist nations, expanding states' rights to protect them from federal control, the inclusion of Russia in NATO decision-making, the need for peacekeeping forces in the Middle East, the problems of nuclear proliferation, terrorism risks in the United States, reorganization of the FBI and CIA, the regulation of internet spam, the death penalty, free speech protection for hate speech, and child welfare reform. Any of these would work.

Take the public policy issue and brainstorm it. This can be done by individuals, teams, or small groups. Analyze the pros and cons of the proposed case idea. Take notes. If you are able to reach a conclusion that the benefits of your position on the issue are greater than the costs (the same simple calculation you would use in a debate), you have the idea for a case.

Step Two. Do advanced research on the issue. Use your notes from the brainstorming session and look for new ideas. Organize your ideas into an outline of an argument. The possibilities include the identification of a problem and its solution, a chronological examination of the development of an idea, a narrative (a story with a moral or ethical point), etc.

Step Three. Use the outline to anticipate the replies from the opposing side. Prepare answers to their arguments.

Step Four. Provide an introduction and conclusion to your presentation. Complete the outline with additional details. You have now completed a comprehensive fact-argument background brief on a policy issue for use as a case. It has an introduction and conclusion, arguments for an interpretation of a topic, and answers to opponent's refutation.

This model of case construction provides many direct and additional benefits for participants. For example, it levels the playing field in your debates against more experienced opponents. One thing that debaters develop over years of debate participation is a reservoir of knowledge about motions and issues. Experienced practitioners are likely to rely on that information during preparation time immediately prior to debates, as well as during the actual contest. For this reason, it is inaccurate to say that parliamentary debaters are exclusively engaged in impromptu or spontaneous argument. In fact, many argument ideas are "scripted," in that the issues have been discussed in previous debates. Experienced debaters often replay the speeches of their debating career, repeating those clever, winning points from previous debates, exploiting lesser-trained or experienced participants who have yet to create their own history of debate practice.

We strongly recommend that debaters and their extended squads build a library of prepared cases for use in tournament debates. This exercise fulfills two major purposes: it prepares debaters to construct a variety of cases; in addition, it ensures that debaters will not be caught wholly unawares and unprepared at tournaments when they are called on to debate the proposition. Using the guidelines for case construction, debaters should generate a series of prepared cases on a variety of topics they are likely to encounter in their competitive debate season. Your prepared case should contain the following components:

- A detailed outline for the first proposition speaker's speech, including an introduction, body (logical argument, with several major points), and a conclusion.
- A list of potential opposition arguments and appropriate answers to these arguments.
- A list of humorous, issue-specific items that can be used to enliven the debate and persuasively convey critical arguments.

Keep these prepared cases in a notebook for reference before your debates. They will help you use your preparation time more productively and efficiently. There is information in each of the following opposition argument chapters on the use of prepared opposition strategies.

Make sure that your prepared cases span a broad range of potential topic areas to maximize their potential applications. You may have to debate issues of environmental policy, education reform, military intervention, fair employment practices, constitutional law, public health, immigration reform, criminal justice policy, and drug policy. You should develop at least one prepared case for each of these topic areas. You should also develop prepared cases that deal with issues of your particular interest.

Advance research should, of course, include research for the opposition side. Opposition teams should prepare arguments on issues that repeat from debate to debate, including research on popular cases, such as gun control, the media, the application of United Nations peacekeeping forces, and trade-offs between the economy and the environment. Debaters should anticipate and research conventional arguments that are frequently used by proposition teams, including core value claims (life, liberty, equality, justice, privacy, order, aesthetics, etc.) and cases they have previously debated.

Finding Evidence

We have already said that good research requires reading a wide variety of magazines, books, and newspapers. Reading for debate is similar in many ways to other reading you may do for classes you are taking or have taken in the past. Since you should expect to read many sources and articles for preparation in parliamentary debate, you will have to develop good skimming and reading comprehension techniques to maximize your efficiency.

Journalists and other authors often craft their writing to make it interesting to their audience. Their care does not always result in articles that are immediately useful to debaters, who must poke through many articles on the same subject in order to construct a good case or a solid opposition argument. The best advice we can give you for critical debate reading and research is this: don't collect facts more or less at random, hoping that they will prove useful at some future point. Every time you collect data, collect it for a specific purpose—for example, to support a case.

Since successful debaters must read a variety of publications, they must develop techniques for skimming the sources they evaluate, gleaning the relevant facts and circumstances as they read. Learn to use keyword identification as you read. Try to identify causal relationships established by authors, conclusions about policy recommendations, and statements of significance (how much does an issue matter and to how many people?). When reading longer articles or books, read the introduction and conclusion first to determine if they will be useful to you. Books, in particular, should be skimmed: read the table of contents, and use the index to identify facts and sections helpful to your research project.

Using Evidence

In parliamentary debate, you are not permitted to read directly from researched materials to prove various points. This rule does not mean, however, that parliamentary debaters should not make informed and well-evidenced arguments. Complete arguments include evidence, that is, historical and contemporary references, examples, analogies and other information to support reasoning. There are many kinds of evidence that debaters can use to prove their points. In many parliamentary debates, as in most discussions, the primary form of evidence is the *example*. Good parliamentary debaters have at their disposal a variety of anecdotes and examples. Examples must be gathered through a process of research and careful note-taking. The goal of research in parliamentary debate is to build a substantial knowledge base from which you can draw support for extemporaneous speeches on a wide variety of topics.

You might, during the course of preparing arguments for various sub-jects, find quotations from various experts. We caution you against trying to reproduce these quotations in parliamentary debates. The substance of the idea ought to "speak for itself," so quotation from others is largely unneces-sary. The practice of quoting an authority may undermine the credibility of the speaker, as the speaker is no longer an authority on the issue but func-tions as a mouthpiece. Rather than quote, for example, the American Heart Association on the most recent statistical details on cigarette smoking mor-tality, it is better for parliamentary debaters to claim that national health organizations, perhaps even noting the American Heart Association, announce that cigarette smoking kills hundreds of thousands of people each year. It is not a direct quotation from an expert authority. It is, however, evidence. It is also well known evidence. The generalization of popular but meaningful information makes it likely that the judge and audience would agree with the evidence, enhancing the credibility of the speaker. Evidence makes the argu-ment and it promotes the speaker's authority.

Consider bringing a selection of texts to a debate tournament to aid in your preparation. Statistical reference texts and other almanacs are a great resource, as they will give you relevant and useful information on a wide vari-ety of topics. You must bring a dictionary to every debate tournament: it will prove invaluable when defining words and interpreting motions during prepa-ration time. You should compile notes from previous debates. Your previous arguments, arguments from your opponents, comments from your coach and from judges and observers, can help you in later debates. You should organ-ize this material and bring it with you for use in your preparation time and between debates.

Finally, we encourage debaters to continue to identify news stories during the course of the tournament. All too often, debate tournaments seem to occur in a news blackout. However, it can be very persuasive to refer an audi-ence or opposing team to a story in that morning's newspaper as support for your argument.

Your research will help you make better, more successful arguments. If you use research appropriately in conjunction with other debate skills, such as argument anticipation and refutation, you will experience more success in your debate performances.

Suggested Exercise

Practice using reference materials to prepare for a selection of topics. Collect research materials that each debate team should bring to a tournament, such as an atlas, a dictionary, and a selection of periodicals on different issues. Your coach or teacher will announce a topic for preparation. Use your preparation materials to gather relevant information for that topic. Debaters should be able to identify support for arguments on the proposition and opposition sides. Try this exercise with multiple topics to practice timed preparation with reference materials.

Chapter 9

Opposition Strategy—
Disadvantages

Introduction to Disadvantages

Proposition teams usually design their cases on a problem-solution model. They identify a problem, thereby showing that there is a *need* for the plan. They then present a solution, or plan, to deal with the problem. This is an effective and logical approach to making a case. It is also a form of argument organization that most people use daily. You have a problem and figure out a way to solve it.

Usually, proposition teams employ a "cost-benefit" approach to show that their plan is a good idea. If you propose a solution to a problem that does not work, or creates another, more serious problem, that solution is not a desirable one. Let's say that you identify a problem—your grades need significant improvement. There are reasonable solutions to the problem. You could study more. You could ask a teacher for help. You could get a tutor. You could pay attention to your daily schedule and eliminate distractions that hurt your school performance, for example, lack of sleep or too much television. There are also unreasonable choices that you could make. You could conclude that there is nothing that might improve your grades and give up. You could cheat on tests. It is a problem and there are a number of possible "solutions"—that is typical of the everyday experience of most people. Some of the available solutions are worthwhile (the benefits are greater than the costs) and others are potentially disastrous (the costs are greater than the benefits). Debaters use this kind of cost-benefit model all the time. In a debate, the benefits are called **advantages** and the costs are called **disadvantages**.

Debaters and judges are constantly in a position of trying to decide which arguments are more important than other arguments, either in terms of significance, probability, soundness of data or reasoning, or some combination of all these factors. We *weigh* these arguments against each other, just as if we placed them on a scale to determine the heavier object, to determine which is the most important. One argument is said to *outweigh* another if it is more significant according to the decision criteria established in the debate.

The proposition team, then, tries to establish that the benefits of their plan will outweigh its potential costs. In other words, the plan has more advantages than disadvantages. This is only logical. One important strategy the opposition team can take to counter this approach is to show that, in fact, the costs of the proposed plan outweigh the benefits. We have already learned some basic techniques for refuting the proposition case. We've seen how to debate attacks on significance and solvency. A solvency turn is one example of an opposition argument that tries to show that the proposition team's plan has more costs than benefits. Another such argument is the *disadvantage*.

A disadvantage argues that the adoption of the plan will cause something bad to happen. In formal debates, opposition teams argue disadvantages when they want to show that adoption of the plan, usually a proposed government policy, will lead to undesirable consequences that are far greater than any potential benefits. Disadvantages are causal arguments, often composed of one or more cause-effect relationships, that show that the plan will lead to an ultimate impact, or negative consequence. This simply means that to prove a disadvantage, you must show that the proposition team's plan will cause something to happen and that it will be bad.

Disadvantages are one kind of indirect refutation of the proposition team's case, and are typically known as *off-case arguments.* Far from being irrelevant to the case, an off-case argument does not directly refute the fundamental arguments of the case proper, i.e., the first proposition constructive arguments. Some opposition arguments directly challenge the major points of the proposition team's case. These arguments may, for example, dispute the factual claims and informed opinions in the opening speech. Many cases, however, do not discuss all possible relevant arguments to the issue hand. A proposition speaker inevitably leaves out some information because of the time limits of the speech or that the ideas may support the opposition position. The opposition may present arguments that indirectly refute the case; that is, they may develop and introduce their own arguments. "Off-case" generally refers to the opposition's forms of indirect refutation, e.g., topicality arguments, counterplans, disadvantages, and critiques.

You have already learned what an *impact* is. Case advantages have impacts. Perhaps the proposition team claims that their plan will save lives, improve the economy, preserve constitutional or human rights, or attain any number of other benefits. Disadvantages also have impacts. Opposition teams may argue that the adoption of the plan may end lives, hurt the economy, threaten constitutional or human rights, or cause any number of other harms. Disadvantages are an oppositional version of advantages.

Opposition teams may, in theory, argue any number of different disadvantages in a given debate. The purpose of these arguments is relatively simple: to prove, at the end of the debate, that it would be undesirable to adopt the proposition team's case.

Suggested Exercise

Identify public policy changes that are proposed by the government in new legislation or regulations. Analyze them for their costs and benefits. Explain the reasons that the costs might be greater than the benefits.

Basic Anatomy of the Disadvantage

It is important to note that disadvantages, like most debate arguments, can be generic or specific. There are, to be sure, generic, or general, problems with many new public policies. For example, there are limited financial, material, and personnel resources. The resources for new policies, regardless of the particular policy, might trade off with resources for established, effective policies. New regulations also inevitably concern businesses. Businesses are increasingly concerned with government bureaucracy and its impact on effective business practices and the economy. Almost any approach to regulation of business practice or the economy (environmental regulations, civil rights reform, occupational health and safety, tax reform, etc.) might negatively affect businesses, investment, and the economy.

There are also specific problems with plans. A proposal requiring new passive safety devices in cars might increase vehicle prices, with the consequence that people will drive their older and more dangerous cars for a longer time before replacing them. In addition, there is evidence that drivers are more reckless if they believe their cars are safer. They are, therefore, more likely to produce accidents with safer vehicles.

Of course, you will need to have many kinds of disadvantages considered and prepared in advance of tournament competition or public events. But you will always have to make these general disadvantages apply *specifically* to the proposition team's case. In this section, we will see how disadvantages work. First, we'll look at some examples to see what disadvantages look like and how they may be argued. Then, we'll offer some vocabulary to use in discussions about disadvantages.

Example #1: Business Confidence

Proposition Plan: The government should increase taxes on corporate profits to generate more money for welfare.

Opposition Disadvantage: "The proposition plan will cause a near-total collapse in business confidence, destroying the economy as a result. The economy is teetering on the edge of collapse right now for a variety of reasons. Although ultimately it will probably pull through, the proposition plan will doubtless reverse this state of affairs and send the economy into a tailspin. The economy is in recession and showing only weak signs of recovery. The stock market is wavering, unemployment is rising, and consumer spending is slowing. A new blow to the economy at this time might be particularly threatening.

Corporate profits are low enough as it is, and we depend on the strength of corporations to pull us out of the current recession. If the proposition plan passes, corporations will not only lose money in the short term, but they will lose confidence in the government for the long term. They will believe that any strong profit showings in the future might be another excuse for the government to tax their profits. They will not believe that the US market is a good place for their long-term interests. This loss of confidence will cause some businesses to go bankrupt and others to flee the country in search of greener pastures.

This will have a ripple effect—other businesses will follow their lead and soon there will be a general economic panic. This has happened in previous recessions in the US and abroad. The net result will be the collapse of the economy. Millions will be out of work and hungry. The money "redistributed" to welfare will not even provide for the poor because so many new poor will be added to the welfare rolls. So, when they collapse the economy, not only won't they solve their own advantage, but they will make matters worse."

Commentary   In this example, the opposition is using a three-tiered strategy to relate their disadvantage to the plan. Notice how the opposition speaker makes three distinct arguments about why the plan will be bad for business:

- Businesses will go bankrupt because they will lose money and fear excessive government involvement in the private economy.
- Other businesses will leave the country because they are losing money here.
- There will not be enough money to redistribute in the form of welfare.

This is a sophisticated strategy for arguing a disadvantage. You should try to relate your disadvantage to the plan in as many ways as possible to make it more convincing to the judge. Also, note how the speaker argues that if the economy collapses, the plan will be unable to fulfill its goals. In essence, the speaker proves that if she wins the disadvantage, the *case will be turned* because it will cause the opposite of what it tries to accomplish. Does the speaker make a persuasive case for the disadvantage?

Example #2: Strategic Substitution

Proposition Plan: The United States Federal Government should stop the production and distribution of land mines.

Opposition Disadvantage: "The proposition plan will cause a strategic shift by military planners. The Pentagon's defense analysts will substitute other weapon systems for land mines, increasing the likelihood of arms races and conflicts.

Military planners use land mines to slow the movements of enemy forces. They are defensive weapons. If this weapon is taken away, these planners will not abandon national security interests; they will simply think of another strategy to accomplish their goals. If defensive weapons are unavailable, they will use offensive ones. This will mean that the military will rely on more powerful weapons, combined with an early-strike strategy. They will do this because without land mines, they will have no way to slow enemy forces. The solution is to strike quickly and with considerable force. This is dangerous. The addition of offensive weapons is known to create arms races, with one side trying to match or exceed the armaments available to the other. Conflict, particularly accidental conflict or war during a crisis, is more likely when troops are on a hair-trigger alert and have first-strike strategies.

Land mines, for all their problems, are defensive weapons that make immediate conflict difficult. They allow nations to take time during a crisis to cool down and open negotiations to solve differences. They give confidence to field commanders that they will not have to use their weapons or lose them— they can be cautious rather than employ immediate and first strike strategies. Land mines defuse arms races. A ban on the production and distribution of land mines is likely to produce a serious conflict and cost many thousands of lives, exactly the opposite of the advantage claimed by the proposition team."

Commentary   Disadvantages serve to show a judge that the world is not a struggle between good and evil. The proposition team will almost always present a powerful and sensible case. That does not mean that the opposition must defend "evil" to resist it. The opposition, despite its name, does not simply argue the "opposite" of the case. In this example, the proposition team has argued that land mines kill innocent people years after combat has ended; in response, the opposition team would not argue that it is desirable to kill innocent men, women, and children with land mines. Rather, the disadvantage shows that the real struggle in the debate is between *competing goods*. The proposition and opposition both want to save lives. Here, the opposition has argued that the proposition case is not a good idea, even in its own terms. It will not protect life. It will make conflicts more likely and more violent.

Would this disadvantage persuade a judge? If so, how would it do so? Can you think of examples of strategic or tactical substitutions by military planners, when weapons have been changed or modified, to provide evidence for the disadvantage?

Example #3: Court Credibility

Proposition Plan: The U.S. Supreme Court should overturn Roe v. Wade.

Opposition Disadvantage: "The proposition plan is terribly disadvantageous. It will destroy the already fragile credibility of the Supreme Court, eliminating the Court's ability to serve as a necessary check on the unconstitutional excesses of the legislative and executive branches.

When the Court overturns Roe v. Wade, it will be in essence admitting that it was wrong for decades about a popular decision. People will have no reason to trust them about future decisions because the Court will be seen as fickle. Unfortunately for the proposition team, this deathblow to the Court's credibility will have lasting and devastating consequences. The Supreme Court is vital to maintaining our system of checks and balances. If they aren't credible, no one will enforce their decisions. The net effect of the proposition plan will be unchecked tyranny of the legislative and executive branches. Might as well use the Constitution to light a fire—it won't be good for much else."

Commentary   One of the strong suits of this disadvantage, as presented, is its strong wording. The speaker uses words like "fickle," "deathblow," and "devastating." In debate, we call this *power wording*—the idea being that you should use striking words with a lot of force whenever possible, as such phrasing helps cement your ideas in the mind of your judge. Notice also that the speaker advances the claim that the "net effect" of the plan will be "unchecked tyranny." This is a setup for the rebuttal, when she will have to prove that her disadvantage outweighs the case impact. How is this disadvantage different from the previous examples? How does the speaker's use of humor at the end of her presentation affect the overall persuasiveness of the disadvantage?

Example #4: Symbolic Action

Proposition Plan: The United Nations should pass a resolution stating its support for fair trade instead of free trade.

Opposition Disadvantage: "The proposition team's plan is a purely symbolic action that will only delay real, lasting, meaningful social change. It is disadvantageous.

"Right now, a variety of social movements are mobilizing to promote fair trade and protest against the corporatist practices of agencies like the World Trade Organization. The plan's action serves as a Band-Aid solution; in other words, it is a superficial solution to a deep and abiding wound. Activist movements are on the verge of reaching critical mass to effect lasting change in the area of fair trade policies. Meanwhile, the proposition team's plan acts to take the wind out of their sails, undercutting the growth and political power of new social movements just as they're about to achieve some of their goals. The question is this: Is it better to have social change from above, by the government, or from below, by the people? The proposition team's plan dictates change from above, and so will fail because it doesn't wait for the all-important consciousness-raising period. It is not as likely to have the kind of political support necessary for genuine change. Plus, it serves as a purely symbolic action, undermining the strength of potentially revolutionary social movements that, left to themselves, would solve the case harms and so much more. Few people will donate or rally to the cause of social organizations if they believe that the problem identified by those groups has already been "solved." The plan is therefore, on balance, not beneficial."

Commentary   The symbolic action disadvantage serves a wide range of interests against a wide range of cases. The core of this argument is that the proposition team's case is basically a purely symbolic, fundamentally toothless action, which is bad because such incremental, cosmetic reform directly undercuts social reform movements that would otherwise produce better solutions to the problem in question. If you were to argue a disadvantage like this, you would have to emphasize that the social movements in question would solve the problem if left to their own devices. Notice how this speaker creates a sense of urgency about the status of the movements. She says that the fair trade movements are "on the *verge* of reaching *critical mass*," thereby communicating to the judge that now is the key time for these movements. The implication is that if the plan were implemented at this unique junction in history, it would have particularly bad consequences. Do you find the presentation of this disadvantage to be persuasive? Why or why not? How does it differ substantively and structurally from the presentations of the previous disadvantages?

Now that we've seen a few examples of disadvantages in action, let's learn some general vocabulary to use when talking about them. Note that these vocabulary words are generally *not* for use in debate rounds. Judges and audiences, in general, will not have a working knowledge of formal debate vocabulary of any kind. Use of excessive debate jargon in your speeches will sound silly and almost certainly lose and confuse the judge. That said, it is also the case that debate, like all other disciplines or activities, has its own jargon and slang. It is often created for the convenience of the participants, who will want and need to communicate their ideas quickly with teammates and coaches. (Remember that there is only a brief preparation time prior to debates. Speech efficiency during this time is essential.)

There are only a few key terms to keep in mind when thinking about disadvantages. The first is the concept of a *link*. In formal debates, a link is the relationship of one's argument to the opponent's position in the debate, as well as the internal chain of reasoning in a complex argument. More specifically, links are how disadvantages apply to a proposition team's case. In the examples above, the *links* to the proposition team's case occur first in the disadvantage. In example #3 above (the court credibility disadvantage), the initial disadvantage link is that an overturn of Roe v. Wade would hurt court credibility.

Disadvantages also have *internal links*. These are just connections in the chain of causal reasoning of the disadvantage. Sometimes disadvantages will have many internal links; at other times, they will have only a few. In the example on strategic substitution, the chain of reasoning includes the following: military planners will respond to the loss of land mines; they will increase offensive weapons; they will place the weapons on high alert. To make disadvantages more persuasive to your judge and audience, keep the number of internal links to a minimum. Judges and audiences tend to get bored, annoyed, and skeptical of long and tenuous chains of reasoning.

Internal links lead, ultimately, to the *impact* of a disadvantage. The impact to an argument is similar to the "therefore" step used in the four-step refutation process: It is the ultimate result of your preceding reasoning. Impacts used above include "tyranny," a "shooting war," and, in the case of the symbolic action argument, "sweeping fair trade reforms."

1. Identify the link arguments used by each of the above disadvantages. How does each argument relate to the specific plan offered as an example?

2. Identify the impact arguments used by each of the above disadvantages. Be specific. Which disadvantages, if triggered, might implicate the proposition team's ability to solve their designated harms? How?

3. Identify the internal links used by each of the above disadvantages. Using a simple flowchart or other diagram, explain what steps each disadvantage must go through in order to reach its impact.

Advanced Disadvantage Anatomy

Disadvantages must have a link and an impact. This is the nature of a disadvantage argument. There are other aspects to arguing a disadvantage, though. For example, if the opposition wants to show that the plan will cause some bad thing to happen, it needs to show that this bad thing is not happening now. Otherwise the argument will be irrelevant. This is true in everyday argument:

> Parent: If you make that face for too long, it'll freeze that way.

> Child: Too late. It's already frozen that way.

Consider the example of the court credibility disadvantage detailed above. The opposition team is arguing that the plan will hurt the credibility of the Supreme Court, which would be bad. What if the proposition team responded by saying that the credibility of the Supreme Court was *already* terrible, especially given the controversial *Bush v. Gore* decision made in 2000? Why would this be a good argument for the proposition team to make?

Think about it: if the proposition team can establish that court credibility is already low, then they have a pretty good shot at disproving the disadvantage. They can show that *their plan* cannot make the problem any worse, and so the disadvantage is not a reason to vote for the opposition team. This kind of argument is called a *uniqueness* argument in formal debates.

Uniqueness is the part of a disadvantage that proves that the proposition plan and only the proposition plan could trigger the impacts. Affirmative advantages can also have a burden of uniqueness: if their harm is being solved now, then there is no unique need for the plan.

Uniqueness means that an argument applies to one, and only one, team in the debate. As a debater, you want only good arguments, advantages, and benefits to apply to your side of the debate and want undesirable ideas, disadvantage, and costs to apply to your opponent. The reason should be obvious. Debating involves a comparison of the ideas of the competing teams. Only those issues that give you an edge will help your arguments compare favorably to those of the other team. If each team in the debate would help the economy earn $1 billion, how could that claim assist in making a favorable comparison of one team against the other team? It cannot. There is no advantage to either team on this issue. Both teams would produce $1 billion and so that cannot be a factor in determining which team is better.

So when we say that disadvantages must be *unique*, we are saying that the opposition team must prove that the causal chain of events is not occurring in the status quo (present system). By extension, the opposition team must show that the plan will uniquely provoke the disadvantageous reaction outlined in the disadvantage argument itself. Opposition teams generally advance uniqueness arguments in their first presentation of the disadvantage. What kinds of uniqueness arguments are made in the disadvantage examples 1–4 listed above?

- **Business Confidence**: The speaker makes a uniqueness argument when she says this: *The economy is teetering on the edge of collapse right now for a variety of reasons. Although ultimately it will probably pull through, the proposition plan will doubtless reverse this state of affairs and send the economy into a tailspin.* This reasoning is a uniqueness argument because the speaker is trying to demonstrate that the economy will recover if left alone, but that the implementation of the plan will disrupt that recovery.

- **Symbolic Action**: The speaker is trying to establish that movements are mobilizing now: "Right now, a variety of social movements are mobilizing to promote fair trade and protest against the corporatist practices of agencies like the World Trade Organization." This statement is a uniqueness argument for the disadvantage because it tries to show that *everything is fine now.*

The concept of uniqueness can be one of the most confusing for beginning debaters. Remember that the opposition wants to prove that the present system is fine now, and that the proposition plan will upset this balance.

Other useful concepts in arguing disadvantages include the concepts of *brink, time frame,* and *threshold.* When we say a disadvantage is on the brink, we mean that it is an immediate possibility. It is on the edge of occurring. An opposition debater wants to claim that the proposition plan is enough to push the chain leading up to the impact over the brink. An example of a *brink* argument can be found in the symbolic action disadvantage presented above: "Activist movements are on the verge of reaching critical mass to be able to effect lasting change in the area of fair trade policies." Some key words here, used to indicate that a brink is near, are "verge" and "critical mass."

The *time frame* is the amount of time it takes for a particular condition to occur, usually (in the case of a disadvantage) its impact. It is usually said that disadvantages with a quick time frame—i.e., whose impacts will happen quickly rather than over the long term—are more persuasive. This is not, however, always true. We examined the issue of time frame more completely in the section on impact analysis and comparison.

Finally, disadvantages often have a *threshold.* A *threshold* is the degree of change necessary to precipitate a particular outcome. In debates about disadvantages, a threshold is usually the degree of change of a plan from current policy that will trigger undesirable consequences. All links, internal links, and impacts have thresholds, i.e., they have a trigger point or tipping point which, when passed, will kick in the next level of the causal chain. To remember this term, think of the threshold of a doorway. You can approach a door all you want, but once you have passed through the threshold, you have unmistakably walked through the doorway. Some phenomena have higher or lower thresholds than others. For example, it may take a lot of doing to make you take out the trash, but very little effort to get you to eat a delicious gourmet meal. Trash removal, then, has a high threshold. Gourmet meal consumption, however, has a low threshold.

All of these words may seem complicated, but in fact they are fairly commonsensical and can be easily remembered and applied once you figure out what makes a disadvantage work. In order to win debates on disadvantages, you'll need to come up with a reliable stable of arguments to deploy on demand. The examples provided in this chapter are a good start, but you'll need a wider variety in order to succeed. How can you come up with good ideas for disadvantages? The best place is to begin with the proposition team's case. Why isn't the plan being done now? Odds are that if the plan is, in fact, a good idea, then someone or something pretty important is keeping it from being done. Some examples might be:

- **Vested interests.** Sometimes powerful political forces conspire to keep certain items off the policy agenda because they stand to lose influence or money. Fossil fuel industries, for example, lobby furiously against legislation to reduce carbon emissions. These vested interests are grounds for a disadvantage: Ask yourself what would happen if these industries were hurt financially or if they felt betrayed by government action that ran contrary to their perceived interests.

- **Financial shortages.** Some policies aren't being pursued now because there isn't enough money to do them, or they are too expensive. Perhaps money is tight and implementing the new policy would result in a tradeoff with another, more desirable, program.

The idea here is to figure out who or what stands to lose if the plan is adopted.

Suggested Exercise

Below are a few examples of proposition cases. Generate a disadvantage argument for each plan. Try to make your link arguments and impact arguments as specific as possible.

- The government should ban the possession of all handguns.
- The United Nations should make all decisions by vote of the General Assembly, rather than letting some decisions be made by the Security Council alone.
- School district zero tolerance policies are justified.
- The USA should recognize Taiwan as an independent state.

Answering Disadvantages

A proposition debater has to learn how to answer disadvantages in a comprehensive and persuasive manner. This task can sometimes be a difficult enterprise, as it is hard to predict what disadvantages the opposition team will argue. Many proposition debaters have great difficulty answering disadvantages in a constructive way. Often, they will simply make one response or ignore the disadvantage altogether, no doubt using the strategy of "ignore it and it'll go away" that works so well for children. Below is constructive, step-by-step advice to proposition teams about how to debate disadvantages.

Step 1: Analyze the Disadvantage

This is the most important part of the process. If you misread the disadvantage, you could fail to answer it properly. You might even answer it in entirely the wrong fashion, and lose the debate. (Don't laugh! It happens to almost everyone sooner or later.) To analyze the disadvantage, you must answer the following questions:

- What's the link? What is it about *your plan*, specifically, that supposedly triggers the disadvantage?

- What are the internal links? The opposition team is alleging that your plan causes something, which causes something else, which causes something bad to happen. Figure out what those internal links are. They are often the weakest part of any disadvantage.

- What's the impact? What is the bottom-line bad thing that the opposition team says will happen?

- How does the impact compare to the impacts of your case advantages? Is it bigger or smaller? Will it happen sooner or later? Is it a one-time event or a systemic problem?

Step 2: Generate Answers to the Disadvantage

Once you've identified the critical components of the disadvantage, you need to generate answers to it. The best place to do this is on your flow (your notes for the debate) or even on a separate piece of paper. Even if you are not planning to number your arguments in your speech, consider numbering them on the page so you can easily check for duplication and relevance. We suggest generating more answers than you will eventually make in your speech and then paring the list down to the best two or three arguments. A few things to keep in mind:

Answering Links   You almost always need to answer the link when debating a disadvantage. Generally speaking, disadvantages come in two kinds: those whose link to the plan is virtually certain, and those whose link is tenuous. When you assess that the link is very strong, don't waste valuable speech time attacking it. Instead, focus your energies on other parts of the disadvantage.

When you think the link argument is tenuous and easily challenged—in other words, that the disadvantage is not relevant to your plan—concentrate your fire at that level of the disadvantage rather than scattering your answers around.

Link arguments come in two varieties: simple (defensive) "no link" arguments and offensive "link turn" arguments. When you argue that there is no link to the disadvantage, you are saying that its relationship to the plan is nonexistent or negligible at best. Phrase your argument in a simple, declarative fashion:

> "On the business confidence disadvantage. There is no link to the plan, because we don't take enough money from corporations to cause a loss in confidence."

Remember that it is the *opposition's responsibility to establish the link to the plan*. As a proposition speaker, you should emphasize this burden to the judge.

You can also make offensive "link turn" arguments. A *turn*, also known as a "turnaround," or, historically, as "turning the tables," is an argument that reverses the position of an opponent. An argument used against you is "turned" when you capture it and it becomes an idea in your favor. Link turns are arguments that attempt to reverse a link established by the other team. For example, if the opposition team argued a disadvantage that said the plan would hurt economic growth, the proposition team might argue a *link turn* by saying that their plan would actually help economic growth. Think about it: what if, by proving that your plan helped the economy, you could argue that saving the economy was actually an *advantage* for your plan rather than a disadvantage? Link turns are powerful arguments.

Answering Uniqueness   Most disadvantages are vulnerable at the level of uniqueness. That is, there are many things that could potentially trigger the impact without the aid or succor of the plan. You need to think of what those things are and cite them, as in this example:

> "They say our plan will collapse the economy, but we disagree. If record unemployment, low consumer confidence, and a burgeoning recession haven't collapsed the economy, then our small, fiscally responsible policy will certainly not accomplish this."

Proposition team uniqueness arguments generally come in two kinds: historical and predictive. Historical uniqueness arguments show that there are present or historical conditions that should have triggered the disadvantage. The economy example given just above is a historical uniqueness argument.

It has the added advantage of showing that the internal link to the disadvantage is *empirically denied*.

When you make a predictive uniqueness answer, you are saying that some thing will happen in the future that will cause the disadvantage. In the case of the business confidence disadvantage above, you might show that the government will adopt more regulations in the future that will be equally, if not more, controversial than the plan. This argument proves that the disadvantage is not a reason to reject the plan, since its consequences will happen with or without the plan.

Debating Impacts   It is **vital** that you debate the impact to disadvantages argued in debates. Even if, in your judgment, the impact is inconsequential or negligible, you still need to say so in your speech:

> **"They say that the plan will increase bureaucracy, but we think that's a small price to pay for lifting millions out of poverty."**

Notice how it is *not enough* merely to say that the impact is small. From a galactic perspective, the Earth is pretty small. You must always say that the impact is small compared to something else, in your case, the impact of your case's advantages.

Just as with links, there are two basic ways to argue against impacts. You can argue defensively, saying that the impact is not really bad, or that other things will reduce it (for example, coming economic reforms or tax changes might stop any adverse economic impact). You can also argue offensively, *turning* the impact just as you might turn the link. An *impact turn* is an argument that tries to reverse an established impact. Using the business confidence example, a proposition team might argue that economic growth is devastating to the environment, thereby *turning* the impact of the disadvantage.

Making Offensive Arguments   It is important to try and have at least one offensive argument against every opposition disadvantage. **BUT (and this is VERY important), you should never argue link turns and impact turns against the same disadvantage.** This unfortunate occurrence is called a *double turn*. When a team argues a *link turn* ("We stop that problem from happening") AND an *impact turn* ("That problem is actually a benefit") on the same disadvantage, they are saying, in effect, that they will stop a good thing from happening. This means that the proposition team is essentially arguing a new disadvantage against its own case. Even if you do not choose to continue arguing your turn in the rebuttals, it is usually a good idea to have turn arguments in your constructive speeches: Turns make it more difficult for opposition teams to conclusively win disadvantages.

Brainstorming Answers   It is difficult to answer disadvantages on the fly, in debates with very little preparation time, but you can do a lot of planning before the debate begins.

- Make a list of common disadvantages for any topic. Use the examples in this book as a starting point for such a list.
- Make a list of disadvantages that apply specifically to your prepared cases. Ask yourself: What disadvantages would I run if I was on the opposition side?

Then, generate a few standard answers for each of the disadvantages on your list. Take stock of your prepared cases and figure out what disadvantages may potentially be linked to them so that you can be ready for prepared opposition teams.

Politicians, social activists, media consultants, lobbyists, public relations operatives, and others involved in policy decision-making regularly engage in this practice. If you want to make your point effectively, you must anticipate the advantages of your idea and points of disagreement likely to be raised by your opponents. You should then prepare answers to their objections. This allows you to argue the idea effectively in full.

Use Your Case   The most important thing to remember when debating disadvantages is to *use your case* to answer them. Your case should be structured in such a way as to address the major opposition arguments preemptively. You can do more than this initial effort, though. You should use your case to make link turn and uniqueness arguments. In a debate where the proposition team has advocated providing comprehensive national health insurance, the opposition has argued that this plan would hurt the economy. What is the proposition's response?

> "They say that our plan will hurt the economy, but this couldn't be further from the truth. The existing lack of comprehensive national health insurance is already hurting the economy and will continue to do so. This is true for a couple of reasons: when people don't have health insurance, they are likely to see a doctor only when they need acute care. Because these people don't have insurance, taxpayers end up footing gigantic bills. Preventative medicine is much cheaper in the

> long run than the painful lack of a system we have now. Also, with a single-payer system, the government will be paying out less in Medicaid/Medicare benefits than it is now. In the long run, we will massively help the economy."

The proposition speaker is using her case to turn back the disadvantage. Notice how she makes a coordinated attack on the disadvantage. She begins by making a uniqueness argument: "The existing lack of comprehensive national health insurance is already hurting the economy and will continue to do so." This argument is designed to show that the harm to the economy is both *ongoing* and *inevitable*. The ensuing explanations are also link turns to the disadvantage. The speaker makes three distinct link arguments: acute care, preventative medicine, and Medicare/Medicaid payouts.

Step 3: Make Your Answers

A final question is this: when you answer disadvantages (and we hope that you will, indeed, answer them rather than merely looking confused at the prospect), how should you phrase your answers? There are at least two schools of thought on this issue, and your manner of debating should always vary based on your audience, judge preferences, and the habits and norms of the community in which you are competing. You may find you want to make a few arguments but don't know how to present them. Don't panic. You have at least two options:

- **Combining**. You can combine your arguments into a cohesive whole, in essence offering a short speech in response to the disadvantage. The above response defending national health insurance is one example of this technique.

- **Separating**. You can also offer your arguments individually, phrasing them as discrete entities. For this technique to succeed, we suggest you number your arguments or use some kind of transitional language to ensure that everyone involved is able to follow you. This technique is discussed in greater detail below.

If you are debating in the USA, either technique is certainly acceptable, although the majority of parliamentary debaters these days seem to separate their arguments for more direct clash and easier note taking. If you are debating outside of the USA, you may find that your judges prefer that you combine your arguments into a more cohesive whole. There are certainly exceptions to this generalization. Many international debaters and international judges prefer the rigorous, specific refutation enabled by separating individual arguments.

This concept of separating your arguments may seem a bit confusing at first, but really it's quite simple. When you generate answers to a disadvantage, you'll end up with a few discrete and potentially unrelated answers. Remember the "symbolic action" argument from a few pages back? You might come up with three different answers and, in lieu of combining them, decide to offer them up as a multi-pronged attack on the disadvantage. You would then end up saying something like this:

"On the symbolic action disadvantage. We have three answers.

1. It doesn't apply to the plan. Our proposal is certainly not a Band-Aid solution. A United Nations push to pressure for fair trade would constitute major progress in the fight for environmental and labor protections.

2. Movements are doomed now. Fair trade movements are struggling now. Just look at the present protests. Sure, they're big, but they don't achieve any consensus for change. In the present system, movements will surely fail to enact lasting change.

3. The plan saves the fair trade movement. Our plan puts wind *into* the sails of the movements by sending a critical signal of support from the United Nations. The resolution of support is a win for movements, giving them a success at a critical time when they must have something to rally around. They will also be able to use the resolution to build larger, more diverse coalitions."

The proposition speaker has taken three discrete arguments and offered them separately, yet as a concerted attack. The first argument is a "no link" attack. The second is a "uniqueness" argument. The speaker concludes with a "link turn." Notice that she has not felt compelled to use debate jargon to talk about her arguments. Avoiding jargon makes her arguments better and more effective.

These arguments are phrased and structured in a very precise manner. Each individual argument begins with a "tag line," or "signpost," a concise summary of the argument that is to follow, also called the *claim*. The reasoning and the evidence follow in the subsequent part of each argument. Why are the arguments structured this way? There are several reasons. First, when you offer a quick summary of your argument, you help the judge and audience to follow your reasoning because they know what to expect. Second, having quick and simple tags for individual arguments facilitates effective note taking. Finally, if you phrase your arguments in this way, you will find it easier to continue them through your rebuttals. You will be able to say to the judge:

> "As to the symbolic action disadvantage. The team from State State still hasn't addressed our argument that this disadvantage plainly does not apply to the plan, which is a large-scale action..."

This way, with only a few words, you and the judge are instantly on the same page. Pity the team from State State (Go State!). Their members are obviously not taking good notes. If they were, they might have clashed directly with your argument instead of ignoring it.

Why would you separate your arguments with numbers or other explicit transitional language? Aside from the reasons given above, many involved in debate feel that this added bit of structure promotes direct clash by facilitating comprehensive refutation of individual arguments. Many debaters, however, have a tendency to get carried away at the "microlevel" of the debate and miss the big picture. It is important to balance attention to individual arguments with attention to the bigger concerns, such as: Why, exactly are you (choose one) a) winning the debate; b) losing the debate; c) wearing that hideous tie?

NOTE: The strategies described above are generally used for answering all kinds of off-case arguments. With disadvantages, counterplans, critiques, and topicality arguments, you will always have the option of combining your arguments or separating them out.

Suggested Exercise

Using the four sample disadvantages listed in the first section (business confidence, strategic substitution, court credibility, symbolic action), generate four answers for each. Assume you are defending the sample case offered in each example. Write out your answers for each disadvantage in both the separated and combined formats given above.

Chapter 10

Opposition Strategy— Counterplans

Introduction to Counterplanning

Traditionally, the proposition team is the advocate of change in a formal debate, while the opposition denies the necessity for change by defending the *status quo*. This model is based on legal argumentation, whereby the prosecution argues for change in the defendant's status (i.e., from free to incarcerated) while the defense argues for no change (i.e., the defendant should remain free).

The ability to defend the *status quo* carries certain advantages for the opposition. The world that exists is well known to the judge and audience. In this respect, the opposition ideas are grounded in the knowledge base and expectations of their listeners. In addition, many people harbor an uncertainty about the future, making them reluctant to support wholesale policy changes. People feel more secure with what they have, even when promised potentially greater benefits in the future. (In this respect, judges and audiences follow the cliché, "A bird in the hand is worth two in the bush.") This is a decided psychological advantage for the opposition. The proposition team has the responsibility to prove that their case is better than maintaining the present system. Many opposition teams find the present system easy to defend, as it is relatively stable and predictable.

By no means is the opposition's strategic arsenal limited to defense of the present system. A defense of the status quo is only one way to undermine the need for, or viability of, the proposition team's case. Another, very powerful option, is the *counterplan*. A counterplan is a hypothetical proposal offered by the opposition that provides a reason to reject the proposition team's plan or proposal. In many ways, it is a thought experiment. A counterplan asks us to consider the following question: if the proposition plan existed, would it interfere with other potential plans that might be more valuable? In economic terms, a counterplan reveals an *opportunity cost*; it shows the choice of the plan would deprive us of a better choice.

In everyday discussion and argument, we argue counterplans all the time without even realizing it. If you are discussing dinner plans with your friends, you do not feel bound to defend the status quo if you disagree, do you? If you did, the discussion would look something like this:

> **Friend: Gee, I'm hungry. Let's go get hamburgers.**
>
> **You: No, let's just not eat.**

Unless you and your friend are on a hunger strike, your statement is likely to be a foolish and unpopular suggestion. Instead, you might counter with a plan of your own:

> **Friend: Gee, I'm hungry. Let's go get hamburgers.**
>
> **You: Let's get Chinese food instead.**

You have just proposed a counterplan. Not only that, by using the word "instead," you have argued that your counterplan is a reason to reject the original plan. We make "instead" decisions between plans and counterplans on a daily basis. For example, every morning we have to decide whether we are going to go to school or work or stay in bed. Clearly, if we stay in bed we cannot go to school or work. Those two options are competitive. That is, they compete for the same resources and time. A counterplan is an "instead" argument for the opposition.

It is also a hypothetical argument. You don't decide whether to go to school or stay in bed by actually going to work and staying in bed at the same time and comparing the results. You *imagine* what it would be like to stay in bed or go to school and *imagine* the costs and benefits of the options. You think about what would be gained and lost—you calculate benefits and opportunity costs. You make a decision in favor of the option that promises greater net benefits.

Counterplans are everywhere in practical decision-making. How do counterplans work in debate? Consider again what the basic role of the opposition team is in any formal debate. Broadly speaking, opposition teams win debates by showing that the proposition team's proposal or position is a bad idea. So what a counterplan needs to do in a debate is show that the judge should not endorse the proposition team's plan; *instead*, the judge should endorse the opposition team's counterplan. How is this accomplished?

First things first: a counterplan, just like a plan, should have a *text* that lays out what exactly the opposition team is advocating as a response to the proposition team's proposal. If the proposition team proposes a particular course of policy action, the opposition counterplan should do the same. If the proposition team proposes a particular stance on values or facts, the opposition's counterproposal should do the same. For maximum effectiveness, it is important that the counterplan (or counterproposal, or counterposition) mirror the proposition team's proposal. It is important to have a text so that the proposition team has a fair chance to debate exactly what it is that the opposition is proposing. This requirement is reciprocal to the opposition's (eminently fair) demand that the proposition team spell out exactly what it is that they are proposing.

Once the counterplan text is written, the opposition needs to figure out why the counterplan is an "instead" option. In formal debate, we call this *competition*. We say that a counterplan is *competitive* with a plan when it *forces a choice* between the two proposals. **A counterplan *must compete* with the proposition team's plan if it is to have a chance of winning the debate for the opposition team.** This is easily illustrated by extending the above example:

Friend: Gee, I'm hungry. Let's go get hamburgers.

You: Let's get Chinese food instead.

Friend: Well, why don't we get hamburgers *and* Chinese food?

You: Oh. Okay.

Here we see that the "Chinese food" option hasn't proven to be a reason to reject "hamburgers." Your counterplan has failed to provide a reason to reject your friend's case. What you need to do is to substantiate your claim of *instead*, which is the claim of counterplan competition. How do you show that a counterplan forces a choice between the plan and the counterplan?

After you present the text of your counterproposal, you must show how your counterplan competes with the plan. In formal debate, we demonstrate counterplan competition using the concept of *net benefits*. That is, in order for the counterplan to be a reason to reject the plan, it must be on balance the best option for action or advocacy. Counterplans compete with plans because they are *net beneficial*. In the ongoing dispute about what to eat, you need to convince your friend that Chinese food is the net beneficial lunch option. There are a few ways you can accomplish this. To establish that the counterplan is net beneficial in this example, you'll have to show that Chinese food is superior to hamburgers—at least in this specific case. There are two basic kinds of arguments you can make to establish net benefits for your counterplan in any situation.

First, you can argue that the plan is a bad idea, i.e., you can find disadvantages to, or solvency problems with, or critiques of the proposition team's plan. In this case, you could:

- Show that eating hamburgers is bad for one's diet (calories, fat, cholesterol, etc...). This argument would be a disadvantage to the plan in that it claims the plan causes some bad effects.

- Show that eating hamburgers would not alleviate your hunger. This argument would be a solvency answer to the plan because it shows that the plan will not solve the stated harm (hunger).

- Show that the assumption that hamburgers are an acceptable food is fundamentally flawed. You could argue (from the perspective, perhaps, of an ethical vegetarian) that consuming meat is always wrong, and that therefore the plan should not be endorsed because of the values it rests on.

Second, you can argue that the counterplan is a good idea. That is, you can find advantages to the counterplan that do not accrue to the proposition team's plan. In this case, you could:

- Show that Chinese food tends to contain more vegetables, allowing you to get more vitamins and servings of healthy greens.

- Show that Chinese food is generally low in fat and cholesterol, making it a healthy cuisine.

All of these arguments serve more or less the same function: they establish that the counterplan is a better option than the plan; it has more net benefits. The result of net benefits argumentation should always be that the counterplan ends up being a reason to reject the original plan.

Because counterplans must be net beneficial, they function in precisely the same way as a disadvantage. Just like a disadvantage, a counterplan must show that the plan will have a cost. In the case of the counterplan, this would be an opportunity cost. The adoption of the plan undermines the opportunities associated with the counterplan. When we argue disadvantages, we are saying that adoption of the plan will cause some bad result. When you say a counterplan is competitive, what you are really saying to the judge is: "Don't vote for the plan, because if you do you will forego this superior policy option."

When we argue counterplans, we are saying that adoption of the plan will cause some bad result. In this case, that bad result is the loss of the superior option of the counterplan.

At one time, it was believed that to compete, counterplans had to be *mutually exclusive* with the proposition team's plan. Mutual exclusivity, simply put, is the idea that the plan and the counterplan literally cannot coexist with each other. There are few circumstances in which you can argue that your counterplan is *mutually exclusive* with the plan:

Friend: Gee, I'm hungry. Let's go get hamburgers.

You: Let's get Chinese food instead.

Friend: Well, why don't we get hamburgers *and* Chinese food?

You: We don't have enough money to get both.

By arguing that both options cannot be done at the same time, you establish that they are mutually exclusive with each other. But you still haven't proven that your option is superior. Mutual exclusivity is not an optimal method for proving counterplan competition. Even if your counterplan is mutually exclusive, it must still be net beneficial.

Another way of thinking about a counterplan is that it is an *opportunity cost* of the plan. An opportunity cost is the sacrifice made when selecting one policy over another. Think of it this way: when you choose a particular course of action, you always forego other opportunities. This happens in everyday life as well as in public policy decisions. If you choose to drive to the movie theatre, you have implicitly rejected the other available means of transportation (bus, dogsled, bicycle, skateboard, rickshaw, etc.). Your choice has *cost* you those other *opportunities*. Every decision has opportunity costs. There are always other things you could do with the time and energy you invest in a particular course of action.

Government officials deal with the implications of opportunity costs all the time. It is the responsibility of public policy makers to evaluate the costs and benefits of policies they implement. Sometimes they have to make tight decisions based on available resources—for example, if there is only a finite amount of resources available to solve a given problem, legislators may have to choose between several options because there is simply not enough money to fund everything. Other decisions are forced because of political pressures, yet have lasting opportunity costs. One such commitment was the decision in Europe to use North Atlantic Treaty Organization (NATO) instead of European defense forces to intervene in Kosovo. The decision to use NATO had many opportunity costs: Europe lost the benefits associated with European military integration as well as the opportunity to use the European Defense force as a legitimate institution. Further, NATO intervention guaranteed the continued involvement of the USA in European affairs, a move that has been criticized by many.

In the end, whether or not you agree that the decision to use NATO was correct, there is no denying that it had clear opportunity costs. In formal debate, those opportunity costs of a potential policy decision are the stuff counterplans are made of. As an opposition debater, you can try to convince the judge or audience that their policy is ultimately undesirable because it necessitates forsaking another, more beneficial, course of action.

As you can imagine, counterplans are a powerful strategic option for the opposition. As a debater, you might quite justifiably be nervous about debating against counterplans. What is to stop the opposition team from simply counterplanning with something that is much, much bigger than your case? Consider this frightening possibility: you begin the debate advocating that a commission should be established to investigate the return of pilfered relics. You think you're doing pretty well, and are pleased with your small case, until the opposition counterplans with a proposal to give massive food aid to starving refugees in Africa. On balance, their counterplan probably solves a bigger problem than your case and saves more lives. What do you do?

First, don't panic. This counterplan does not compete with your proposal. The two policies are *cooperative* rather than competitive, i.e., they do not resist each other and instead can (and probably should) work in concert with each other. Both policy options can (and probably should) be pursued. Remember that it is the burden of the counterplan to provide a reason to reject the proposition team's plan. A counterplan must be *counter* to the plan. If the policies can cooperate—if they do not compete—then the counterplan is *not a reason to vote against the proposition.*

The proposition team needs to test the counterplan to see if it competes— and then clearly communicate to the judge their argument that it does not. In formal debate, we call this kind of argument a *permutation*. In its simplest sense, to *permute* means to combine. When we permute the plan and the counterplan, we experimentally combine them in our imaginations to test how competitive the counterplan is.

Just as a counterplan tests whether the plan provides a compelling reason to change the present system, so the permutation tests whether the counterplan provides a compelling reason to reject the plan. The ability to argue permutations is the first line of proposition team defense against opposition team counterplans.

When you defend the motion, you should always attempt to permute the opposition counterplan. The permutation argument needs to be advanced at the first opportunity your team has to respond to the counterplan. Permutations do not need to be complicated; in fact, they are most effective when they are simply phrased. In the example above, where your team has argued for relic return and the opposition has argued for food aid, you can simply phrase your permutation argument as follows:

> "Their counterplan is simply not competitive with our plan. It does not *counter* our case. In other words, it is another public policy. It might prove that the opposition team has opinions, but it does not mean that their opinions undermine the case as presented. We can demonstrate this with the following permutation: it would be possible and net beneficial to do *both* the plan and the counterplan. You can give back relics *and* give food aid. Thus, the counterplan does not provide a reason to reject the plan."

Notice that this argument does more than just advance a permutation. It also provides a theoretical justification for the permutation, and in doing so attempts to teach the judge a little something about counterplan competition. Theoretical justification is an important component of the argument. Remember that many or most of your judges and audiences will be extremely unfamiliar with the formal debate terms we use here. There is, ultimately, no real need to use the word "permutation" to talk about this critical proposition team argument. However, the vocabulary is useful shorthand for the more developed discussions about counterplan theory and practice that follow later in this chapter.

Counterplan Topicality

Before we move on to discuss types of counterplans, we should offer a few thoughts on counterplan topicality. Some people believe that counterplans have to be nontopical. They argue that to challenge the topic effectively, the opposition team can defend only nontopical action. We believe that this philosophy is fundamentally bankrupt. The *plan* is the focus of the debate. As long as the counterplan is counter to the plan, it is a legitimate subject for discussion. In a debate, the plan becomes the embodiment of the resolution—it is a living interpretation of the topic. Once the plan is the interpretation of the topic, any policy that's not the plan is *automatically not the topic*. Consider: you would never say that a disadvantage about the topic is illegitimate because it is about the topic; yet, folks say this kind of thing all the time about counterplans. Let us emphasize again: The *plan is the focus of the debate*. It is said that topical counterplans are unfair because they force the proposition team to debate against the topic. This is untrue. Once the case for the topic has been made using the plan and its advantages, anything that counters that case, topical or not, is intrinsically counter to the topic.

Suggested Exercises

1. Pretend that you are defending a proposition case that has the United Nations pay reparations for its failure to stop the genocide in Rwanda. Prepare and deliver a permutation argument for each of the following counterplans:

- Counterplan: The USA should pay its back dues to the United Nations.
- Counterplan: The Organization of African Unity should develop an autonomous self-defense force to deter future conflicts.
- Counterplan: The European Union should adopt a policy to intervene in future African conflicts.

2. Below, find a list of different actions. For each action, think of at least three opportunities you would lose if you were to take that action.

- Intervene, as the government, to stop a strike by workers in the airline industry.
- Criminally penalize chemical industries for water pollution.
- Restrict the transfer of copyrighted music on the Internet.
- Support World Trade Organization authority to arbitrate trade disputes.

Types of Counterplans

Just as there are many types of proposition team cases, there are many different types of counterplans that you can learn to use strategically and effectively. Counterplans fall into two basic categories: those that are *generic* and those that are *specific* to the plan you are debating. A *generic* counterplan is one that can be argued in a wide variety of debates against many different types of proposition cases. A *specific* counterplan is targeted directly at the case or plan you are debating against. This distinction, while important, may be a bit misleading in this way: Generic counterplans must *always* be tailored to the specific proposition plan. Without a strong element of case-specific competition, they will usually fail to persuade your judge because they will not *clash* directly with the proposition team's case.

To say that there are many different proposition cases is a gross understatement. In the first appendix to this book alone, you will find more than a thousand potential topics for debate. For each of these topics, there are at least dozens of potential topical cases, all of them different—even if you were to use the strictest interpretation of each topic. As a parliamentary debater, you will have to be prepared to debate an enormous variety of specific cases and plans. To be consistently successful on the opposition, then, you will need some generic strategies that can apply to *types* of plans. Generic counterplans are indispensable for this endeavor. We will discuss several generic counterplans and explain how they can be used against a variety of cases.

Agent Counterplans

One thing that almost all plans have in common is that they all have an *agent of action*. That is, every proposal requires someone or something to carry out the proposition team's recommendation. In the USA, the agent of action is usually the U.S. Federal Government. Sometimes, proposition teams will specify their agent even further and argue that a specific *branch* (legislative, judicial, executive) or *division* (i.e., the Environmental Protection Agency, Bureau of Indian Affairs, Department of Justice, etc.) of the federal government should implement their proposal. In Europe, it is common for proposition teams to say that their proposal should be enacted by a national government, or perhaps by the European Union or the United Nations. This specification in the plan is curious, given that it is rarely mandated by the resolution for debate.

In any case, no matter what the justification, most proposition teams do specify (and are *expected* to specify) the agent of action for their plan.

This specification gives the opposition more than adequate grounds for what is called an **agent counterplan**. An agent counterplan is a counterplan that argues that *the plan the proposition team implements through one agent of change should instead be implemented through another agent of change*. So, for example, if a proposition team argues that the USA should provide free malaria medication to children in Central America, you might propose a counterplan to enact the basic mandates of the plan through a different agent:

> Counterplan: The World Health Organization should provide free malaria medication for children in Central America.

At first glance, it appears that this counterplan does not compete with the proposition team's plan. After all, it is possible to act through both the World Health Organization and the U.S. government. But would such cooperative action be net beneficial?

To resolve this question, you'll have to think back to the comparison between hamburgers and Chinese food we laid out in the previous section. Remember that there are two basic kinds of net benefits arguments you can make in debates: You can argue that the plan is bad and you can argue that the counterplan is good. In this case, since the difference between the plan and the counterplan is the agent of implementation, you'll want to stick to net benefits arguments having to do with the respective agents. So you'll need to generate a few arguments *attacking their agent of action*. You might phrase your attack like this:

> "There are a few reasons that the USA is a poor actor for this policy. First, the USA has a history of using these kinds of humanitarian campaigns as cover for military, covert, or other bad and dangerous interventions. Just look at how they use food aid as an excuse to deploy troops and stage covert operations. Second, the USA has a bad record when it comes to malaria prevention in particular. After the dangerous pesticide DDT was banned in that country, they proceeded to export and promote it for malaria control worldwide. Surely we don't want to risk these kinds of consequences."

After you have argued that the agent of action designated by the proposition team is bad, you'll need to defend your own agent of action. You need to show that your proposed alternative agent will do a good job of addressing the harms specified by the proposition team. You might phrase your defense like this:

> "The World Health Organization would be at least as good as the USA for the distribution of malaria medication and treatment. The WHO has extensive experience in organizing and carrying out broad international health campaigns. They also have extensive international support and can draw on a wider range of international resources and volunteers. The USA is comparatively limited in these regards."

When defending this kind of counterplan or any other kind of counterplan, you need to advance both of these kinds of arguments. To win your point that your counterplan competes with the proposition team's plan, you must argue *both* that the plan is bad *and* that your counterplan is good. Once you have made these arguments for your counterplan's competition, it is appropriate to offer some kind of summation that explains to the judge why the counterplan is a reason to vote for the opposition team. This summation might look something like this:

> "The bottom line is that the USA is a poor agent for this course of action. Our counterplan will better solve the problems of malaria in Central America, while avoiding all of the terrible costs historically associated with the USA's actions. Thus, when weighing your options in this round, you should prefer our counterplan and support the opposition team."

This summation should be made early and often throughout the opposition speeches in the debate round in order to set up the final *decision calculation*, or final reason to vote, that you present in your last opposition rebuttal.

When planning what kinds of arguments to make to defend your counterplan, always anticipate what your response will be to the proposition team's inevitable permutation of your counterplan. In this case, the proposition team will no doubt argue that you can and should distribute malaria medication using both the USA and the World Health Organization. While the proposition team is probably right that you *could* act through both agents, they are not necessarily right that you *should* act through both agents. You are questioning net benefits. What are some arguments you can make against this permutation? For the most part, you have already made them. If you can show that there are affirmative reasons *not* to prefer the proposition team's agent of action, then all of those reasons function as *disadvantages to the permutation*. That is, they are reasons that the permutation (just like the plan) causes bad things to happen. All the reasons that it is bad to use the USA as an actor *still apply to the permutation*, thus the permutation is not net beneficial. Instead, it is better to prefer the counterplan alone than the combination of the plan and the counterplan.

Agent counterplans are very useful tools for opposition teams. The above example shows how you can argue for agents other than the USA, but the same basic method applies to all agent counterplans. When thinking about agent counterplans, you should be creative. Consider using different agencies within the same government. For example, if the proposition team advocates using Federal Bureau of Investigation counterterrorism agents, you might recommend that the plan be done by the Central Intelligence Agency instead. If they say the plan should be done by the legislature, think of some reasons why the executive branch or the judicial branch might be a superior actor. One way to master agent counterplans effectively is to come up with a list of common agents of action. Then generate arguments about why each is a bad agent in general as well as in some specific areas of public policy. Finally, generate arguments about why each is a good agent in the same categories. This way, you will always be prepared to counterplan with an alternate agent.

No discussion of agent counterplans would be complete without a section on what we call the **states** or **sub-national governments** counterplans. These are a specific subgroup of agent counterplans that try to delegitimize the need for federal action by showing that sub-federal action is superior to the proposition team's reliance on the federal government. This counterplan originated in policy debate in the USA as a way to test the affirmative's (proposition team's) use of the U.S. Federal Government as an agent of action. Opposition teams can *counterplan* with state action, saying that action by the 50 states would be superior to federal action.

This type of counterplan can be used with great success when discussing other regions of the world. Opposition teams can argue that provincial, decentralized, or other nonfederal government entities should enact the plan's mandates instead of the federal government. To be net beneficial, these sub-national counterplans must show that federal action in the area of the plan is bad. Frequently, opposition teams running this counterplan will also claim that their policy is better suited to redress the proposition case's harm area because states or provinces are better positioned (via efficiency, experimentation, enforcement, or whatever) than the federal government to help those in need.

When you are defending the proposition, you will need to be prepared to defend your agent of action so that you don't lose debates to agent counterplans. To do so, you will need to have prepared at least three sets of arguments. (1) You need to be able to argue why *your specific agent is the best one for the task at hand.* (2) You will also need to have a variety of arguments against other potential agents. (3) You must have a developed defense of your permutation argument. One thing to consider about permutations to agent counterplans is this: frequently, it is the case that having two agents work at the same problem will produce a kind of *double solvency,* i.e., the permutation could potentially solve the designated problem doubly well. Consider the example of the USA vs. the WHO in malaria prevention. If both agents worked at the problem, it might be solved more quickly and with greater coverage than if either acted alone. The permutation could save more lives than either the plan or the counterplan alone. If you could win this argument, you could argue that the counterplan was therefore not net beneficial.

What would you say, as the opposition team, if the proposition team advanced this "double solvency" argument in defense of their permutation? Here, the debate gets more complicated. The important thing to remember is that you must *weigh the issues* and their associated *impacts.* We will discuss techniques for this process in the chapter on rebuttal skills. For this specific argument, you would do well to answer that the WHO will solve the problem well enough on its own, and that the potential risks of involvement by the USA in the project *outweigh,* or are more important than, the potential benefits of extra solvency.

Suggested Exercise

1. Below we have listed a few common agents of action and a corresponding public policy area. For each agent, generate three arguments for why this agent would be a *good* actor in the specified area. Then come up with three arguments for why this agent would be a *bad* actor in the specified area. Provide as many specific examples as you can.

• USA—peace negotiations in the Middle East

- United Nations—peacekeeping operations
- Corporations—environmental pollution
- USA—War on Drugs
- Britain—sanctions on Iraq
- European Union—immigration
- World Trade Organization—labor law

Study Counterplans

Often, proposition teams choose to advocate a course of action in an area where the existing research or available information is substantially unclear as to either the causes of the harms or the correct way we should proceed to redress these harms. This confusion happens all the time in complex issues of public policy. In these cases, a good option for the opposition team is to propose a *study counterplan*. The study counterplan is a generic counterplan that says that instead of acting in the specified area of the proposition or the proposition team's case, we should instead study the problem some more to find the most desirable course of action.

This counterplan is a great option for opposition teams, because it applies to a wide variety of propositions and specific proposition team cases. When you argue a study counterplan, you need to establish that there is great controversy over the area the proposition case deals with. You need to prove that a study is the appropriate course of action to pursue in this problem area.

Public policy advocates routinely decide to study rather than pursue a more direct course of action. For example, recently in Illinois, the governor was confronted with the need to make a decision about that state's death penalty. Much new evidence revealed disturbing inconsistencies in the application of the death penalty in that state. In fact, several convictions had been overturned as new evidence came to light. Many critics argued that because of inconsistent applications and dubious due process protections, the governor should act to ban the death penalty in Illinois. Instead of taking this course of action, the governor decided to declare a moratorium on the death penalty and *study* its application to find a way to reform death penalty policies and procedures. This action is a real-life example of deferring to a study counter-plan. The governor decided that he did not have enough information to make a decision about banning the death penalty, and *instead* decided to study the problem to reach the optimal solution.

When should you use study counterplans? There are two basic circum-stances in which they are eminently useful tools for the opposition:

• when the solution can be optimized

• when there is inadequate information for decision making

Study counterplans can try to optimize a solution for the problem outlined by the proposition team. When the proposition team confronts a difficult problem with a dubious solution, you should consider using a study coun-terplan. Argue that the counterplan is net beneficial because it will create the information necessary to choose the best solution for the problem at hand.

Study counterplans are also useful when you can show that the proposi-tion team is acting on inadequate information. In most societies, even relatively open democracies, the information necessary to make an informed decision about a problem is difficult to find and often highly classified. All too often, debaters (just like journalists and other public policy opinion makers) simply do not have all the information they need to draw an informed conclusion about the topic at hand. For example, on most foreign policy matters, the classification of information (keeping information from the public by label-ing it "top secret") prevents reasonably informed decision-making by the gen-eral public. If you can establish that this is the case in your debate, if you can show that the proposition team may *literally* not know what they are talking about, then you may be able to win your argument that a study counterplan is the superior course of action.

You need to be careful and specific when writing the text of your study counterplan. In general, it is vital that you have an *actor*—a commission that will do the actual studying. You will also need to have a designated *length* for the study—usually, anywhere from six to 18 months, although it could be longer or shorter depending on your assessment of what is needed. Finally, you need to make sure that the counterplan mandates some sort of action at the study's end. If the proposition team's plan was to have the U.S. Federal Government abolish the death penalty, for example, your study counterplan might look like this:

> Counterplan: The U.S. Federal Government should immedi-
> ately impose a moratorium on the death penalty. A blue-ribbon
> commission should be appointed to study how the death
> penalty is applied, with special attention paid to inconsisten-
> cies in due process and ethnicity-based application. This study
> will last 18 months, and subsequent policy action will be based
> on recommendations of that commission. Opposition speeches
> will clarify intent.

Notice the last sentence, "opposition speeches will clarify intent." It is a useful phrase to include at the end of any counterplan text, because it creates leeway for the opposition team to interpret their counterplan in light of any objections or requests for clarification that the proposition team might offer.

As a proposition team debating against a study counterplan, you have a few options. Initially, you should always defend your course of action with as much specific and recent information as you can. Try to show that there is no need for a study—that you have enough relevant information to make the decision now. You should also argue that study would take too long and fail to resolve critical harms that are happening right now. Try to show that there is an affirmative reason to adopt your proposal *now*, rather than waiting for a potentially inconclusive study to reach a dubious conclusion. Finally, you should argue that the results of the study would be biased. Ask the opposition team who will be on the commission. Ask them who will appoint these members. Argue that their so-called "blue-ribbon" commission will most likely reflect the dominant paradigm—precisely the thing your plan tries to combat.

As the opposition team, plan in advance for your answers to these questions and arguments. On the issue of specification about the commission's content, consider directing the same questions back at the proposition team. Ask them who will be implementing *their* plan and how those people will be chosen. Insist that your counterplan be held to the same standards of specificity as the plan.

Suggested Exercise

Imagine that you are debating on the opposition. The proposition team's plan says that the government should build a large, central-ized, underground storage facility for nuclear waste. You think you can prove that there is a substantial risk that such a facility might cause lasting environmental damage. You decide to argue that the government should study these potential consequences before deciding on a course of action. Write the text for your counterplan, using the above example as a model.

Consultation Counterplans

We will discuss one final type of generic counterplan, *consultation counterplans*. This type of counterplan argues that we should consult another relevant actor as to whether or not the proposition team's plan should be implemented. That alternate actor is therefore given a kind of veto power over the adoption of the proposition team's plan. If the alternate actor says yes, the plan is adopted. If the alternate actor says no, the plan is not adopted.

Let's say that you are debating a proposition team that advocates the following plan: NATO should expand its membership to include the Baltic States. This plan is ripe for a consultation counterplan. When you try to find grounds for a consultation counterplan, think to yourself: what actors might be angered or otherwise substantially hurt by adoption of the plan? In this case, the obvious answer is Russia, a nation that has in the past made threats about what might happen if NATO were to expand without explicit consultation. As the opposition team, you might counterplan this way:

> Counterplan: NATO will consult with the Russian government on the issue of expansion to include the Baltic states. Implementation of expansion plans will be made contingent on Russia's explicit approval. Opposition speeches will clarify intent.

You should argue that the counterplan is preferred because it does not anger Russia. In this situation, it would be appropriate to argue some sort of improved NATO-Russia relations disadvantage or better integration of Russian influence in NATO, claiming that argument is an advantage to the counterplan. What do we mean by this?

In this case, you could probably also argue convincingly that the plan would anger Russia substantially because, by not consulting them, it would send a message that Russia was cut out of the communications loop or was otherwise not substantively important enough to be consulted on the matter of NATO expansion. We say that the counterplan *solves* or *avoids* the risk of the disadvantage link because it does engage in active consultation, as opposed to the plan, which continues to act in a unilateral and headstrong manner. The consultation counterplan thus competes.

What to do if you are the proposition team? The wisest course of action is usually to argue that the counterplan will, in effect, preclude implementation of the plan, because the relevant actor will say *no* in consultation. You should disarm the opposition by arguing that Russia will say no and that the counterplan will never in fact implement the mandates of the original plan. Then, all you need to do to win the debate is to prove that the impacts of the case outweigh the impacts of the Russia disadvantage.

The consultation counterplan applies especially well to very small proposition team cases. These "small cases" are cases that do not have very large advantages. The reason that this counterplan works well against "small cases" is because those cases do not have large advantages to weigh against the risk of the opposition's comparatively large external net benefit.

Suggested Exercise

Below find a list of potential actions. For each action, pick an actor to consult about that action and explain why this actor should be consulted. In effect, you are here writing a consultation counterplan and constructing a disadvantage to non-consultation. Explain why that actor should be consulted and what might happen if not consulted. Be specific.

- environmental regulations
- setting wage standards
- immigration reform
- elimination of racial profiling
- pulling out of the World Trade Organization

Specific Counterplans

We have discussed several types of generic counterplans. You may have figured out by now that even the label "generic" is misleading for these counterplans, which must always be substantially adapted to the proposition case they are designed to defeat in any given round. A second type of counterplan is a *case-specific (or plan-specific) counterplan.* These counterplans are adapted very specifically to respond to the particular aspects of the proposition team's case or plan. These counterplans fall into three basic categories: counterplans that compete based on solvency, counterplans that neutralize advantages, and exclusionary counterplans.

Opposition teams can argue counterplans that compete based on substantial, exclusive grounds. These counterplans usually go in the so-called *opposite direction* of the proposition team's plan. For example, if the proposition team argues that more government regulation is the best solution to environmental pollution, an opposition team might productively argue that a superior solution would be a deregulation counterplan. There is in fact a substantial debate about the comparative virtues of government-based as opposed to market-based solutions to environmental problems. The advantage of the market-based counterplan is that it goes in the opposite direction of the proposition case's mandates and becomes a competitive alternative. On the opposition, you can make a good case for why deregulation addresses the given harm better than regulation. The exercises below encourage you to come up with your own arguments to substantiate both sides of this debate.

The important thing to remember about this sort of counterplan is the possibility of a permutation. What is the logical permutation to be proposed by the proposition team? It is both to regulate and to deregulate to solve the harm. On the opposition side, you should argue that this permutation is incoherent and infeasible—one could not conceivably regulate and deregulate the same policy area at the same time. Argue that the judge must choose one option, and then try to prove that deregulation is the superior option using the method already demonstrated earlier:

- Show that their plan is bad. In this case, show that regulation is a bad solution, perhaps because it causes bad consequences or simply fails to solve the designated problem.

- Show that your counterplan is good. In this case, prove that deregulation gains multiple advantages and solves the problem better than regulation.

• Weigh the potential costs and benefits. In summation, show the judge that, *on balance,* deregulation is the superior alternative because it redresses more significant harms than regulation.

This counterplan is not the only one of its kind. Other examples of comparisons include: unilateral vs. multilateral action, criminal vs. civil penalties, or compulsory vs. voluntary incentives.

Suggested Exercises

1. Make three arguments that show why government regulation is the best way to solve environmental problems such as air and water pollution.

2. Make three arguments that show why deregulation and its subsequent reliance on corporate action is the best way to address environmental problems such as air and water pollution.

Exclusionary Counterplans

A final type of case-specific counterplan is the *exclusionary counterplan.* A fairly advanced type of counterplan, it is an extremely powerful weapon for the opposition. Sometimes proposition teams will argue plans with several different mandates or components. You may have arguments against some, but not all, of their mandates. In this case, you might want to consider using an exclusionary counterplan. An exclusionary counterplan endorses some, but not all, of the proposition team's plan. This type of counterplan competes, based on arguments about why the excluded parts of the plan are bad. Exclusionary counterplans are a way for the opposition to focus the debate back on areas they might be more familiar with, or on areas they feel are more advantageous for them to discuss.

Public policy makers endorse exclusionary counterplans all the time. For example, when the U.S. Congress was debating new air pollution and emissions regulations for automobiles, they were considering adapting sweeping reforms applying to all vehicles. Then someone proposed light truck exemptions from that legislation. The legislation with the exemption was, after some debate, adopted.

As an opposition debater, think of exclusion counterplans as "the plan, except..." In order to win that your exception is net beneficial, you have to win a disadvantage related to the specific topic or item that you exempt from their plan. Let's say that the proposition team argued the following plan:

> **The U.S. Federal Government should restrict the export of all pesticides currently banned for use in that country.**

You might happen to know that some of these pesticides have uniquely beneficial aspects for the economies of other countries. The Mexican timber export industry, for example, is extremely reliant on the pesticide chlordane to kill termites in their lumber stacked for export. Also, DDT is very useful for malaria eradication. You could exempt one or both of these pesticides in your counterplan:

> **The U.S. Federal Government should restrict the export of all pesticides currently banned for use in that country except for chlordane and DDT.**

The net benefits to your counterplan would be arguments about why it would be good to continue limited exports of chlordane and DDT.

As a proposition team, your best defense against exclusionary counterplans is good, careful plan writing. Don't write mandates into your plan that you aren't prepared to defend. In this pesticide example, it might have been wise not to use the word "all," as this word arguably gives the opposition team plenty of ground to argue their exclusionary counterplan.

Chapter 11

Opposition Strategy —Critiques

Introduction to the Practice of Critiquing

Arguments are like houses in that they rest on foundations. Recall that in the chapter on argumentation we detailed how arguments are constructed: they have supporting premises, reasoning, and evidence.

Complex arguments, like the kind made in the body of a proposition team's case, are composed of many different, smaller arguments that unite to make a cohesive whole. A proposition team's case, therefore, rests on a fairly broad foundation composed of other arguments and the support that those arguments rely upon. While this broad foundation can render a case fairly stable, it can also be the undoing of a proposition team's case if approached correctly by the opposition team.

You may have had the occasion to play the popular block-stacking game Jenga. In Jenga, many small blocks are stacked on each other, cross-hatched to make an irregular square tower. Participants remove blocks until someone is unfortunate enough to remove the block that causes the whole structure to come crashing down. That load-bearing block is a fundamental, even critical, part of the whole structure of the tower. Many of the other blocks are essentially trivial, and can be treated as such. They can be added and removed with no cost to overall structural stability.

As with Jenga, so it is with arguments. All arguments make assumptions and leaps of reasoning. Some of the assumptions are more critical than others for the overall stability of the argument. Consider the following example: you are taking a class with a section on ancient civilizations at your school. Your assignment is to write a comprehensive report on one of the Earth's ancient civilizations. After weeks of hard work, you turn in your best work—

a history of Atlantis. The teacher gives you a failing grade. Horrified by this turn of events, you go to her and ask why. She says that there *were* some things about the paper than impressed her. For example, she was excited and intrigued by your detailed and informed discussions of native Atlantean foods, dances, and cultural practices. She thought that your position on Atlantean civil-military relations was quite innovative. In fact, it was a spectacular paper. There was just one small problem: there was no such civilization as Atlantis. Oops. You made a fundamental assumption that turned out to be incorrect. (Jenga!)

Some assumptions, like the Atlantis assumption, are just plain wrong. Others are both wrong and dangerous. Imagine that you and a friend arrive in San Francisco for a sightseeing tour. You've never been to the city, but you hear that it's lovely. After leaving the airport, you rent a car and take the map offered by the attendant. Since you are better behind the steering wheel, you drive the car while your friend navigates. After a little bit of driving, you notice that the streets you are on don't quite match up with the streets on the map, but you assume that's just because you are lost. You are very lost. You are so lost, in fact, that while trying to get to Berkeley you drive into the Bay. As you are sinking, you realize the problem: The map you were given, that you assumed was correct, was in fact a map of Chicago. Oops. You made a fundamental assumption that turned out to be incorrect and dangerous. (Jenga!)

Debate arguments make assumptions that are incorrect and potentially dangerous all the time. But debate rounds are not (perhaps fortunately) like Jenga. It is very rare that you will be able to identify a single assumption which, when pulled out and examined, will bring down the entire position of the other side. However, the investigation and criticism of fundamental assumptions are invaluable parts of debate for both the proposition and opposition sides. The goal of this chapter is to show how the practice of critiquing arguments (that is, examining the underlying assumptions of arguments) and their accompanying fact sets can be used strategically in debate.

You have already learned that the most effective way to refute an argument is *not* by simply providing an assertive counter-claim. Arguments are most effectively refuted from within their own substance; that is, sophisticated debaters know that *arguments are best unraveled by focusing on the language, reasoning, underlying assumptions, interpretations, and proofs of the opponent.* We answer arguments in this way all the time. When you answer a disadvantage, you attack its reasoning, testimony, and proofs.

In academics or public policy analysis, the practice of criticism is everywhere. One important thing to remember about argument critique is that it is all about where you look, and from what perspective. You may have heard the old story about the three blind men who are called to examine an elephant. One feels its side and determines that it is a piece of luggage. Another feels its foot and says it is a stool. A third feels its tail and calls it a snake. They are all wrong, of course, but from their perspective they are correct. In this story at least we know there is an elephant and so are not worried about the possibility of implementing policies based on these incomplete worldviews. In public policy decisions, however, it is not so easy to identify the elephant or even to know that there is an animal being examined in the first place.

The closest thing to an elephant we have in any formal debate, at least from the perspective of the opposition, is the presentation of the first proposition speaker. That presentation is not only (if it can be considered to be so at all) a suggestion of an important value, an identified fact, or a sound public policy. Rather, it is a kind of text to be interpreted and analyzed. Every element of the speech has underlying assumptions, which may be examined and criticized.

This idea of speeches as texts is important, and one that is critical to understanding how the practice of critique works in debate. If the proposition team's case is a kind of text, it is therefore up for interpretation just like any other text. The proposition team's case should not necessarily be thought of as a set of true facts. It is, however, usually presented as such. This presentation should pose no great barrier to a critical opposition team who want to reinterpret the proposition team's presentation in a manner that will help them to achieve victory in the debate.

Let's see how critiquing is done in practice. When presented with a particular fact set (this simply refers to the set of facts and opinions that make the argument for you or your opponent in the debate), people from different intellectual and cultural traditions and social and ideological perspectives will inevitably look at it differently, with different results. We know this is true with complex decisions. Judges with significant legal training often disagree with other judges about an interpretation of the law. They each try to follow the law but their perspectives are different and so their understanding of the law is different. Parents and children do not always see eye-to-eye on the same issues because of the differences in their age, peer group influences, and knowledge. Even good friends of the same age disagree about movies, fashion, and food. This is because their histories, identities, cultural influences, and interests are sufficiently different. In debates, an effective student can use these differences in perspectives to find the basis for argument clash and criticism.

The recognition of multiple perspectives can be an good place to start when critiquing arguments. Let's take the example of the death penalty to see how this works in practice. Here's a description of a state of affairs, one that could very easily be a component of any number of proposition team cases:

> **A man is arrested for killing someone. After being given due process, appropriate prosecution, and trial in front of a jury of his peers, he is found guilty of murder. Once his appeals have been rejected, he is executed.**

Individuals will respond differently to this set of facts.

A critic who argues from the perspective of the Critical Legal Studies (CLS) movement, a legal reform movement in the USA arguing that the legal system is biased in favor of the wealthy, might point out that what this description leaves out is an examination of the part played by money and class.

She might argue that the poor are more likely to be arrested and indicted for any number of crimes, including murder. Among other factors, the net worth of defendants directly determines what kind of lawyer will defend them: an overworked public defender or a specialized private attorney. Finally, she might suggest that the jury was most likely *not* a jury of his actual peers. At worst, this description might be dangerous because it seeks to paint as neutral a criminal justice process that is fundamentally unfair and unjust. Several fundamental components of the description have been substantively undermined by means of this criticism. The critic has shown that it makes faulty assumptions about the world (echoing the example of the Atlantis paper) and that its presentation is dangerously misleading (echoing the example of the map of Chicago). If she chose, the critic could probably make a convincing case for disregarding or rejecting the description on these grounds.

This exercise is what it is like to practice criticism in debate. When you focus on the underlying assumptions of your opponents' arguments, you are engaged in criticism of their arguments. The practice of critiquing arguments can have tremendous power in contemporary parliamentary debating, and has quickly become a crucial type of argument for opposition teams. We will discuss how critiquing can be used by the opposition side in a debate and then conclude with some general advice about the practice of criticism.

When the proposition team makes their case, they are presenting a text for analysis and interpretation. This text usually consists of a few basic components:

- a description of the present state of affairs
- an explanation of how that state of affairs causes a problem
- a proposal (the plan)
- an explanation of how the proposal will solve the given problem
- an explanation of how the proposal might solve other problems

All of these components, as well as their various combinations, are potential grounds to be mined for criticism. On the opposition, you can criticize the proposition's text on any number of grounds.

Suggested Exercises

1. Take a series of debate motions. Investigate the arguments for and against each motion from different perspectives. How would someone poor think about the proposition? How would an immigrant? What about the President of the United States? A farmer? A citizen from Brazil? The owner of a corporation? Are you able to appreciate the world from several of these perspectives? Are there some you cannot even begin to know?

2. Take a series of debate motions. Consider a specific debate motion from two contrasting perspectives: an employer and an employee, a patient and a doctor, a leader of a nation and a leader of the United Nations, a student and a teacher, a vegetarian and a hunter, a prisoner and a prison guard. Do different roles produce different ideas? Do the ideas clash with each other? Are there good arguments for each perspective?

Language

Initially, you can address the proposition team's case by criticizing its language. Traditionally, we learn that language is fundamentally neutral, a kind of "container" with no particular value of its own. There are many social theorists who disagree with this perspective. They argue that the language that we use has real effects on what we perceive to be "reality." Here are some questions to consider:

- Does it matter if you refer to a given nation as part of the "Third World"? From a certain perspective on global affairs, it certainly matters. The language of "Third World" assumes a hierarchy of civilizations and thereby creates assumptions of inferiority and superiority (and it is better to be "first" than "third.")

- What happens when you call someone an "alleged criminal"? All too often, the power of the word "criminal" overcomes its modifier "alleged" to type the individual in question as a presumed lawbreaker, whether or not that person has, in fact, committed a crime. Although individuals are claimed to be "innocent until proven guilty," this idea is frequently reversed once a person is called criminal, even an "alleged" one.

- What kinds of cultural and historical associations do we have with the word "black"? There are a myriad of ways that, at least in the West, "black" is a negative modifier—think about the "black arts," "black magic," or what it means to call someone "black-hearted."

- How do you talk about a civil disturbance? Do you call it a "riot" or an "uprising"? Is there a difference between the two? When we think about a "riot," we think about directionless, senseless violence and destruction of property and lives. When we think about an uprising, we think about a specifically political event that is targeted to achieve social change or at least to "rise up" against some oppressive set of circumstances.

The worldview that holds that language is itself more or less meaningless can and should be called into question. All too often, policy decisions are justified with language that may reveal unsound or particularly distasteful hidden agendas.

When you critique the proposition team's case, you will have to prove at least two things in order to win the debate on the basis of your criticism. You will have to uncover a fundamental assumption of the proposition's case, and you will have to disprove the validity of that assumption to win the debate. How is this done in practice? There are as many ways to structure your argument as there are potential criticisms to be made in a debate round. Generally, you will need to prove at least the following components of your argument:

- The proposition team makes assumption X.
- Assumption X is bankrupt (or dangerous, or patently silly, or shamefully weak) for the following reasons...
- Successful criticism of Assumption X wins us the debate because...

Let's look at the example of the critique of "development." Many, many public policies are framed using the language of development. In the USA, a good bit of foreign aid is funneled through the Agency for International Development (US-AID). Money and assistance is given (by the US-AID and by other agencies and other nations) to countries who are often explicitly referred to as "underdeveloped" or as "Lesser Developed Countries." These countries are understood to be in need of "development." What is, exactly, to count as "development" is an interesting question. Development is understood to be exemplified by the so-called "developed" countries—those countries, including Europe, Japan, and the USA, which have reached their fully formed status. The implication is that some countries need development because they are not like a set of other (industrialized, consumer-based) countries.

There are many that critique the deployment of this language of "development" to describe and attempt to solve social problems. It is said, in the first place, that the language of "underdevelopment" misunderstands the nature and causes of real harms in specific parts of the world. What is the cause, for example, of high infant mortality? Is it because there are not enough well funded medical facilities in a given nation? Or is it because that nation is not enough like its "developed" cousins? These questions matter quite a bit for the business of interpretation and criticism. It could be, for example, that the way the problem is framed obscures other ways of thinking about it while lending an air of legitimacy to the proposed solution. The language of "development" might be said to betray a fundamental misunderstanding of the present while *at the same time* dangerously obscuring other problems and their causes. Further, if the harm is misunderstood, then how can the proposed solution be said to "solve" it in any meaningful way? "Solve *what?*" you might ask. "If we have proven that you don't have any idea what the problem is, then what possible currency could this appeal to solvency have?"

Critics of the language of "development" have argued that the idea of "development," inherited and refined as it is from the legacy and practice of colonialisms and imperialisms, is itself responsible for many of the most trenchant problems in so-called "underdeveloped" countries. From this perspective, it follows that using "development" aid to alleviate the problems of "underdevelopment" might be a bit like using sewer water to clean an open wound. In practice, development assistance often fails to achieve its stated goals. It has often been said to perpetuate dependency on donor states, further impeding economic and social self-sufficiency. In this respect, development assistance may achieve the *opposite effect* of what its advocates intend—not creating development at all, but rather furthering the state of "underdevelopment."

It is probably easy to imagine a proposition team using the language of "development" to justify their proposal. They might propose giving food and farming aid to some nations defined as "developing." They might call the aid "development assistance." They might even talk about the responsibility held by all "developed" nations to help along their less-privileged cousin states. The proposition team would have a harm—famine. They would have a plan—development aid. They would try to show that their plan dealt with the problem.

As an opposition team, your work would be cut out for you. You could argue that the case's implicit and explicit relationship with the language of development reveals some fundamental flaws in the proposition team's reasoning and presentation. You could argue that:

- They fundamentally misunderstand the problem, and thus their statements of harms should be disregarded.
- This misidentification of the harm undercuts any appeal to solvency that they might make.
- Their proposal is part of the problem rather than part of the solution.
- Their proposal will *at best* be unable to ameliorate the problem. *At worst*, their proposal will simply make things worse rather than better. Thus, there is a net solvency turn for the opposition.

Of course, you would want to flesh these arguments out by giving much of the analysis and explanation offered above, but the basics of your argument should still be fundamentally clear. Should you choose to criticize the proposition team's embrace of a difficult or objectionable type of phrasing, value, or thinking, you will usually try to make all of these arguments (a-d) as evaluative statements that detail why your criticism matters.

We are reluctant to advance a specific *model* for advancing critical arguments. As you might have gathered by now, there are different approaches to argument design and execution. You might structure your argument as in the following example:

A. **The proposition team frames and advances their policy using the language of "development."** They propose giving food and farming aid to some nations defined as "developing." They call the aid "development assistance." They even talk about the responsibility held by all "developed" nations to help along their less-privileged cousin states.

B. **The language and concept of "development" is bankrupt and dangerous.** It presumes that there is a single appropriate model for national development. As we know, cultural, geographical, economic, religious, and political differences mean that the processes of national development will mean different things in different places. Western-style development, which often involves large capital projects and labor-saving business techniques, is often inappropriate for other countries, which have large unemployed or marginally employed populations. "Development" may improve the economy for the few people in charge of mining operations and agribusinesses but labor saving technologies replace hundreds of thousands of workers with machines, increasing poverty, hunger, and despair. In other words, development works, if what is meant is economic improvement for the few. But the many pay the price for development's "success."

C. **Because we successfully criticize the language and concepts of "development," we win the debate because:**

1. They fundamentally misunderstand the problem, and thus their statements of harms should be disregarded. [explain]

2. This misidentification of the harm undercuts any solvency they have. [explain]

3. Their proposal is part of the problem rather than part of the solution. [explain]

4. Their proposal will *at best* be unable to reduce the problem. *At worst*, their proposal will make things worse rather than better. [explain]

This is just one suggestion for how this argument could be advanced in a formal debate. You could certainly flesh it out or cut it down. You could also loosen the structure of the argument, turning it into a more unified attack without an explicit structure. We show how the argument works as a structured idea only to show the relationships between its components.

Values

In addition to criticizing the language of the proposition team's proposal, you can also criticize the assumptions it makes about values. Sometimes we think about values as abstract entities without a direct relationship to policy choices. This tendency is a fairly dangerous way of thinking about values: they are not just disembodied concepts like "dignity," "freedom," "justice," "liberty," "order," "security," "democracy" and "safety"; they are also the prime movers for our policy and personal decisions. In the chapter on topic interpretation, we discussed the relationship between values and policy choices. It is, in theory, possible to think about a value in the abstract, but you can't think about a policy without reference to values. Without values (in essence, a justification for the "good"), there is no basis for policy action.

How can you productively criticize the proposition case's allegiance to particular value structures? First, you need to pinpoint a fundamental value that seems to support the proposition team's case. Then, you need to criticize that value. Finally, you need to show how your criticism of that value proceeds to undermine or unravel the proposition team's case. In this respect, value criticism is very similar to criticism based on the language of the proposition case. Let's walk through an example to see how this works.

The proposition team opens their speech by detailing a problem that exists in the present system: there is tremendous violence in the Middle East, specifically violence between Israelis and Palestinians. They then present a specific proposal to minimize conflict: the USA should send peacekeeping troops to the Gaza Strip and the West Bank to help quell the violence. Finally, they argue that the presence of these troops will deter and prevent conflict, thereby keeping the peace.

It is possible to criticize this presentation. The value presented is "peace." You could argue that the proposition team's proposal relies on an implicit belief in the value of violence, that is, the use of a military force as a "solution" to social problems, and is thus inconsistent with its own value system.

Consider that the harms described by the proposition team all have to do with the existing armed conflict between Israelis and Palestinians. The understanding here, at least according to the proposition team, is that violence is something to be avoided and prevented, or at least stopped. As an opposition debater, you can concede these fundamental harms and argue that the proposition plan fails to redress them and in fact might make the problem much worse. The proposal, after all, *deploys the military*, assuming that it is right or acceptable or even feasible to use force to make peace, an assumption that is contested by hundreds of years of thinking about non-violence and the practice of non-violent resistance.

One critical question to ask of the proposition team is this: how is it, exactly, that the presence of troops serves to deter conflict? The answer, of course, is that the troops are a threat of further force. This threat, it can be argued, is itself a kind of violence: a regime that keeps the peace by means of threats condones a violent arrangement, and one that may inevitably produce violence in the future. The fact of this inconsistency alone, however, is not necessarily a sufficient reason to reject the plan. You must also show how the proposal fails on its own terms. One way to do this might be to show that the presence of troops will only escalate the level of conflict rather than reducing it—as has been the case in the U.S. intervention in Somalia, Russian intervention in Afghanistan, American intervention in Vietnam, Cuban military deployments to Angola, and British troop deployments in Northern Ireland. Foreign military intervention has a nasty habit of raising the stakes for the local forces intent on victory. There is, therefore, a decent possibility that the plan will make the problem worse.

You might also voice a principled objection to the use of force, thus advancing a kind of *value objection* to the proposition team's proposal. Using an adaptation of the model given above, your argument might be structured something like this:

A. The proposition team's case relies on the use of violence. They deploy troops to the Middle East and argue that those troops will be good because they will deter conflict. Deterrence, however, is just code for threatening behavior.

B. The idea of using violence to stop violence is bankrupt and dangerous. [explain]

C. Because we successfully criticize the proposition team's use of violence, we win the debate because:

1. The plan contradicts the essence of the case. If they are right about violence being bad, then they lose the debate because their proposal is intrinsically and necessarily violent. Their proposal is part of the problem rather than part of the solution.

2. Their proposal will *at best* be unable to reduce the problem. *At worst*, their proposal will simply make things worse,

> inevitably risking a wider conflict. Thus, the opposition ought
> to win the debate. [explain]

Note that the parts where we have written "[explain]" are the places in the argument outline that you will need to fill in to make the argument complete. This kind of value critique tries to show that the proposition team's value claims are at odds with the course of action they propose.

Another kind of value critique investigates the proposition team's values for inconsistencies. Our value concepts are often so broad that proper investigation can reveal troubling internal inconsistencies. Take the example of "liberty." Although just about everyone supports "freedom" in its abstract sense, they rarely support it without qualification. Few human societies, for example, recognize that there is a universal freedom to kill. This value means that "freedom" is generally only accepted with the qualification that one has freedom as long as it doesn't interfere with the freedom of others. This qualification may make sense in the abstract but often makes little sense in its social application. In a desert society, your freedom to consume fresh water necessarily conflicts with the freedom of others to consume fresh water. In a tight job market, your freedom to select a desirable job interferes with the freedom of someone else to have that position. There is thus an inevitable conflict of rights inherent in the very concept of liberty.

When debating on the opposition, you will frequently encounter proposition cases that claim to protect "liberty" or "freedom" as abstract values. One way you can counter this kind of case is to argue that although the case is in favor of liberty, there is no liberty they can really identify as a value, since the very concept of liberty is itself internally inconsistent and thus fundamentally incoherent.

A third kind of value criticism shows the conflict between two or more values. In our discussion of impact comparison, we talk briefly about the relationship between the values of liberty and equality. These two values are often in conflict in society. Ask yourself: Are we free to discriminate at school or work? After all, schools and workplaces are often privately owned (for example, a private school, or a corporation). If we were to support liberty unconditionally and at all costs, we would have to also support the right of business owners and school directors to discriminate against whomever they chose. This practice of discrimination, however, is seldom tolerated in societies that support equality.

In these circumstances where values are in conflict, you need to construct and defend a value hierarchy in which you argue that one value is a dependent, diminished, inferior value compared to others. A *hierarchy* is simply a preferred ranking system. We create hierarchies all the time—top ten lists, "close" friends, and preferred clothes. In debates, value hierarchies are constructed—you want to defend one or more values against less preferred values associated with your opponent. You might argue that equality is more important than liberty because of the historical exclusion of minority groups from voting and political participation in the United States. You might also claim that equality is a value preferable to liberty because the failure to provide equal treatment amounts to a denial of citizenship to those victims of discrimination. This denial of citizenship could be said to undermine the liberty of the victims of discrimination, thereby justifying your use of a hierarchy of values against your opponent's case.

All of these are ways of arguing against the values that inform and structure the proposition team's case. It is important to note that when you argue against the case and its values, you are *not* arguing against the values held by the proposition team members themselves. After all, it is unlikely in the extreme that you even know what values they hold personally, let alone which of those values might match up with those present in the arguments they advance. Our point here is to encourage you to think more about how values are applied in a policy context. The pursuit of liberty can provide us with any number of freedoms in civil society, but unlicensed freedom can also allow for child pornography or sex tourism, so they are not necessarily an unqualified good.

You may have already noticed that the distinctions between language and value criticism are less than well defined. The examples we have used make this pretty clear: the criticism of the use of the word "development" is also a criticism of the values embraced by the proposition team's case.

Thinking

A third kind of criticism questions the kind of *thinking* that informs and organizes the proposition team's presentation of their case for the motion. This is arguably the most sophisticated kind of criticism one can advance in debate, yet it is also the most loosely defined.

When you critique the thinking of a proposition team's case, you are essentially saying that the way they are thinking about their problem, solution, or both is essentially bankrupt or dangerous. This conclusion might be true for any number of reasons. Perhaps their perspective on an issue is outdated, biased, or fundamentally incomplete. Maybe their method for approaching the problem fails to take into account critical factors that would, if accounted for, radically change their approach and its results. Perhaps, because of gaps in their thinking, they misidentify the causes of the problem they attempt to solve. We will walk through a few examples of criticisms of thinking to show how this might work in practice.

You can refute the proposition team's case by criticizing the way of thinking that makes the case possible in the first place. We are taught in science and social science classes to think of methods of study or examination as more or less neutral. Methods of thinking, particularly in science, have been traditionally understood to be fundamentally neutral. We do not think that a chemistry experiment is "biased." But your perspective or approach does in fact greatly change what it is that you see when you examine a given fact set or argument. Many theorists have argued that our *methods* and ways of thinking should be subject to the same kind of criticism as our results.

One public policy issue that pops up often in debates is the problem of population control. The conventional story about the world's population problem is fairly evident, and goes something like this: there are simply too many people on the planet and, therefore, there are not enough resources (food, fuel, drinkable water, television, Pokémon cards, etc.) to go around. This problem is getting worse all the time, as resources (with the help of technology) at best only increase arithmetically, while population increases geometrically (A maitre de's worst nightmare, perhaps: "Malthus, party of 2?" "Malthus, party of 4?" "Malthus, party of 16?") Population is the problem, according to this way of thinking about the issue. If the number of people continues to grow, then there will not be enough resources to go around and people will starve, or else they will fight each other for control of valuable resources, or else they will starve while they fight each other for control of valuable resources. The proposed solutions, therefore, attempt to remedy this by doing something about population, usually by giving out some combination of family planning techniques. This solution is said to deal with the problem very neatly: if there are fewer people, then there will be more even distribution of resources.

Many people have advanced compelling critiques of this way of thinking about the problems of population control and resource allocation. It is said that this conventional thinking on population grossly mischaracterizes the real causes of resource shortages. Think about existing patterns of global resource distribution. It is the case that a small percentage of the world's population uses a gigantic percentage of the world's available resources. The average European, Japanese, Canadian, or U.S. citizen, for example, uses a vastly larger amount of resources than the average Guatemalan or Somali citizen does. It may be the case that there are not enough resources to go around, but it is important to ask *why* this is so. Perhaps there are not enough resources to go around because of unjust patterns of resource allocation and consumer use and *not* because of population.

If this is the case, we must ask a follow-up question: Why, then, are resource shortages blamed on population excesses rather than on the excessive and unjust consumption patterns practiced by a certain segment of global society? Critics suggest several motives for this shift in blame. It all has to do with assumptions about the way the problem is analyzed. For example, it is not necessarily in the interests of thinkers in industrialized nations to be critical of their own consumption habits. Also, we may assume that patterns of distribution and consumption naturally or more or less inevitably exist and there is not much that can be done or should be done. This assumption may mean that the proposition team's proposed solution—providing for family planning and fewer people—is part of the problem because it fails to address the real causes of resources shortages.

Also, the proposition team's presentation may be a rationalization for continuing the practices that have created the problem in the first place. In other words, their proposal may allow industrialized nations to continue to consume resources disproportionately.

By this point, you can probably see how this critical dispute might play itself out in a debate. The proposition team makes a case for increasing family planning aid. They say that there is a problem: too many people, not enough resources. They say there is a solution: family planning and population control. They say that their solution addresses the problem: it reduces the total number of people.

Your reply: the proposition team does nothing to correct resource problems. The maldistribution of resources is not caused by overpopulation and cannot be eased by family planning assistance. They will waste resources on family planning that governments could better spend on other social problems.

They allow nations to rationalize greedy overconsumption, increasing pollution and other costs of too much resource use. The proposition team will reduce the population in countries that need labor. Agricultural production in many countries requires large labor forces to produce sufficient resources. Family planning will reduce the population and domestic production will decrease, making it even worse for the people of those nations.

You will be able to argue that the thinking that supports the case is so fundamentally flawed that their solution could make the state of affairs worse rather than better. Using the model we've modified for the other critique arguments, you might frame your initial opposition argument like so:

A. The proposition team's case relies on a particular way of thinking about the population problem that is wrong and dangerous. [explain]

B. Because we successfully criticize their thinking about resource allocation and population control, we win the debate because:

1. They fundamentally misunderstand the problem, and thus their statements of harms should be disregarded. [explain]

2. This misidentification of the harm undercuts any advantage. [explain]

3. Their proposal is part of the problem rather than part of the solution. [explain]

Sound familiar? It should. The format we're using is more or less the same—all you need to do is fill in the details depending on your particular argument and the specifics of their case argumentation. Critiques of thinking, done properly, can nullify every aspect of a proposition team's case.

Responding to Critiquing

Disadvantages and counterplans are specific argument types with predictable components. Thus we are able to offer fairly predictable and stable advice to proposition teams regarding a basic method of answering these kinds of arguments. When you are debating against a disadvantage, for example, you will answer the link, the uniqueness, and the impact. When you debate against counterplans, you will try to show that they do not compete or are not net beneficial. Critique arguments are not as predictable as disadvantages and counterplans.

The best advice we can give you is to *think*. Take the opposition's argument seriously and try hard to answer it on its own terms while still using the bulk of your case as leverage against it. Remember: Critique arguments will usually try to take your case and turn it against you.

When you think about the opposition's critique argument, try to consider it in policy terms. Identify the way in which it is consistent with, rather than in opposition to, the case. Let's say that you make a case for limiting the government's power in a particular area. The opposition criticizes your approach because they say that you focus inappropriately on the government as a solution to the problems of the state. In this instance, you should argue that the opposition's criticism is fully consistent with your case presentation. You should say that there is no way to eliminate the state other than to have the state eliminate itself.

Many critique arguments are ahistorical. That is, they presume that there's been no thinking about the issue prior to the debate, when it's possible that in fact the proposition team *has* considered the subject of criticism and has decided to introduce the plan *based on* that consideration rather than in spite of it. Let's look at an example. Imagine that you make a case for increased environmental protection. Your advantage claim might be that adoption of the plan would save many human lives. In response, the negative team might critique your case's alleged association with *anthropocentrism*. Anthropocentrism is a view of the world that is centered on humans. Many environmental advocates, particularly those affiliated with the so-called "deep ecology" movement, criticize a human-centered approach to environmental issues. Anthropocentrism is said to be detrimental to environmental philosophies and policies because it promotes the idea that the nonhuman world is only valuable insofar as it is useful to protect human life, a point of view that is arguably at the center of the current environmental crisis. The opposition team's criticism, therefore, is potentially very serious—they say that you are only protecting the environment to save humans and thereby reproducing the central error of previous environmental policy.

What should you say? You should say that you have certainly considered the serious issues of anthropocentrism. You could argue that you do, in fact, favor policies that protect all creatures, even inorganic matter (not just humans, that is). It is, perhaps, just that the particulars of *this* case happen to protect humans. The criticism is therefore ahistorical and has no foundations for its questioning of the ideas associated with the case.

The critique arguments outlined in this chapter are fairly sophisticated. They are also, alas, not necessarily representative of the majority of critique arguments that appear in debates. As a competitive debater, you will hear many substandard disadvantages, counterplans, and critique arguments. To this end, we want to offer a few general things to consider when debating critiques:

- It is *vital* that you figure out, *before* you answer the opposition team's critique argument, what the implications of their criticism are for your case. In other words, if they win their criticism, why does it therefore follow that they win the debate? After the opposition's presentation of their argument, if you cannot identify why the critique is a reason to reject your case, you should *ask* using a point of information. This way you will be able to debate the implications of the criticism.

- Often the most vulnerable part of any opposition critique argument is its implication. Any assumption of any argument can be criticized, but only the most fundamental assumptions of a proposition case are essential to ensuring the case does not collapse. Remember Jenga? If the opposition team only criticizes non-essential or non-fundamental assumptions of the proposition case, the structure will remain intact and chances are you will still be able to convince the judge that your case achieves a clear and decisive advantage over the present system.

- Some opposition critique arguments may have only a loose relationship to your case, and you should point this out. Some teams will make a point of criticizing a broad system of thought—e.g., colonialism, statism, patriarchy, capitalism—of which the proposition case (if it is complicit at all) is only a small part. The opposition team will argue that the case should be rejected because of its association with this larger and dangerous system of thought. In these cases, you should certainly maintain that your case is barely, if at all, related to the overall philosophy being critiqued, and that even if the opposition is right that capitalism (for example) is always bad, it does not therefore follow that the plan is bad. Call this error in reasoning what it is: the fallacy of division. Pressure the opposition team to apply their argument specifically to the mechanics and contentions of your case. Instruct the judge not to vote on the argument until the opposition meets at least this minimal burden of proof.

- Use your case. We talked about the need to use your case as a weapon to fend off or turn disadvantages earlier. You should also use your case to fend off or otherwise respond to critique arguments. Use your case to demonstrate your advantages. Challenge the opposition team to show that the consequences of adopting the plan would be worse than the harms that would be redressed. Use empirical examples from your case to show that the way you're thinking about the world is, in fact, sound.

Above all, don't panic. Read up on various perspectives on national and international issues. Be conscious of the perspective you employ when you design your case and be ready to defend it as well as its most fundamental assumptions. Just as you design your case to answer common disadvantages and counterplans, so too should you design your case to anticipate and answer common critique arguments. Argument anticipation is one of the hallmarks of successful debaters on both sides of a topic and at any level of experience.

Suggested Exercise

Select and describe a case. Have debaters, working in teams or small groups identify underlying criticisms of language, values or thinking that might apply to the case. Debaters should describe these issues to others, noting the reason the criticism undermines the case.

On That Point!

Public Debate

Individuals need the opportunity to engage each other in forums that promote discussion of issues of controversy and concern. These engagements can encourage more formal participation in local community politics and social activism, as well as teach respectful conflict resolution. Public parliamentary debate is an appropriate forum for achieving these goals.

Parliamentary debate is uniquely capable of supporting public debate projects. With its combination of critical analysis of public policy issues, dynamic participation interaction, and format flexibility, it provides an informative and enjoyable experience for general audiences. Drafting topics of immediate local or national concern can appeal to the needs of civic and community groups, political organizations, and the media. The format is easily modified to include the voices of a general audience. Public parliamentary debates provide opportunities for questions, statements, and floor speeches from the audience. Of course, the format is also adaptable for class presentations.

The following is a sample format for public debates that may be used in the classroom or for a general audience, such as those in school assemblies. Five students participate in the debate. Four of the students will argue the case for and against the motion for debate—two will be on the proposition team, arguing for the topic, and two will be on the opposition team, arguing against the proposition team's case. One student serves as the moderator. The debate format might look like this:

Moderator: Introduction of format, participants, and topic: 3-minute speech

First proposition speaker: 5-minute speech

First opposition speaker: 5-minute speech

Moderated question and comment time with the audience: 12–15 minutes

Second opposition speaker: 3-minute speech

On That Point!

Second proposition speaker: 3-minute speech

Moderator: Conclusion: 1-minute speech

You should, of course, adjust the speaking times limits to suit your needs and the needs of the audience. Consider starting with shorter debates and increasing speech times as students become more experienced.

Notice that this format uses several different types of speeches. The moderator, for example, delivers informative speeches about the event. She explains the format for the audience, noting that the audience will be able to ask questions and make comments during the debate. (Audiences are more likely to listen carefully if they are able to participate in the discussion.) She introduces each of the speakers. She provides a very brief summary of the topic, perhaps explaining its importance or the reason that it was selected for the debate. She also gives a conclusion, thanking the participants and the audience and announcing any future events. If it is agreed in advance, the moderator may also take an audience vote to determine the winner of the debate.

Each team has an opening, or constructive, speech and a closing, or rebuttal, speech. These speeches serve the same purposes as they would in any regular parliamentary debate. In the rebuttal speeches, debaters should include final opinions on the information from the audience question and comment period in addition to the usual summarization and explanation of why their side is winning the debate.

The audience is actively involved in the debate. After the constructive speech for each team, the audience may participate, asking questions or making arguments challenging the claims of the debaters. Statements and questions from members of the audience should not last more than 1 minute. They should be directed to one of the two teams. Only one person on a team should give an answer. The speaker should have 30 seconds for an answer. If the moderator decides that the question or comment deserves a reply from the other team, she may ask one speaker from the other side to comment. This comment should last no more than 30 seconds. The moderator should keep time during the audience question and comment period and ought to limit the replies of the debaters strictly. This is an opportunity to listen to the opinions of the audience. The moderator should make sure that the audience is heard. After all, each of the speakers has an uninterrupted speech to make her points known to the audience. The speakers do not need additional speaking time that should

On That Point!

properly go to the audience. If there is more time available for the debate, it should go to the audience question and comment time, to ensure that as many members of the audience as possible have had a chance to make a point.

Topics may be announced just prior to debates (typically 15–20 minutes), or they may be announced days, or even weeks in advance. Set topics, announced several days before a contest, allow research, argument analysis, and practice debates in anticipation of an event. This procedure is appropriate for novice debaters and other new participants. Set topics are good for public debates, because audiences will know what to expect from the debate and the debaters will be exceptionally well prepared.

Exercise

Prepare a public debate on the topic "This House supports a living wage." There are four attached articles with information for and against this motion, although there is considerable additional material on the Internet and in periodicals. Select teams for the debate and a moderator. Each team should have one constructive speaker and one rebuttal speaker. We recommend that you underline or highlight quotations that you think might be useful in a debate about the assigned topic. Transfer relevant quotations onto note cards or paper so you can use their accumulated evidence in the public debate. These notes are an "argument summary sheet," a guide to the anticipated arguments for and against the topic. A summary of the most important and debatable points on either side of the controversy will help students answer the most challenging issues raised during the debate but are no substitute for thorough understanding of the topic.

On That Point!

Introduction to ACORN's Living Wage Web Site

Welcome to ACORN's living wage website. What you will find here is a brief history of the national living wage movement, background materials such as ordinance summaries and comparisons, drafting tips, research summaries, talking points, and links to other living wage-related sites.

Visitors to the web site should keep in mind that there is no magic formula for a successful living wage campaign. Every campaign is different—dependent on the campaign leaders and their constituencies, local politics and power dynamics, the campaign coalition's interests and scope, resources, experience, timelines, local and regional economies, etc.

Clearly, there is much to learn about running a living wage campaign that cannot be contained in a web site. However, as the movement chalks up wins, and leaders and organizers gain experience and become more savvy, we are building a body of material and experience that should be shared among living wage organizers everywhere.

ACORN and Living Wage

The Association of Community Organizations for Reform Now, or ACORN, is the nation's oldest and largest grassroots organization of low and moderate income people with over 100,000 members in over 30 cities. For over 30 years, ACORN members have been organizing in their neighborhoods across the country around local issues such as affordable housing, safety, education, improved city services, and have taken the lead nationally on issues of affordable housing, tenant organizing, fighting banking and insurance discrimination, organizing workfare workers, and winning jobs and living wages.

Over the past three years, ACORN chapters have been involved in over fifteen living wage campaigns in our own cities, leading coalitions that have won living wage ordinances in St. Louis, St. Paul, Minneapolis, Boston, Oakland, and Chicago, Cook County, IL and Detroit. Our current campaigns are going on in Philly, Albuquerque, New Orleans, Little Rock, Dallas, Washington D.C. and Sacramento.

In addition, we have established the Living Wage Resource Center to track the living wage movement and provide materials and strategies to the new campaigns that are cropping up everywhere.

In November of this year ACORN will host the second National Living Wage Training Conference in Baltimore. The first conference, in Boston in 1998, drew over 70 folks representing 35 different living wage campaigns across the country to learn from each other about elements of a living wage campaign such as building local coalitions, doing research, working with city council, developing message and responding to the opposition, preparing for living wage implementation fights, and using living wage campaigns to build community and labor membership and power.

We encourage campaign organizers to contact Jen Kern at ACORN's National Living Wage Resource Center at 617-740-9500 for more materials, to discuss specific campaign strategy, and to get referrals to experienced living wage organizers who have been or are currently involved in living wage campaigns in cities all over the country.

NOW AVAILABLE: A comprehensive 180-page guide for organizing living wage campaigns. This guide—authored by David Reynolds of Wayne State University Labor Studies Center with the ACORN Living Wage Resource Center—includes profiles of successful campaigns, chapters on how to build a coalition, conduct research, draft an ordinance, and plan larger electoral strategy. To order *Living Wage Campaigns: An Activist's Guide to*

On That Point!

Building the Movement for Economic Justice send a check or money order for $12 (payable to ACORN) to 739 8th St. SE, Boston, MA 02122.

The Living Wage Movement: Building Power in our Workplaces and Neighborhoods

In 1994, an effective alliance between labor (led by AFSCME) and religious leaders (BUILD) in Baltimore launched a successful campaign for a local law requiring city service contractors to pay a living wage. Since then, strong community, labor, and religious coalitions have fought for and won similar ordinances in cities such as St. Louis, Boston, Los Angeles, San Jose, Portland, Milwaukee, Detroit, Minneapolis, and Oakland—bringing the national living wage total to 50 ordinances. Today, more than 75 living wage campaigns are underway in cities, counties, states, and college campuses across the country. Taken collectively, these impressive instances of local grassroots organizing are now rightfully dubbed the national living wage movement, which syndicated columnist Robert Kuttner has described as "the most interesting (and underreported) grassroots enterprise to emerge since the civil rights movement...signaling a resurgence of local activism around pocketbook issues."

In short, living wage campaigns seek to pass local ordinances requiring private businesses that benefit from public money to pay their workers a living wage. Commonly, the ordinances cover employers who hold large city or county service contracts or receive substantial financial assistance from the city in the form of grants, loans, bond financing, tax abatements, or other economic development subsidies.

The concept behind any living wage campaign is simple: our limited public dollars should not be subsidizing poverty-wage work. When subsidized employers are allowed to pay their workers less than a living wage, tax payers end up footing a double bill: the initial subsidy and then the food stamps, emergency medical, housing and other social services low wage workers may require to support themselves and their families even minimally. Public dollars should be leveraged for the public good—reserved for those private sector employers who demonstrate a commitment to providing decent, family-supporting jobs in our local communities.

Many campaigns have defined the living wage as equivalent to the poverty line for a family of four, (currently $8.20 an hour), though ordinances that have passed range from $6.25 to $11.42 an hour, with some newer campaigns pushing for even higher wages. Increasingly, living wage coalitions are proposing other community standards in addition to a wage requirement, such as health benefits, vacation days, community hiring goals, public disclosure, community advisory boards, environmental standards, and language that supports union organizing.

Although each campaign is different, most share some common elements. Often spearheaded by ACORN, other community groups, union locals, or central labor councils, living wage campaigns are characterized by uniquely broad coalitions of local community, union, and religious leaders who come together to develop living wage principles, organize endorsements, draft ordinance language, and plan campaign strategy. The campaigns usually call for some degree of research into work and poverty in the area, research on city contracts, subsidies and related wage data, and often cost of living studies.

In addition, the strength of living wage efforts often lies in their ability to promote public education through flyering, petitioning, rallies, demonstrations targeting low wage employers, low-wage worker speak-outs, reports,

220

On That Point!

and press conferences. Because most current living wage campaigns seek to pass legislative measures, campaigns also include lobbying and negotiations with elected officials such as city and county councilors, the mayor's office, and city staff.

Living Wage campaigns also provide opportunities for organizations that work to build a mass base of low income or working people to join up, organize, and mobilize new members. Community organizers and labor unions can look to build membership during the campaign with neighborhood door-knocking, worksite organizing, house visits, neighborhood and workplace meetings, petition signature gathering, etc. and after the campaign on workplace and neighborhood living wage trainings, implementation fights with city agencies, and through campaigns targeting specific companies to meet or exceed living wage requirements.

So, what makes a collection of local policy decisions merit the title of a national "movement"? In short, both the economic context that gives rise to these efforts and the nature of the campaigns themselves make them important tools in the larger struggle for economic justice.

First, consider the economic realities facing low income people today: the failure of the minimum wage to keep pace with inflation (it now buys less than it did in the 1960's); the growing income gap between the rich and the poor; massive cuts in welfare and downward pressure on wages resulting from former recipients being forced into the labor market with no promise of jobs; the growth of service sector jobs where low wages are concentrated; the weakening of labor unions; rampant no-strings-attached corporate welfare that depletes tax dollars while keeping workers poor. The list goes on. Living wage campaigns have arisen in response to all these pressures.

Given this context, living wage campaigns have the potential to have benefits that go beyond the immediate benefits to affected low wage workers and their families. Wherever they arise, living wage campaigns have the potential to:

• Build and sustain permanent and powerful community, labor, and religious coalitions that promote greater understanding and support of each other's work and create the potential to influence other important public policy debates

• Provide organizing opportunities that strengthen the institutions that represent and build power for low and moderate income people: community groups, labor unions, religious congregations

• Serve as a tool of political accountability, forcing our elected officials to take a stand on working people's issues, as well as engaging low and moderate income people in the political process

• Build leadership skills among low-income members of community organizations, unions, and congregations

• Raise the whole range of economic justice issues that gave rise to the living wage movement and affect the ability of low income families to live and work with dignity and respect

Despite the concerted efforts of business interests who consistently oppose these campaigns, "living wage" has become a household word and an exciting model of a successful local grass-roots strategy. With new campaigns springing up every month, this movement shows no signs of slowing down. *We encourage you to join in the fight.*

On That Point!

Real Evidence Refutes Business Scare Tactics

This document was prepared for a campaign in Philadelphia. However, the arguments still hold true for campaigns elsewhere.

Everywhere these living wage campaigns arise, businesses are there to fight them. It will be no different in Philadelphia. You will hear the same arguments here as we've heard whenever wage raises are proposed: businesses will leave town, businesses will pass on their labor costs to the city and/or consumers, businesses will employ fewer people, less-skilled employees will be hurt, etc. None of these arguments have proven true, yet the business lobby continues to present them as fact.

The truth is, all evidence suggests that prevailing wage and living wage policies help low-wage workers and their families without adverse effects on business and the local economy, or increasing city spending in any significant way. Below are some specific responses to common arguments of living wage opponents:

"Philadelphia doesn't need a living wage ordinance."

"Businesses will leave the city—or not locate here—if we put new burdens on them."

"A living wage ordinance would cost the city too much money."

"A living wage ordinance would cause job loss."

"A living wage ordinance will cause inflation."

"A living wage ordinance will create unnecessary regulations and more bureaucracy."

"No one is trying to support a family on less than $7.90. Most low wage workers are well-off teenagers."

Low wage workers aren't "worth it"— The problem is low skilled workers, not low wages. What's needed is more education and training, not a wage hike.

Requiring a minimum wage will "hurt those its intended to help" (minorities and low income young workers) because they will be locked out of jobs.

"Philadelphia doesn't need a living wage ordinance"

- **Twenty-nine percent of all Philadelphia workers make less than $7.60 an hour** (According to the Current Population Survey Outgoing Rotation Group, analysis by Economic Policy Institute). **The current federal poverty guideline is $7.90 for a family of four** (U.S. Department of Health and Human Services). There is widespread agreement that this poverty figure is nowhere near enough to support a family.

- In Philadelphia, like everywhere else, workers' wages have been stagnating or shrinking as CEO salaries and profits rise. In Pennsylvania between 1989–1995 both family income and hourly wages plummeted, with low-wage workers getting hit the hardest, experiencing a decline in hourly earnings.

- A full time minimum wage worker— and there are tens of thousands in our city—now earns just over $10,700 a year, thousands of dollars below the poverty line. People simply cannot live on $5.15 an hour.

- A recent study based on federal, regional, and local expenditure data found that a full time worker supporting just one child in Philly would need an hourly income of at least $9.93 just to cover basic needs. For a full time Philadelphia worker with two children, that "basic needs" wage jumps to over $13 an hour.

- Service sector jobs—where low wages are concentrated and which this ordinance targets—are growing faster than any other employment segment.
- And each year the City of Philadelphia—through PIDC (Philadelphia Industrial Development Corporation), PCDC (Philadelphia Commercial Development Corporation), the Commerce Department and the Mayor's Office hand out millions of dollars in economic development assistance to businesses and agencies and spend millions more in contracts to private companies to perform services and provide goods to the city. And often these agencies dole out the dollars with no strings attached—no requirements or accountability from companies to create family-supporting jobs.

WE NEED TO MAKE SURE THAT THIS MONEY IS RESPONSIBLY BEING PUT TO WORK CREATING LIVING WAGE JOBS FOR PHILADELPHIA RESIDENTS. And with the new law, Philadelphia would send a strong message to business that it cares about its citizens and is committed to investing their tax money wisely—in businesses that do the same.

"Businesses will leave the city — or not locate here — if we put new burdens on them."

- Historically, businesses always make a lot of noise when wage increases are proposed—threatening to lay people off, shut down, move out of the city,—but experience with the economic evidence from both federal and state minimum wage increases has taught us that when push comes to shove, the vast majority of businesses adjust professionally and continue to operate normally and profitably. This makes sense, given:

- The vast majority of low wage workers are employed in industries that are tied to their locations, and find it difficult to leave. Only 24% of low wage workers are employed in more mobile manufacturing jobs (which typically already pay more than the proposed living wage); the other 76% are concentrated in service industries which must be near their customers to operate profitably.
- For example, restaurants will not pass up the lucrative business of serving meals to Philadelphia residents because of a higher minimum wage, and they cannot leave the city limits and retain that business. Stores will not pass up the market provided by Philadelphia consumers, and they need to be here to enjoy it. Personal services must be provided to people where they live, and the government must continue to employ people here.

This is the favorite argument of business against proposals to raise wages or provide other pro-worker benefits—yet it has never proven true.

- The living wage ordinance would cover only those businesses that have chosen to accept over $50,000 of city money or benefit from large City contracts, and will not apply retroactively. No business is "forced" to take a handout from the City.
- A 1996 and subsequent 1998 update study of the impact of the Baltimore Living Wage Ordinance found that—contrary to claims that the ordinance would drive out business, business investment in the city actually increased substantially in the year following passage. In addition, Baltimore contractors PRAISED the living wage legislation in interviews because it "levels the playing field" and "relieves pressure on employers to squeeze labor costs in order to win low-bid contracts."

- The modest living wage requirements are simply not enough of a drawback to outweigh Philadelphia's business advantages. Business decisions are based on access to markets and transportation systems, infrastructure, education and skill level of the available workforce, and overall quality of life—things that our City has going for it. Businesses that can profit in Philadelphia will remain here, with or without the new law.

In fact, Living Wage Good for Business

While opponents try to cast living wage as anti-business, the truth is that living wage ordinances have the potential to boost business:

- First, putting more money in the pockets of low wage workers means more money spent in our local economy at neighborhood businesses and fewer tax dollars needed for housing subsidies, medical assistance, and other public benefits for the working poor. For example, a study of the estimated impact of the Los Angeles Living Wage Ordinance study predicts a 50.4% reduction in the amount of government subsidies received by affected workers and their families, as well as growth in spending, home ownership, and small business markets in areas of the city where affected workers are concentrated.

- In addition, there is evidence that decent wages have the potential to reduce employee turnover, increase productivity and lower training and supervision costs for businesses. Higher wage floors also encourage more business investment in training, technology, and other productivity enhancers.

- Importantly, a living wage ordinance would support "high road" businesses already paying a living wage and prevent "low road" businesses from undercutting them by paying poverty wages.

"A living wage ordinance would cost the city too much money."

- The proposed measure does not directly impose any extra costs on the City of Philadelphia. What it DOES do is direct our tax dollars to address the problems that really DO cost the City money: poverty wages and underemployment.

- Research—and common sense—tell us that when people are paid enough to support their families, they no longer rely on public assistance in the form of Medicaid, food stamps, and other programs (increasingly provided to the working poor) that come at taxpayer expense. In addition, they pay more taxes and buy more goods and services in the local economy, stimulating growth of neighborhood economies. (A recent study from Chicago calculates the higher cost of keeping families at minimum wages than paying a living wage.)

- Experience in Baltimore indicates that costs to the city were negligible:

- The real cost of city contracts **decreased** since the ordinance took effect.

- The cost to taxpayers of compliance with Living Wage was minimal (17 cents per person per year).

- The value of business investment in Baltimore **increased** substantially in the year after passage of the Living Wage ordinance.

- Similarly, an economic analysis of the proposed Los Angeles Living Wage Ordinance concluded that the ordinance could be implemented while causing no net increase in the City budget, no employment loss and no loss of city services to the residents of Los Angeles.

- In addition, other academic studies prompted by Living Wage proposals in Chicago and Los Angeles predicted that the cost of such an ordinance to the city would pale in comparison to both the total city budget and—most importantly—the benefits to workers, families and neighborhoods. Even if—in response to the living wage ordinance—contractors passed the full value of increased labor costs directly on to the city (in the form of higher bids for contracts), the resulting cost to the city would represent a tiny fraction of the overall city budget. Yet we all know of projects that have been proposed by the mayor and other city officials that not only have a much higher ticket price but are far less important to the survival of Philadelphia's working families than the guarantee of decent pay for work.

- The basics of competition dictate that contractors in fact **will not** pass on their full labor costs to the city, but rather make necessary adjustments to keep functioning profitably in the city. The Baltimore experience supports this fact (see above).

- While opponents argue that a living wage costs too much, we say that living in Philadelphia costs too much for low wage working families. ACORN's study entitled Left Behind: The Real Cost of Living in Philadelphia—based on an accepted economic model for calculating a basic needs budget using local, regional and federal expenditure data—revealed that a Philadelphia family with only one child would require almost $10 hourly wage to meet basic needs.

"A living wage ordinance would cause job loss."
Although businesses love to threaten job loss, evidence of wage increases in cities and states tells us that this is not a real fear.

- The vast majority of economic research concludes that there is little or no disemployment effect associated with such wage increases.

- Most recently, a study released last week by the Economic Policy Institute concluded that last fall's minimum wage increase raised earnings for low-income working families and did so without jeopardizing jobs. The raise produced gains for four million workers, two-thirds of whom are adults, not teens as antis had claimed. At the same time, the increase did not cause employers to eliminate jobs held by entry-level workers. Black and Hispanic teens were the biggest beneficiaries.

- Take into account that since the federal minimum wage was increased last year, unemployment is at a 40 year low.

- The proposed ordinance only raises wages for a limited number of employees—those that work for a city contractor or subsidized employer. None of these companies are forced to accept public subsidies or make any changes in their payroll size.

- Because the ordinance will put more money into the hands of low wage workers, it has the potential to help rebuild our poorest communities and possibly spur job growth.

- Contractors interviewed as part of the Baltimore study did not report that they decreased their payrolls in response to the living wage requirements.

- The success of prevailing wage laws for construction firms contracting with the government can be considered a predictor of the effect of living wage legislation. These laws have created stability in the construction industry, encouraged training, and provided career opportunities with no adverse effects on employment or local economies.

"A living wage ordinance will cause inflation."
This is simply a scare tactic that hardly merits a response. In the words of John

Schmitt, a labor economist with the Economic Policy Institute in Washington, D.C:

"The fact is that we have seen and will continue to experience price increases in cities and nationwide driven by a series of factors of the larger economy that have little or nothing to do with the minimum wage. In reality, proposed efforts to raise wages of America's lowest paid workers will function to help wages catch up with price increases that are happening independent of wage fluctuation."

We all know that inflation is constantly on the rise, whether low wage workers get an increase or not. Blaming inflation on those who make the very least is nothing short of shameless.

"A living wage ordinance will create unnecessary regulations and more bureaucracy."

• The proposed ordinance is quite modest in scope and imposes few that are not already regularly kept by businesses.

• The Baltimore study showed the living wage regulation there did not discourage companies from doing business in Baltimore at all. Administration of the ordinance was estimated to have cost 17 cents per taxpayer in the first year—arguably a price worth paying to encourage jobs and responsible development in our city and to realize the savings from a lightened burden on social services needed by impoverished workers.

• The proposed living wage ordinance would only affect a limited number of businesses—those that choose to accept a substantial contract or financial subsidy from the City—not the entire Philadelphia-based business community.

The businesses covered are only those that have asked for and been granted public assistance either through a contract or subsidy. No one is forced to accept a public subsidy. At bottom, if a business wants to avoid bureaucracy and regulation in any form, the most effective way to do so would be to forsake the public trough.

• We are talking about public tax dollars. We have a right to expect accountability with respect to the use of our own money—to require that it benefit our community, not just business profits.

• In the absence of such an ordinance, the city does very little to insure the public tax dollars it invests in businesses . We have no evidence that has actually increased our tax base, provided decent jobs, or benefited commerce in the city. Any good business person expects some level of oversight to insure a return on his or her investment. Why should our city and her citizens expect any less?

• Extensive research of business investment and location decisions concludes that differences in regulatory structures are of little or no consequence to corporate decision-makers. Instead, firms are primarily concerned with worker skill levels, well-maintained infrastructure, transportation, access to markets, and overall quality of life.

• In our country, a mother unable to support her own children independently is subject to a litany of rules, regulations, and eligibility requirements in order to receive public assistance (and those regulatory requirements have increased dramatically under the new welfare law)—Why shouldn't we expect businesses seeking public assistance to be regulated?

• Businesses have historically tried to escape doing what is right by complaining about the "burden" of "regulation". Remember Child Labor laws? The minimum wage? Safety and Health regulations?—all of these were important **regulations** designed to protect the safety, health and well-being of workers. Businesses fought against these too.

It is the job of citizens and public officials to look out for the needs of the citizenry—not just sacrifice what is right to "lighten the burden" on corporations.

- No "regulatory burden" on businesses as a result of this simple, responsible legislation could match the daily burden forced on Philadelphia workers who work full time and still can't support their families adequately.

"No one is trying to support a family on less than $7.90. Most low wage workers are well-off teenagers"
Although a familiar refrain of opponents, this is simply not true.

- The fact is that people in Philly **are** struggling to support families at very low wages and even on the minimum wage. In fact, about 75 percent of minimum wage earners are over 20 years old, and more than 70 percent are lower income people. Before this last federal increase, the average minimum wage worker brought home over half of his or her family's earnings, and roughly 40% of minimum wage workers are the only earners in their families.

- In Philadelphia alone, 170,000 workers over the age of 19 toil for less than $7.60 an hour.

- Low wage workers are a major part of our workforce. They watch over our children, clean our offices, provide essential services in our daily lives, and care for our aging parents.

Low wage workers aren't "worth it"—The problem is low skilled workers, not low wages. What's needed is more education and training, not a wage hike.
It's certainly true that we need more education and training. We need better public schools, and real training programs connected to real jobs, and we

need to make sure that working people can afford to send our children to college. **But all the training in the world doesn't help if there are no jobs that pay decent wages.** It is worth noting that over the last 20 years, the number of workers with college degrees has nearly doubled, and the U.S. now has the highest percentage of college graduates in the world. The growing number of college degrees hasn't stopped the growing income gap between the richest and everyone else. Only raising wages can.

Requiring a minimum wage will "hurt those its intended to help" (minorities and low income young workers) because they will be locked out of jobs.
Nonsense. Low wage employers make this same argument every time wage increases are proposed, and it has never proven true. The same businesses that now hire young workers will still need those jobs done, and the same pool of young workers will continue to apply for and fill those jobs. Low wage workers of all races and ages stand to gain the most from an increase in the minimum wage.

Besides, it should be obvious that the folks opposing this increase are the same folks who oppose all federal minimum wage increases and most other worker benefits. They also represent some of the richest, most profitable corporations in the country, dependent on their low wage workers. Are we really supposed to believe these people care about young, minority workers?

In short, as Economist Mark Weisbrot stated after researching the issue in Connecticut and Baltimore, "The claims made by business interests concerning proposed corporate responsibility legislation simply cannot stand up to empirical or theoretical scrutiny. They are contradicted by the experience of other states, by voluminous evidence concerning business location decisions and by the basic laws of economics."

On That Point!

Monday March 26, 2001, The Guardian

It's time for a living wage

An invisible and miserably paid workforce helps companies with public contracts to make millions

Madeleine Bunting

When you arrive in your office this morning, the carpet will have been vacuumed, the bins emptied and the desk cleared of its old polystyrene coffee cups. Do you ever think about the life of the person who clears up your mess, and whether they were thinking of their kids back home asleep as they cleaned? They are an invisible workforce, the only sign of whose presence is the cleanliness and order they leave behind. In London, you occasionally catch glimpses of them, after a very late night out or a very early start, as they stand at bus stops at 5am in the morning; they are usually women and often black.

This workforce is notoriously difficult to unionise. It shifts from contract to contract, working in different offices in different teams. The army which floods into central London to clean and cook 24/7 is at the sharp end of a reorganisation of labour relations across both the public and the private sector brought about by contracting-out and privatisation.

We know little about them, they know a little about us. Disturbingly, the brutal politics of class, race and exploitation are masked by "the peace of mutual indifference" as the sociologist Richard Sennett phrased it in a recent essay on the decline of urban civic culture. What that means for the cleaners and cooks, is that the arrival of one of the handful of global business services companies which suck up all the contracts, is signalled by closing the tearooms. Then they set up a part-time shift system, so the overlap with fellow employees is reduced to a minimum.

Tony Blair and Gordon Brown hail this as "flexible working" and "best value" and show a quixotic blindness to how this form of invisible, flexible global capitalism corrodes human relationships—the very social capital which New Labour professes to being so concerned about. Robert Putnam, the US guru on the subject, is in Downing Street tomorrow, the latest in a flow of big thinkers to offer advice. But New Labour, fearful of a conflict with big business, takes the traditional right-wing route of ignoring the economic causes of civic decline, and pins the responsibility firmly on the individual. Labour rhetoric treats us as a nation of lazy couch-potatoes, and subjects us to sermons on the walk-by culture.

But look what happens when someone does get off the couch. Rosie (her name has been changed) has had enough. She's worked as cook for an east London hospital for 10 years, and the contract has now been taken over by Compass Granada. Her verdict is: "They don't know anything about catering, us girls tell them how to run things. I wish they'd stayed on the motorways." She objects to being moved from contract to contract, she objects to the permanent understaffing which results in frequent arguments with the management. And, she objects to her pay, £6 an hour for a 39-hour week, with little left over after the rent and bills. She often ends up working seven days a week and double shifts to make ends meet, yet she counts herself as one of the lucky ones, whose conditions are legally protected. Those getting new contracts and doing the same work can earn as little as £4.75 an hour. Rosie, now in her fifties, is exactly the kind of essential worker who is now being forced out of central London

On That Point!

through a combination of low wages and high housing costs.

Rosie is one of hundreds who have joined the Living Wage campaign organised by Telco (the East London Community Organisation) and Unison, to be launched next week. The campaign is based on a US model where a new generation of organisations, drawn initially from faith communities and human rights groups and subsequently teaming up with unions, have succeeded in getting "living wages" as a condition of contracts with public authorities in scores of US cities.

The Living Wage campaign's first target is the Greater London Authority's £3bn budget, but if the condition was built into every public contract, they argue, it would have a bigger impact on poverty across the east of London than any of the huge regeneration grants the government routinely pours into the area. So what is Labour's response? Here is a grassroots organisation working with some of the most marginalised groups, tackling poverty: it hits all Labour's favourite buttons. Yet, so far, not one local Labour MP has agreed to turn up to the launch of the campaign. Financial secretary, Stephen Timms, a long-time supporter of Telco, admits privately he's sympathetic, but can't publicly endorse a challenge to the minimum wage. Only Nicky Gavron, London's deputy mayor, to her credit, has promised to sign up.

The Living Wage campaign exposes the bind Labour is in. It is an excellent instance of Gordon Brown's much-trailed "renewal of civic society" and his proclamation of a "new era—an age of active citizenship and an enabling state" earlier this year. But what he envisaged was nice, malleable volunteers running toddler groups for Sure Start rather than those women gaining the confidence to challenge the whole system which consigns their children to poverty in the first place. A curiously

macho muscular language of weight-lifting has crept into poverty policy: Brown boasts of New Labour's lifting women and children out of poverty—but woe betide anyone uppity enough to want to do it for themselves.

Worst of all is how Rosie's low wages are a massive rip-off on us, the taxpayer. Prem Sikka of Essex University has compiled a top 50 list of companies with the highest differentials between the pay of the top and the bottom. Based on 1998–99 figures, Compass Granada came 19th; the highest paid director earned £1m and the average wages among the workforce were £11,000. Another big player scooping up government contracts is Rentokil Initial: the highest paid director was on £1.5m, compared to £9,000 at the bottom. Between 1990–99, Rentokil Initial's profits soared from £74.6m to £541.1m.

These kinds of profits are not a mystery of the market. In large part, they're made of our money. Firstly, it is our taxes which pay, through the local authorities, hospitals and schools, for the contracts with the like of Rentokil Initial and Compass Granada. Secondly, when those profits don't translate into living wages, it is our taxes, again, which pay for the tax credits, benefits and low-cost housing which are necessary to subsidise their employees. Plus there are the things which get missed off a balance sheet such as stress, but most importantly, the dignity and self-worth of people like Rosie in earning a decent wage for themselves so they don't have to rely on Mr Brown's muscles.

If the Living Wage campaigns can work in the US, hardly known as a model of good labour relations, it can work here. It's about time the taxpayer, let alone Rosie, got a bigger pay-back from the companies making millions out of public contracts. And here is an excellent opportunity for New Labour to show what to do with active citizenship when it sees it: support it.

On That Point!

This article appeared in The Los Angeles Times *on April 1, 1999.*

Keep Goose That Lays Golden Eggs

The Government should stay out of the labor market. Setting living wage standards is counterproductive.

By Diana Furchtgott-Roth

America's economy leads the world. The Dow hovers around 10,000, unemployment is at a record low of 4.4% and last quarter's GDP growth rate was 6.1%. So why is there a movement afoot to kill the goose that is laying the golden eggs —to replace our system of market pricing for wages with a socialist ideal of setting wages according to some arbitrary system of value?

These days the socialist ideal is manifesting itself in a push for a so-called "living wage" for low-income Americans and "comparable worth" or "pay equity" for women. Claiming that the federal minimum wage of $5.15 is too low, many municipal governments have instituted mandatory living wages ranging from $6.25 to $9.50 per hour plus benefits. The Los Angeles living wage is currently set at $7.39, and any company doing business with the city has to pay it to workers as contracts come up for renewal.

It's already illegal to pay different wages to men and women who do the same jobs, but the AFL-CIO and the feminists are going further: They are pushing for comparable worth or equal pay legislation in 22 states, so that men and women who do different jobs "of equal value" would be paid the same. These groups are planning a blitz of events around the country on Equal Pay Day, April 8.

A new study by the AFL-CIO and the Institute for Women's Policy Research asserts that women face a wage gap of $3,000 or $4,000 per year because they have chosen different jobs from men. But setting wages by cost-of-living indices or by others' earnings makes no sense because wages are affected not only by the supply of workers but by the demand for different services. Job requirements affect only how many workers are willing to take jobs, not how much the employer is willing to pay for the work product.

Look at a large firm such as Boeing. Boeing could not hire a single Ph.D. in engineering for under $75,000. But it could hire all the Ph.D. historians it wanted for $30,000. The jobs appear identical: doctorate required, must do research, write memos, attend boring management meetings. So why are the salaries so different? Is it some insidious, pernicious plot? No. The demand for any occupation is derived from the value of the goods and services produced, which is why football players are paid more than lacrosse players.

The facts are clear: artificially raising wages reduces the number of workers employed. Even worse, it hits hardest at new entrants to the labor force by preventing them from getting their feet on the bottom rung of the career ladder and working their way up. Many workers are entry-level, but they do not stay that way for long. If raising minimum wages truly improved incomes, why not just increase the minimum wage dramatically and save on investments in education, training, technology and infrastructure?

In our technology-oriented global economy companies have many choices about numbers of workers hired and plant location. Higher wages mean that companies change their production processes to use more machines and fewer workers, or shift production to countries with low wages. Naturally, this isn't going to happen tomorrow, but it will happen the next time the company has to decide whether to hire that extra person or build that second plant.

The American economy is steaming ahead. But today's new job opportunities render union membership unnecessary, and it has been steadily declining, from 24% of wage and salary workers 25 years ago to just 14% today. It's in the interests of union management to try to reverse this trend by falsely promising members artificially high wages.

And a false promise it is, because these wages cause more job losses than they put money in pockets: union members generally earn above minimum and living wages, so they don't profit from the increases; they are primarily blue-collar workers, who would fare poorly under comparable worth schemes. The best system for union members and for all Americans is to keep the goose that lays golden eggs and keep the government out of the labor market.

Chapter 12

Points of
Information

Introduction

Most debate formats give debaters an opportunity to question or challenge
the arguments of the opposing debate team. This usually means that there is
a period of questioning or cross-examination during the debate. For several
minutes, one or more debaters are permitted to examine, or ask questions,
of an opponent, usually after she has finished her speech. For example, a
speaker might deliver a seven minute speech for her side of the topic and, at
the end of the speech, remain standing at a desk or podium for another two
or three minutes of questioning by the other team.

Points of information make parliamentary debate different from other
forms of debate. In parliamentary debates, points of information are used
instead of the cross-examination of a speaker. Points of information are presented during an opponent's speech. The "interruption" of a speech is unusual
in debating, although it is more common in other argument settings. Most
people are familiar with a lawyer, rising to her feet, interrupting her opponent by saying, "I object!" The lawyer follows the objection with an argument—she might claim that the lawyer for the other side is harassing a witness
or breaking the court's rules of evidence. The objection is presented to a judge
and the judge rules for or against the objection.

Parliamentary points are used in a similar way, except a point is made to
the speaker "holding the floor" (delivering the speech at the time). The speaker
may accept the point or refuse it. If the point is accepted, the debater making
the point may ask a question or make a statement, as long as she does so within
fifteen seconds. The speaker holding the floor answers the point, using as
much or as little time and argument as she thinks is necessary. The judge does

not rule on a parliamentary point. In fact, the judge does not make any comments about it during the debate. The judge may consider the information or argument from parliamentary points in deciding the result of the debate or evaluating the performances of the debaters.

Points of Information

A point of information (a. k. a., "POI," pronounced as P-O-I) is a brief statement or a question to a point then being made by a speaker. The point must be made quickly and clearly—a debater is usually given fifteen seconds to successfully make a point. A debater makes just one point at a time. A debater may not ask a follow-up question or begin a conversation with the speaker. By accepting a point of information, a speaker is agreeing to allow the person on the opposing team to interrupt her speech for one statement or question. It is considered rude or unfair for the person making a point to try to make more than a single point or use more than fifteen seconds of time.

In the American parliamentary debate format, points of information are allowed in the first four speeches of the debate— these are also known as the constructive speeches (the speeches are also known as the first proposition speech, first opposition speech, second proposition speech, and second opposition speech). Points of information are not permitted in either the proposition or the opposition rebuttal speech. In addition, parliamentary points are not permitted during the first minute or the last minute of a speech. This is also known as "protected time." It is an opportunity for a speaker to introduce and conclude a speech without any distraction or interruption.

The timekeeper, often the judge of the debate or a person selected to keep time for the debate, will signal the debaters and let them know when they may make points of information. After the first minute of each constructive speech, the timekeeper will make a noise and let the debaters know that protected time has ended and debaters may now make points. The timekeeper usually knocks on a table or desk, claps her hands once, or makes some other appropriate or discreet noise. The timekeeper will make a similar noise with one minute remaining in each of the constructive speeches. This lets the debaters know that protected time has started for the last minute of each speech and that they may not interrupt the speaker with a point.

In the American parliamentary debate format, points of information are not allowed in either the proposition or opposition rebuttal speech. In the British parliamentary debate format, points of information are permitted during any of the speeches in the debate but, just as in the American version, there is still a minute of "protected time" at the beginning and end of each speech.

Points of information are actually a request to a speaker by an opponent to give some speaking time to the opponent so that the opponent may ask a question or challenge a part of the speech. When a point of information is accepted, the speaker holding the floor agrees to give some of her speaking time to the opponent. This means that the timekeeper does not stop the time for a point of information. The point of information comes from the allotted speaking time of the person holding the floor. If the speaker allows too many points from the other side, she may find herself without enough time left in which to make an effective speech. For example, if a speaker is delivering a seven-minute speech and a person on the opposing team makes a point of information at the first opportunity (one minute after the beginning of the speech or with six minutes of the speech remaining) and the point is accepted, the time will continue to run. If the point is made in fifteen seconds and the speaker replies to the point for fifteen seconds for a total of thirty seconds ("but I participate in debate because I thought there would be no math"), the speaker holding the floor will have five minutes and thirty seconds remaining in which to present an argument she had planned to deliver in six minutes.

Points of information may be announced and presented in different ways. One popular method is to rise from your seat and face the person speaking, and, at the same time, say, for example, "Point of information," "Information," or "On that point." Another way to make a point is to rise and not say anything at all. The fact that you are standing is a signal to the speaker that you would like to make a point of information.

The person speaking holds the floor during the time of her or his speech. That means that the person speaking is the only one who is authorized or permitted to speak at that time and the speaker must agree to share her time with any other person. The speaker, therefore, may take the point of information or refuse the point.

If the speaker agrees to take a point, she simply says "I'll take the point," or "Yes." If the speaker accepts your point of information, you make your point and sit down.

You might want to ask a question:

Speaker: Schools that have uniforms for students have better discipline and lower crime rates than school without uniforms.

Opponent (rising from her seat): On that point.

Speaker: I will take your point.

Opponent: What studies show that uniforms reduce crime among student populations?

You might make an argument:

Speaker: Schools that have uniforms for students have better discipline and lower crime rates than school without uniforms.

Opposing Speaker (rising from her seat): On that point.

Speaker: I will take your point.

Opposing Speaker: The majority of schools that have uniforms are private schools. The private schools expel their problem students to the public schools. That is the reason that schools with uniforms are likely to have better discipline and lower crime rates.

Additional statements or follow-up questions by the debater making a point are out of order. You cannot make more than one point at a time. After all, the speaker only recognizes you for a single and brief point of information. When a speaker accepts a point of information, the speaker should carefully listen to the point and make a decision about the best way to answer it.

A speaker should be patient during the presentation of an opponent's point of information. Although points of information are brief, a fifteen second point of information may seem like a long time, particularly if the speaker has much to say and little time to say it. To the interrupted speaker, it always seems that the amount of time taken by an opponent to make a point greatly exceeds the fifteen seconds.

To determine how long fifteen seconds can be, parliamentary debaters might consider an experiment in which they pinch themselves, or hold their breath, or otherwise perform an uncomfortable task for a timed fifteen-second period. Any debater who tries such an experiment will believe that fifteen seconds is not a brief or insignificant time.

The speaker does not need to accept a point of information. The speaker may refuse to take a point. This is not only acceptable but may be a good strategy at a key point in a speech. A speaker might refuse a point of information with a brief phrase (for example, "Not at this time" or "No, thank you"). On some occasions, particularly if the opposing team has attempted many points, a speaker may use a more direct approach. A speaker might reject a point of information with a quickly and strongly expressed "No" or may not even respond orally, but alternatively gesture with a downward wave of her or his hand to indicate that a debater rising for a point of information should sit down. If the person speaking declines to accept your point of information, you must sit down immediately.

Points of information are directed to the opposing team in a debate. "Friendly" questions to your partner or, in the four-team format, to another team arguing the same side of a motion, are not permitted. Each debater should both make and accept points of information. If you fail to make any points, it will seem that you are incapable of challenging your opponent's arguments. You will also not seem to be actively involved in the debate. This might hurt your credibility with the judge.

If you do not accept any points of information, it may appear to the judge that you fear your opponents or their arguments. On the other hand, if you accept too many points of information, you might lose control of your speech. The distraction and continuous interruption might undermine the many good arguments you might want and need to present to establish your team's position in a debate. As the English-Speaking Union's guidebook explains: " Offering points of information, even if they are not accepted, shows that you are active and interested in the debate. Accepting them when offered shows that you are confident of your arguments and prepared to defend them. A team that does neither of these is not debating."

Strategic Uses of Points of Information

Points of information are a powerful tool. They direct the judge's attention to the more relevant issues of the debate. They provide opportunities for dynamic and direct clash with opponents. Informational points are opportunities for displays of wit, humor and style.

Statements or Questions?

Parliamentary points may be statements or questions. In college debating in the United States, for example, the National Parliamentary Debate Association has codified the use of informational points as statements or questions:

> A debater may request a point of information—either verbally of by rising—at any time after the first minute and before the last minute of any constructive speeches. The debater holding the floor has the discretion to accept or refuse a point of information. If accepted, the debater requesting the point of information has a maximum of fifteen seconds to make a statement or ask a question. The speaking time of the debater with the floor continues during the point of information.

If you can use either a statement or a question to make a point, a statement is a preferred. A declarative statement shows command of the facts. A question more likely indicates your lack of knowledge about one or more issues and appears to be a request for information from the speaker holding the floor. A question, therefore, places the person making a point in an inferior or weaker position. You may ask a question but the speaker has the answer. In this exchange, speaker will seem to have the upper hand. This is particularly unfortunate in debating contests, where judges and audiences usually conclude that the most credible speakers are winning the debate. It is not good practice to make your opponent look as if she is winning the debate simply because you have questions and she has all the answers.

Too many debaters try to convert their statements to questions for the purpose of making a point of information. You may be able to challenge the information from a speaker in a direct way.

> Speaker: "The death penalty is an effective deterrent to murder. Research has consistently shown that states with capital punishment have lower murder rates."
>
> Opponent: "On that point. [The point of information is accepted by the speaker holding the floor] That research also shows that states that actually use the death penalty have growing rates of murder and that it is the states with an unused death penalty that have decreasing murder rates. States may lower their murder rates, just as long as they do not use the death penalty."

This point of information challenges the factual claims of the speaker, undermining the argument claim that the death penalty deters crime.

You could also "convert" this point of information and press forward with the following question:

> Opponent: "On that point. [The point of information is accepted by the speaker holding the floor] Isn't it true that states that actually use the death penalty have growing rates of capital crimes and that states with an unused death penalty have decreasing murder rates?"

The question simply does not challenge the speaker's facts in the same way as the earlier example. The question might imply that the opponent is unsure of the facts and genuinely needs information from the speaker. To answer this question, the speaker only needs to repeat or otherwise confirm a portion of her speech. The predictable answer to the respondent's question:

> Speaker: "Of course that isn't true. As I already said, the opposite is the case."

The transformation of powerful statement to weak question is poor practice. In this example, the point of information does not undermine the speaker's argument in favor of the death penalty. In fact, it reinforces the point made by the speaker, that is, that the death penalty deters murder. The opponent seems unsure of the facts and needs to ask a question about the death penalty. The speaker repeats her earlier argument, making it appear that she is correct and that the opponent is not really paying attention to the substance of the debate.

In addition, the question makes it harder for the opponent to refute the argument effectively at a later point in the debate. The opponent has seemingly undermined her own credibility—the question reveals a lack of knowledge about death penalty deterrence. It would be difficult to establish an equally credible argument regarding knowledge of the deterrent effect of capital punishment after asking a question indicating you might not be sure of the facts.

In a debate, the credibility of the speaker is essential to a judge's appreciation of the factual material. A judge is more likely to agree with the more credible speaker. In this example, an opposing team's argument about the deterrent effect of the death penalty would have little chance against not one, but two, authoritative claims that the death penalty deters murder. And one of those claims would have been heard as an answer to a question during an interactive portion of the debate— one of the infrequent opportunities for the debaters to "square off" and confront each other about the debate's facts. In this circumstance, a judge would be hard-pressed to agree with the opponent. There are good opportunities to ask questions of your opponent. You should ask questions, when it is in your interest. If a point of information can be made either by a question or a statement, however, make the point with a statement.

Applications for Points of Information

There are five reasons to use points of information. Points are used to gain understanding of the issues presented by an opposing side; to seek agreement on the core issues of the debate; to evaluate factual material; to advance the arguments of the side raising the point; and to undermine the arguments of the opposing side.

Seeking Understanding   A point of information can be used to understand your opponent's arguments. In a debate, you must understand your opponent's arguments in order to answer them. It is not possible to answer arguments with which you are unfamiliar or about which you are uncertain. Points of information can be used to discern the key issues of your opponents' argument.

Informational points may be used to examine a topic's interpretation, the details of a policy, the technical details of products and technologies, and more, as seen in the following examples.

> "The topic for the debate is 'Bury it.' Could you explain how taking DNA from corpses in criminal investigations supports the topic?"

> "Your say that the United Nations ought to use peacekeeping forces to protect human rights. Would you use military forces for every violation of human rights, regardless of location of the violation or the degree of the violation? For example, would you send forces to China because of the arrest of a single political dissident?"

> "Please describe, in a known human language, what it is you mean by the phrase 'dispositional intrinsicness counter-permutation?'"

> "The World Health Organization is responsible for international smallpox eradication. What is the WHO's position on eradication of the smallpox virus at remaining sites at which there is smallpox and how is it carrying out that policy?"

> "I understand your claim that a 'suture,' as explained from the synchronic gaps in a signifying chain, might lead to narrative dismemberment. What I don't understand is your other statement that the suture effect on a hypertextual subject in the international binding of the docuverse might lead to diachronic discourse closure or link function fragmentations. Please explain the latter."

Points of information may clarify or simplify the issues of a debate. Debates are not occasions for disagreeable people to be unpleasant to each other for an hour, if only to spare other people from their social problems.

Establishing Agreement   Debates involve disagreement but they surely include issues of agreement as well. The clever debater (you) will want to identify issues of agreement in your debates. Agreement on some issues, particularly on insignificant and trivial matters, might allow you to focus the issues of the debate on more important matters. It is in your interest to successfully mark points of agreement.

In a debate on the motion, "This House prefers liberty to equality," an opening proposition speaker might dramatically influence the outcome of the debate, or cause considerable confusion, unless there is a clear definition of "liberty." There are many conceptions of liberty, some of which are at odds with each other.

The opposition team must do something to focus the discussion on a limited definition of liberty if they are to refute the case successfully. Agreement—established with a point of information—may be the solution.

> "Point of information. [The point of information is accepted by the speaker holding the floor] Can we agree that liberty, in this debate, should be understood as the independence of the individual from control by the state?"

When points of information clarify issues of agreement, they remove issues from a judge's consideration so that the debaters are able to concentrate on more important and decisive matters.

Evaluating Facts   Interesting claims about history, government, economics, politics, and culture are often introduced in parliamentary debates:

> "There are fifty nations in NATO."

> "It is not possible to have unemployment and inflation at the same time."

"The most underdeveloped European country is Hawaii."

"The United Nations was established in 1850, at the conclusion of the First World War."

The listed claims are, quite obviously, inaccurate. There are other, less obvious, factual inaccuracies in many debates. Many debaters present facts with a knowledge base that includes a healthy dose of misinformation, half-truths, gossip, rumors, innuendo, hearsay, official government and/or corporate propaganda, quasi-royal decrees, slander, puffery, eyewitness accounts, hyperbolic realities, voodoo simulacra, carnie wisdom, folk psychology, psychic hotline notations, tarot pronouncements or a personal belief system. On some occasions, there are even false claims in debate topics. (Adonis is the god of vegetation, not love!)

Points of information are a superb opportunity to examine the "facts" of a debate. You might question the truth of your opponent's information, reconsider the historical record, or analyze the relevance or importance of noted examples and exceptions to those examples.

Advancing Your Own Argument   A successful debater might be able to advance her own argument during points of information with a little bit of help from her friends. This is best accomplished with a cooperative point, that is, one that avoids the confrontational, strident, skeptical or accusatory tone often accompanying points of information in a heated debate.

As most professional interrogators (police, lawyers) are aware, unfriendly questions or statements are easily anticipated and often resisted by witnesses. Many points of information are decidedly unfriendly:

"Point of information. You, madam, are deceiving the good ladies and gentlemen assembled. As sure as I have an active brain wave, there are fifty nations in NATO."

"On that point. I knew Jack Kennedy. I worked with Jack Kennedy. And you, sir, are no Jack Kennedy."

A better strategy might be a "leading" statement or question, designed to encourage your opponent to speak at length on an issue.

To present a point of information, which might advance your argument in the debate, you should begin by anticipating the arguments that will come up in a debate. Argument anticipation is a key to successful debating. Anticipation is important in all competitive contests—athletics, board games such as chess and backgammon, card games, and other academic competitions (Model United Nations, academic decathlon, etc.).

Your success in competitive contests presumes that you will identify the moves that an opponent might make and that you will make effective counters to those moves. In an athletic contest, this means that one might anticipate a physical move by an opponent and use a misdirection to avoid her. In a board game, such as chess, victory is typically based on a player's ability to anticipate the direction of play eight, nine, ten or more moves in advance of the actual movement of the pieces. In debates, consistent success requires anticipation of the issues that will be argued in the contest. Effective debaters should "know," with some degree of confidence, many of the issues that will be introduced in a debate prior to the opening speech of the debate.

How can a debater anticipate opponents' issues and, subsequently, their own replies to those arguments? It is a relatively simple. You should initially consider the arguments that you will introduce in the debate. Then imagine the way that your opponent will respond to each of your arguments. Ask yourself the following question: "What will they say when I make this argument in the debate?" The answers to this question will successfully reveal many of your opponents' arguments.

Once you have identified the likely replies to your arguments in the debate, it is then necessary to consider the moves you will make to answer your opponents' main points. At this point, ask yourself the following question: "What will I say when they present their answers to my first arguments?" This, of course, will provide the next set of appropriate arguments. These two modest yet vitally important questions ("What will they say when I make this argument in the debate?" and "What will I say when they present their answers to my arguments?") will help you prepare for all the speeches of a debate.

In this way, much of a debate can be "scripted" prior to its start. This does not mean that you will know all the arguments before a debate. After all, it is extraordinarily rare indeed to anticipate all of your opponents' arguments successfully. A number of unanticipated issues will be part of every debate. At the same time, "scripting," or argument anticipation, helps any person prepare for a debate.

Advancing an argument through a point of information relies on argument anticipation. In a debate, you will successfully anticipate some of your opponents' arguments and prepare your answers to them. You would like to make sure that you are able to introduce your arguments with necessary legitimacy and credibility.

You should make a point of information that will appear to be friendly and to which your opponent will want to respond. The point will get your opponent to speak. In fact, your opponent will not just speak to the point—your opponent will "embrace" the properly worded friendly point.

In the following example, we will presume that the proposition team has presented a case arguing that the United States Federal Government should significantly expand its school breakfast and lunch program, providing nutrition supplements to needy children:

> Opponent: "Point of information. But the federal school breakfast and lunch program doesn't provide a comprehensive diet. It doesn't even include dairy, does it?"
>
> Speaker: "Yes, it does include dairy. It provides all the necessary components of a daily nutritional supplement."

In this example, you, as respondent to a speaker holding the floor, have introduced a point of information that has encouraged the speaker to say precisely what is needed to advance your arguments indicating that:

> **1. Dairy products exacerbate the incidence of childhood asthma;**
>
> **2. The inclusion of dairy products reduces immunity to bacterial infections. As dairy farmers add antibiotics to livestock feed to protect their herds, the medication is passed, through the consumption of dairy products, to consumers and the addition both generates antibiotic-resistant strains of germs and increases the tolerance of the immune system to particular drugs, reducing the effectiveness of antibiotics; and**
>
> **3. Many children, particularly those of African or Asian descent, are lactose intolerant. A "dairied" diet is unhealthy and inedible for many of the children for whom the federal school breakfast and lunch program is designed.**

These issues, anticipated before the debate, are secured with a point of information. The speaker for the proposition, in reply to the point of information, has established a clear relationship between the plan of action in the opening speech, a plan endorsing a significant increase in the federal school breakfast and lunch program, and a diet that includes dairy products. This relationship, or "link," is more than enough to serve as a foundation for the opposition arguments listed here, as well as many more. The opposition team is now in a superior position to advance its own arguments in the debate because a point of information encouraged the proposition team to speak on an issue in a way that was predictable, and favorable to the opposition.

Undermining Your Opponent's Argument   We will begin this section on points of information and note that this last task, undermining your opponent's arguments, is the most challenging of all. Points of information are different from the Spanish Inquisition or Salem Witch Trials. The opposing side must have the approval of the speaker holding the floor to make a point. Only one point may be made at a time— there are no opportunities for a series of questions or an open discussion with the speaker. The speaker may choose to answer the point or might refuse the point and ignore the issue entirely. In other words, you are not in a strong position to get a confession, admission, or disclosure from the speaker. It is highly unlikely that you will be able to undermine a speaker's arguments consistently. There are, however, some opportunities to counter the claims of the speaker effectively.

A challenge to the logical construction of an argument (an investigation of causality or a showing of an argument fallacy, for example) might undermine the point of the speaker. In a reply to a proposition speech on the need for foreign aid to Africa to promote economic growth and relieve human misery, you might offer the following point:

> Opponent: "On your point on aid to the Sudan. The cause of human misery in the Sudan is a drought and a civil war between Christians and Muslims. Foreign assistance will do nothing to stop hunger and disease because the civil war interferes with the distribution of aid. These new projects will only increase the violence of the civil war, as participants struggle for the few incoming dollars."

In this case, the point might prove that more foreign aid will increase the violence of the civil war, decreasing opportunities for economic growth and development, making matters worse for the people of the Sudan.

Avoiding the "Rule of Three"

There is no "Rule of Three." Some debate coaches teach as if such a rule exists. It does not. Let us clarify: there is no "Rule of Three." No such rule. Number of "Rules of Three" in parliamentary debating—zero. Why, then, is it important to discuss a non-existent rule? Because some debate coaches do believe that such a rule exists. So do a number of judges. Unfortunately, some debaters perpetuate the myth of its existence. It is, therefore, important to understand what it is and how one might avoid it.

Some debaters, coaches, and judges, primarily but not exclusively in the United States, believe that a speaker holding the floor is obliged to accept three, but no more than three, points of information. Some of them extend the fanciful rule in this way—they believe that a team may make only three attempts to request points of information during any speech. Neither version of the "rule" is accurate.

Debate teams may attempt any number of points of information during the non-protected time of opponents' speeches (that is, after the first minute of the speech and before the last minute of the speech). You are not limited in any way in the number of attempts. This is because the speaker holds the floor and must approve any points of information. The speaker may accept or refuse points in a strategic manner during her presentation. The speaker controls the introduction of points of information from opponents and does not need the protection of a formal rule.

In practice, many debaters in the United States train their judges and coaches in the "Rule of Three." Debaters are likely to reply to points of information this way:

"I will take your first question."

"I will take your second question."

"I will take your third and final question."

This over-rehearsed, mechanically delivered set of replies offers rather poor instruction to inexperienced judges. To begin, these replies presume that points of information are questions, which is wrong: as noted previously, points of information may be either statements or questions (and clever debaters would prefer to make their points of information in the form of statements).

This approach also makes the error that the speaker holding the floor in the debate controls the number of attempts that might be made by the opposing side. Although the speaker is able to accept or refuse points, the speaker is not authorized to dictate the number of attempts made by another team. The opposing side may, if they desire, continue to make attempts. This could be necessary. The fact that a speaker holding the floor might decide to refuse later points during her speech does not mean that there will be no need for informational points. The speaker might present confusing arguments, inaccurate facts, or unclear details of a product or public policy.

Because points of information are often poorly presented, it can be in the speaker's best interest to accept more than three points of information. Sometimes opponents will meekly quibble with the argument claims and evidence of a speaker. In these circumstances, it is in the interest of the speaker to accept more than three points. This is an opportunity for you to demonstrate superior argumentative ability. It does not make sense to limit the number of points of information to "three," when taking more points will help improve the odds of winning a debate or gain favor with the judge. Debaters should be free to raise points and accept or refuse them at will. Practice and debate convention might suggest that taking three points during a speech is good form, but this is in no way an obligation of a debate format.

Manner During Points of Information

Attitude   Debates are, by nature, adversarial. Competition potentially increases the anxiety of participants and the tension between teams. Points of information, because they constitute an interactive portion of the debate, are an occasion for tension and conflict. Debaters should present points of information in a clear, relatively dispassionate manner. This recommendation applies equally to the person making the point and the speaker holding the floor. Debaters must keep in mind that points of information are not an opportunity to vent frustration on the opposing side. Rather, they are an occasion for further communication with the judge.

A debate judge is likely to hold both parties (the person making the point of information and the speaker holding the floor) responsible for the breakdown of effective communications during points of information. It is unwise to antagonize the judge with unreasonable, petty, immature, mean or small-minded behavior.

As in any setting, communication in debates is effective when the message is delivered to the appropriate decision-maker. In the overwhelming majority of debates, the decision-maker is a single judge or a panel of several judges. (There are exceptions, including decisions by a vote of the full audience.) Debaters should make every effort to provide information to the decision-maker. It will undoubtedly be the case that there is little satisfaction in speaking with an opposing side in a debate. For one thing, they **oppose** you. Your appeals to their rationality, humanity, or general decency are likely to fall on deaf ears. They are extraordinarily unlikely to concede the debate to you.

This means, of course, that you should focus attention on the person or persons actually making a decision on the outcome of the debate. The presentation of a point of information, although directed to a speaker holding the floor, is an opportunity to transmit supplemental information to the judge. The superior debater should employ points of information that will use the other side's anticipated responses as part of a strategy to communicate with the judge. Our suggested approach—information to the judge rather than to the speaker holding the floor—is more likely to reduce hostile or impotent communication during attempted points.

Gesticulation   Local conventions will determine the forms for the presentation of a point of information. These forms include, but are not limited to, the following:

- A person attempting a point of information will rise.
- A person attempting a point of information will rise and say "Point of information."
- A person attempting a point of information will rise and extend an open hand.
- A person attempting a point of information will rise and extend an open hand and say "Point of information," or "On that point."
- A person attempting a point of information will rise and extend one open hand, while placing the other hand on her head.
- A person attempting a point of information will rise and extend one open hand, while placing the other hand on her head and say "Point of information."

Unnecessary or inappropriate gestures can confuse an audience. You may see debaters who place their hand on their head while attempting a point of information. This is a gesture left over from British Members of Parliament attempting to keep their wigs on, and is not necessary in modern parliamentary debate.

The initial attempt of an informational point ought to be subtle—you should rise and make no other verbal or physical moves. If the point is refused, the second attempt should be more demonstrative, for example, you should rise, saying "Point of information" in a clear, loud but measured tone. If the second attempt is also refused, the third attempt might add an extended open hand, a gesture clearly asking, perhaps imploring, the speaker to recognize you.

If your first attempt in the debate throws in every statement and gesture in the known POI world—hands outstretched and on head with an additional verbal cue that you are delivering a "point of information," you have undercut your ability to escalate the presentation of points of information, making it less likely that your later points will get addressed. Save the ballet for those times during opposing side speeches when a point of information **must** be made.

Responding to Points of Information

To be brief, be brief. Points of information should not distract from your message as a speaker. Even relevant points may not require much of an answer. They may not have sufficient importance or significance. Replies should not last much longer than the time used to make the point.

Be brief but be clear. Let the judge know that you understand the objection or question and that you have presented a fully satisfactory reply. Do not continue with your speech if the judge is not convinced of the reply—she will continue to think of (perhaps obsess over) your reply, reducing your ability to communicate the next set of arguments in your speech effectively.

Avoid the rhetorical traps of the ineffective speaker. For example, you should avoid refusing points by saying "Not at this time." (It only encourages your opponent to rise moments later. "Is this a good time?" Or moments after that. "Is this a good time?" "Not at this time." Or nanoseconds after that. "How about now? Is this a good time?" "Not at this time." It is quite obviously better to say, "No," or "No, thank you." Direct. Clear. Evident. Do not worry. Their feelings will not be hurt. And they will learn to say the same to you.)

Take points during argument transitions. This minimizes the distraction of the point. First, complete your argument. At the conclusion of your argument, pause, just briefly, to create some rhetorical space for a point of information. (You are, in effect, inviting a point of information at this time, for your own convenience.) Before the introduction to your next major argument (perhaps after you have detailed one advantage of your plan and before you move on to the next), if an opportunity presents itself, take a point.

Opponent: On that point.

Speaker: No, thank you. [The speaker holding the floor refuses to take the point. The opponent sits and the speaker continues with her presentation.] In conclusion, the risks of chemical and biological weaponization and proliferation are today greater than the risks associated with the use of more traditional weapons of mass destruction and terror—nuclear weapons. I will now take your point.

This tactic reduces points of information to those times in the speech with the least distracting or confusing effect. In addition, it is often the case that your opponent has forgotten the point by the time she is called to stand and deliver. Making your opponent seem forgetful and ineffectual is a real plus:

Opponent: On that point.

Speaker: No, thank you. [The speaker holding the floor refuses to take the point. The respondent sits and the speaker continues with her presentation.] In conclusion, the risks of chemical and biological weaponization and proliferation are today greater than the risks associated with the use of more traditional weapons of mass destruction and terror—nuclear weapons. I will now take your point.

Opponent: I forgot it. That's okay. Go on. I don't have a point.

Points of information are often the allies of the speaker holding the floor. After all, you are the speaker **holding the floor**. It is possible to dismiss the point as an empty gesture from a confused opponent. It is possible to use the point to your strategic advantage (that is, almost any direct and effective reply is typically counted as a victory—they raised an argument point and you succeeded in addressing it).

These tactical advantages are available to you because you hold the floor. The point of information is a valuable tool but it is a limited one. Speakers have the time to respond to well-expressed points and should be ready to do so.

Suggested Exercises

1. Have a teacher or coach present a case study or historical example on a topic of their choosing. Students should analyze the example, identifying counterexamples and/or supporting examples for the case study.

2. Debaters should divide into two teams of equal numbers of debaters (it may be any number but the exercise works best with four to six debaters per side). One debater should present a seven-minute speech on a narrow motion. The teams should then alternate sides, delivering points of information in turn. Each debater must to make a point within a set period of time (typically, fifteen or twenty seconds). No points may be repeated. If a debater repeats or is otherwise unable to make a point, she is removed from the competition. Debaters are removed for frivolous points as well. At the conclusion of the speech, another round begins with the remaining competitors. The last side with participants wins the contest.

Chapter 13

Rebuttals and Humor

Introduction

Debate requires the development of many skills at once. In addition to all of the skills you have already learned about, you will have to refine your rebuttal skills. You will also need to work on your ability to use humor effectively in debates. In this chapter, we will discuss these skills and suggest some methods for strengthening them.

Tips for Rebuttals

The purpose of rebuttal speeches is to give your side a last chance to explain why you should win the debate. The rebuttal speech is an opportunity to summarize and extend your critical arguments in the debate, summarize and refute the arguments of the other team, and show why, given the arguments that have been advanced in the debate, your side wins. Rebuttals are not the time to make new arguments. New arguments are for constructive speeches. Rebuttal speeches may include new examples, but you should refrain from introducing new lines of argument. In other words, it is appropriate for each team's rebuttal speaker to have new analysis of the *already established and important arguments* of the debate. It is also fine for the rebuttal speakers to present new examples to support for the arguments that were *first introduced in the constructive speeches* of the debate. The rebuttals are the closing speeches of a debate that is ongoing. They follow on and are limited by the arguments that have gone before. These final speeches cannot be considered as just another opportunity to make a good point for your side of the debate. A rebuttal speaker may only present a logical continuation of the established arguments.

Rebuttal speeches must contain a substantial element of refutation. Some debaters see the rebuttal speech as an opportunity for grand, summarizing gestures and little else. While summarizing the debate is an important element of any rebuttal speech, rebuttal speakers must also refute the arguments made by the other team in their most recent speech or speeches in order to win the debate. The effective rebuttalist must play offense and defense. If you only summarize the debate in your final speech, you risk losing the debate on the details of arguments advanced by the other team.

On the other hand, you should try to avoid the opposite mistake of rebuttal speakers: too much attention to detail and not enough attention to the "big picture" of the debate. Some rebuttal speakers invest all of their time in refuting the arguments of the other team and extending their own arguments without providing any meaningful summary of the debate or the reasons why they think they should win the debate. This is a mistake, because you need to communicate to judges why, given all of the arguments that have been made, your side should win.

A lot of impact assessment happens (it is to be hoped) in the final rebuttals of a formal debate. Rebuttals present you with your last chance to impress the judge with your command of the issues at hand. Many debaters, perhaps echoing socially maladjusted behaviors learned in primary school, will try too hard to impress the judge ("Ooh, please pick me, teacher! I'm ever so smart!") by trying to win every single argument in the debate. This strategy ignores one of the most valuable rebuttal techniques you can employ: the fine art of strategic concession. Good debaters know when to concede arguments to strengthen their overall position. In impact debates, you can use a version of strategic concession to solidify your winning position. The key phrases to use are:

> **"Even if we lose this, we still win because…"**

> **"At worst, they're just winning that… but this still doesn't trump our position because…"**

What these phrases have in common is that they *take seriously* the possibility that the other team might be winning some of the arguments in the debate. The "even if" argument is one of the most powerful phrases you can use in a rebuttal speech:

"Even if they win their argument that our plan increases government spending, we still win the debate because we have
proved that spending is worthwhile";

"Even if we lose this particular advantage, we still win the debate
based on the cumulative strength of our other advantages";

"Even if you think this link turn argument is tenuous, the fact
remains that they haven't *ever* answered it."

When assessing impacts in rebuttals, it is important to use "even if" and other
related phrases to realistically compare arguments for evaluation by the judge
or audience.

Humor and Heckling

Parliamentary debates are engaging and dynamic events. Unlike most formal
speaking engagements and other forms of academic contest debating, they
are designed to encourage speech interruption from the opposing side of the
motion (for example, points of information) and the assembled participants
and audience (with verbal and non-verbal heckling).

In all formats, humor and heckling play important roles in parliamentary
debate's dynamism. Humor has striking persuasive power in an oral presentation. It motivates the audience to engage in critical listening. The audience,
including judges for the contest, wants to be entertained as well as informed.
Debates go on for too long to be nothing but a dull recitation of facts.

Humor not only connects the speaker with the judge and audience but
also enhances the credibility of other arguments in a presentation. The use
of humor is popularly associated with higher-level critical thinking skills and
intelligence. This association of humor and wit with intellectual sophistica-
tion reflects favorably on a speaker's other, and frequently rational, lines of
argument.

Debaters should prepare to use humor in the same way they might prepare
to express an opinion on historical, political or social events. Research and
practice are keys to the effective use of humor in speeches.

There are hundreds of texts providing reference material for humor.
Dictionaries of humorous quotations are available. Websites collect the
malapropisms of political figures and celebrities. Periodicals such as *The Onion*

(www.theonion.com) offer models of humor, including, in its headlines, surprise, satire, and irony.

Surprise: Man Accidentally Ends Business Call with 'I Love You'

Satire: Depression Hits Losers Hardest

Irony: Sculptor Criticized for Turning Women into Objects

The hardest working people in show business are stand-up comedians, who toil for many hours to craft only a few minutes of material. Debaters do not need to devote similar effort, but some preparation is required. Debaters are not expected to make the same kind of presentation as a comedian. For this, debaters ought to be thankful. Debate audiences, starved as they are for any sort of entertainment, are a receptive crowd for subtle wit and drollery. It is not necessary to be "laugh out loud funny" to be a hit in the debate world.

A speaker should use humor at the beginning of her speech, certainly within the first 30 seconds. Early use encourages critical listening on the part of the assembled judges and audience as they eagerly await the next funny bit. It doesn't have to come until two or three minutes later, at the point of the speech at which they believe you might have already exhausted your treasure chest of jokes. Some wit or cleverness toward the end of the speech is also appreciated: merely a few clever lines, some prepared in advance and some extemporaneous comments rising from the clash in the debate, should suffice for an entertaining speech.

Heckling is also an important part of parliamentary debating. If you have doubts about this, spend some time watching the British Parliament in session—there are always many different kinds of heckling. In debate, you may engage in supportive heckles of your partner, perhaps by knocking on your table to support her after she makes a particularly good point. You might also say (in a relatively quiet voice) "Hear, hear" to emphasize your agreement with your partner's point or even a point made by the opposition. You may also heckle the opposing team, but should not engage in rude behavior. Audience members should be encouraged to heckle responsibly, as well. Heckling is an important part of parliamentary debate all over the world, and it can make debates fun and interesting.

On That Point!

Open Forum Debate

Involving many people in a debate or discussion is a good way to ensure that multiple points are raised and many issues are discussed. It is possible, even desirable, to have a debate that engages an entire class of students on an issue in controversy. This kind of exercise requires some preparation and careful topic selection, but is well worth the investment of time and energy.

To have a classroom debate, you will need a topic that is broad enough to interest the entire class. In this section, we have included two articles on the topic of opening borders. Although these articles deal only with issues related to the USA's borders, the topic is certainly important for any other nation's immigration policy. We suggest that you choose the topic a few days in advance of the actual debate, so that all the students will have an opportunity to investigate the topic on their own.

For the debate, the class (this works with groups as large as 30) should be divided in two, with half of the students representing the proposition side, and the other half representing the opposition side. In addition to the debaters, you will need a moderator and at least one person to serve as the "scribe" for the event. The teacher or coach is probably the best candidate for moderator, at least the first time you try this exercise, but you may want to switch moderators periodically so that everyone has a chance to try this challenging task.

The "scribes" for the event have the task of tracking the arguments in the debate. They should do this on the board so that everyone can keep track of what arguments have been raised and which arguments have been refuted.

The job of the moderator is to ask provocative and directed questions of the participating debaters. As with the panel discussion exercise, the job of the moderator is also to help ensure that everyone has a chance to speak. The moderator should not, however, dominate or direct the discussion too forcefully. The debate itself may be conducted in either of two ways:

- An **open session**, where the two sides alternate turns expressing opinions on the topics; or

- A **closed session**, where each side has a certain number of speakers in a designated order who address the points for discussion.

Either format works well, and has its own advantages. The class debate is basically an example of group analysis of an issue. It should demonstrate both the breadth and depth of the issues on the topic.

During the course of the debate, as each side in the debate raises points, the scribes should write basic summaries of those points on the board. As the other side answers those points, the scribes should note the answers to each point. This will help everyone involved in the debate to keep track of what issues have been raised and which issues still need to be addressed. After the designated time for the debate is over (usually 30 minutes, depending on the size of the group), the moderator or another participant should lead a discussion about which side had the stronger arguments in the debate and why those arguments were stronger.

═══════════ Exercise ═══════════

Have a classroom debate according to the guidelines given in this section. Using the articles reprinted below or other articles you find on your own, debate on the topic "This nation should open its borders."

This article first appeared in The San Diego Union-Tribune on August 3, 2001. Copyright Ben Zuckerman and Stuart H. Hurlbert. Reprinted by permission of the authors.

Is Overimmigration in the U.S. Morally Defensible?

By Ben Zuckerman and Stuart H. Hurlbert; Zuckerman is a professor of physics and astronomy at UCLA. Hurlbert is a professor of biology at San Diego State University. Zuckerman and Hurlbert are directors of the non-profit, public interest group Californians for Population Stabilization.

President Bush and Mexican President Vicente Fox are now at the poker table deciding how many persons from Mexico currently residing illegally in the United States will be given amnesty this year, a first step in Fox's plan for an open border between the two countries. Not to be left behind, Senate Majority Leader Thomas Daschle has raised the stakes and proposed amnesty for all illegal immigrants.

Meanwhile, we read the latest Census Bureau figures showing a U.S. population increase of 33 million during the 1990s, which exceeded the bureau's projections by 6 million persons and is the largest decadal jump in U.S. history. The Census Bureau now projects that, by the end of the century, U.S. population might exceed 1 billion, even in the absence of an open border with Mexico. Most of these 1 billion will be immigrants yet to arrive and their descendants.

President Fox is one of numerous powerful persons and groups lobbying

On That Point!

for continued and even increased high levels of immigration to the United States. Two such groups are (1) the Democratic Party, which believes, probably correctly, that a majority of immigrants will vote Democratic and (2) some Republican business interests who understand that massive immigration depresses wages and provides additional consumers of products and services.

Today, we would like to speak on behalf of three multitudinous, but "voiceless" groups in America who are harmed by massive immigration.

The first group is the poorest segment of the U.S. population. Independent studies by the Rand Corporation, the National Academy of Sciences, and the Center for Immigration Studies all show that today's policy of overimmigration negatively impacts the economic well-being of the poorest Americans. A summary discussion by James Goldsborough appears in the September/October 2000 issue of Foreign Affairs. Needless to say, poor Americans are not the people who set our immigration policies.

In addition to the strictly economic considerations, overimmigration has had disastrous consequences for the quality of education available to poor inner-city Americans. No wonder that poll after poll shows that a strong majority of poor Americans want to see immigration levels reduced.

The second voiceless group consists of indigenous non-human species. The Nature Conservancy's comprehensive new book "Precious Heritage"—foreword by Harvard conservation biologist E. O. Wilson—depicts the high correlation between U.S. endangered species and areas with rapid, immigration-driven, population growth, including California, the Southwest and Florida. It is not hard to see exploding human populations eating up land that indigenous species have lived on for countless millennia.

This is quantified in a recent analysis by environmental/resource planner Leon Kolankiewicz and public policy analyst Roy Beck, titled "Weighing Sprawl Factors in Large U.S. Cities." This report, and two others devoted specifically to California and to Florida, show dramatically that massive human sprawl in the Southwest and Florida is due not to poor urban planning, but rather almost entirely to rapid population growth.

The connection to immigration? Here in California, for example, analysis of our state government and U.S. Census Bureau statistics indicates that about 90 percent of California's population growth during the 1990s was due to immigrants and their children.

The third voiceless group is people and other creatures not yet born who have no control over decisions being made today. An excellent analogy is China. In the 1950s and 1960s the Chinese government encouraged high fertility which peaked at 6.5 children per woman in the mid-1960s. This irresponsible policy caused China's population to surpass 1 billion by 1980.

One consequence is the Draconian one-child-per-woman policy instituted around 1980. Thus, present and future generations of Chinese families are paying the price for previous short-sighted government policies. Rapid population growth cannot be turned off like a faucet and the Chinese population is projected to continue growing for at least another 30 years, at which point it will be about 1.5 billion, in spite of the present harsh fertility policies. Current immigration policies are propelling the United States to a 22nd century population of over a billion. This will leave Americans then in the same nasty situation as the Chinese are in now. High fertility or overimmigration, the outcome—too many people—is all the same.

Zuckerman can be reached via e-mail at ben@astro.ucla.edu. Hurlbert can be reached via e-mail at shurlbert@sunstroke.sdsu.edu.

On That Point!

This article was originally published in the January 2002 edition of The World and I

Keep the Borders Open
by Jacob G. Hornberger, February 2002

In times of crisis, it is sometimes wise and constructive for people to return to first principles and to reexamine and reflect on where we started as a nation, the road we've traveled, where we are today, and the direction in which we're headed. Such a reevaluation can help determine whether a nation has deviated from its original principles and, if so, whether a restoration of those principles would be in order.

It is impossible to overstate the unusual nature of American society from the time of its founding to the early part of the 20th century. Imagine: no Social Security, Medicare, Medicaid, income taxation, welfare, systems of public (i.e., government) schooling, occupational licensure, standing armies, foreign aid, foreign interventions, or foreign wars. Perhaps most unusual of all, there were virtually no federal controls on immigration into the United States.

With the tragic and costly exception of slavery, the bedrock principle underlying American society was that people should be free to live their lives any way they chose, as long as their conduct was peaceful. That is what it once meant to be free. That is what it once meant to be an American. That was the freedom that our ancestors celebrated each Fourth of July.

Let's examine the issue of immigration because it provides a good model for comparing the vision of freedom of our ancestors with that which guides the American people today.

In economic terms, the concept of freedom to which our Founders subscribed entailed the right to sustain one's life through labor by pursuing any occupation or business without government permission or interference, by freely entering into mutually beneficial exchanges with others anywhere in the world, accumulating unlimited amounts of wealth arising from those endeavors, and freely deciding the disposition of that wealth.

The moral question is: Why shouldn't a person be free to cross a border in search of work to sustain his life, to open a business, to tour, or simply because he wants to? Or to put it another way, under what moral authority does any government interfere with the exercise of these rights?

Most Americans like the concept of open borders within the United States, but what distinguished our ancestors is that they believed that the principles of freedom were applicable not just domestically but universally. That implied open borders not only for people traveling inside the United States but also for people traveling or moving to the United States.

One important result of this highly unusual philosophy of freedom was that throughout the 19th century, people all over the world, especially those who were suffering political tyranny or economic privation, always knew that there was a place they could go if they could succeed in escaping their circumstances.

The American abandonment of open immigration in the 20th century has had negative consequences, both morally and economically. Let's consider some examples.

Prior to and during World War II, U.S. government officials intentionally used immigration controls to prevent German Jews from escaping the horrors of Nazi Germany by coming to America. Many of us are familiar with the infamous "voyage of the damned," where U.S. officials refused to permit a German ship to land at Miami Harbor because it carried Jewish

On That Point!

refugees. But how many people know that U.S. officials used immigration controls to keep German Jews and Eastern European Jews from coming to the United States even after the existence of the concentration camps became well known?

Indeed, how many Americans know about the one million anti-communist Russians whom U.S. and British officials forcibly repatriated to the Soviet Union at the end of World War II, knowing that death or the gulag awaited them?

Ancient history, you say? Well, consider one of the most morally reprehensible policies in the history of our nation: the forcible repatriation of Cuban refugees into communist tyranny, a practice that has been going on for many years and that continues to this day.

Let me restate this for emphasis: Under the pretext of enforcing immigration laws, our government—the U.S. government—the same government that sent tens of thousands of American GIs to their deaths in foreign wars supposedly to resist communism, is now forcibly returning people into communism.

We have seen the establishment of Border Patrol passport checkpoints on highways and airports inside the United States (north of the border), which inevitably discriminate against people on the basis of skin color. We have seen the criminalization of such things as transporting, housing, and hiring undocumented workers, followed by arbitrary detentions on highways as well as raids on American farms and restaurants.

We have seen the construction of a fortified wall in California. This wall, built soon after the fall of the ugliest wall in history, has resulted in the deaths of immigrants entering the country on the harsh Arizona desert. Would Washington, Jefferson, or Madison have constructed such a wall?

We have come a long way from the vision of freedom set forth by our Founding Fathers.

Let's consider some of the common objections to open immigration:

1. *Open immigration will pollute America's culture.* Oh? Which culture is that? Boston? New York? Savannah? New Orleans? Denver? Los Angeles? I grew up on the Mexican border (on the Texas side). My culture was eating enchiladas and tacos, listening to both Mexican and American music, and speaking Tex-Mex (a combination of English and Spanish). If you're talking about the danger that my culture might get polluted, that danger comes from the north, not from the south. America's culture has always been one of liberty—one in which people are free to pursue any culture they want.

2. *Immigrants will take jobs away from Americans.* Immigrants displace workers in certain sectors but the displaced workers benefit through the acquisition of higher-paying jobs in other sectors that expand because of the influx of immigrants. It is not a coincidence that historically people's standard of living has soared when borders have been open. Keep in mind also that traditionally immigrants are among the hardest-working and most energetic people in a society, which brings a positive vitality and energy to it.

3. *Immigrants will go on welfare.* Well maybe we ought to reexamine whether it was a good idea to abandon the principles of our ancestors in that respect as well. What would be wrong with abolishing welfare for everyone, including Americans, along with the enormous taxation required to fund it? But if Americans are in fact hopelessly addicted to the government dole, there is absolutely no reason that the same has to happen to immigrants. Therefore, the answer to the welfare issue is not to control immigration but rather to deny immigrants the right to go on the government dole. In such a case, however, wouldn't it be fair to

exempt them from the taxes used to fund the U.S. welfare state?

4. *Immigrants will bring in drugs.* Lots of people bring in drugs, including Americans returning from overseas trips. Not even the harshest police state would ever alter that fact. More important, why not legalize drugs and make the state leave drug users alone? Is there any better example of an immoral, failed, and destructive government program than the war on drugs? Why should one government intervention, especially an immoral, failed one, be used to justify another?

5. *There will be too many people.* Oh? Who decides the ideal number? A government board of central planners, just like in China? Wouldn't reliance on the free market to make such a determination be more consistent with our founding principles? Immigrants go where the opportunities abound and they avoid areas where they don't, just as Americans do.

6. *Open immigration will permit terrorists to enter our country.* The only permanent solution to terrorism against the United States, in both the short term and long term, is to abandon the U.S. government's interventionist foreign policy, which is the breeding ground for terrorism against our country. No immigration controls in the world, not even a rebuilt Berlin Wall around the United States, will succeed in preventing the entry of people who are bound and determined to kill Americans.

More than 200 years ago, ordinary people brought into existence the most unusual society in the history of man. It was a society based on the fundamental moral principle that people everywhere are endowed with certain inherent rights that no government can legitimately take away.

Somewhere along the way, Americans abandoned that concept of freedom, especially in their attachment to such programs and policies as Social Security, Medicare, Medicaid, income taxation, economic regulation, public (i.e., government) schooling, the war on drugs, the war on poverty, the war on wealth, immigration controls, foreign aid, foreign intervention, and foreign wars—none of which our founders had dreamed of.

The current crisis provides us with an opportunity to reexamine our founding principles, why succeeding generations of Americans abandoned them, the consequences of that abandonment, and whether it would be wise to restore the moral and philosophical principles of freedom of our Founders. A good place to start such a reexamination would be immigration.

Chapter 14

Judging Debates

Introduction to Judging

One of the things that distinguishes debate from simple argument is that in debate, you are trying to persuade a third party—sometimes, many third parties, if there is a panel of judges or an extended audience. In parliamentary debates, the judge is the person who is responsible for deciding who wins and loses a debate. Depending on the arrangements made in any particular debate, the judge may also be the timekeeper, moderator, or Speaker of the House. They may assign a range of points and rankings to individual debaters or teams of debaters. After a debate, judges will offer reasons for their decisions. They will explain their decisions on paper ballots, to be distributed to the participating teams at the conclusion of the tournament. Judges may also provide oral critiques after the debate, when they explain their decisions in the debate and offer advice and criticism to the participating debaters.

Of course, not all debates are judged in a formal way. Many debates are audience-oriented events, where no formal decision is ever rendered or announced. When you are an audience member for any debate, you are still, in a sense, a judge. Even if the audience doesn't make a formal decision, they are still evaluating the participants' performance. So whether you end up judging formal, competitive, tournament debates or judging debates as an audience member, you will need to know some basic skills for judging.

If you are a competitive debater, we recommend that you try to find opportunities to judge debates yourself. You might volunteer to judge debates for younger students or to referee practice debates between other members of your squad. This experience is an invaluable teaching tool for aspiring debaters. Practice in judging will be a great teaching tool.

Debaters should respect their judges. Consider that your judges are volunteering their time or working for little pay to listen to you debate. Without the involvement of judges, debate tournaments would certainly not happen. That said, it is inevitable that you will encounter judges with whom you will disagree. Your best response is to listen carefully to their decisions and try to understand why they voted the way they did. Just as everyone has different political and cultural opinions, everyone has different opinions about how to decide who wins and loses a debate and why. It is not uncommon for two judges in the same debate to vote for different sides, or to vote for the same side, but for different reasons. It is also not uncommon to be thoroughly convinced that you won a debate, only to find out afterwards that your judge disagreed with your assessment.

Some debaters treat judges as if they were only passive receptacles for information. This is a dim view to take of judges, who should be treated as active participants in the debate. Just as you may educate the judge about certain issues, they may in turn educate you about the practice of debating. Keep an open mind, and above all, do not behave in a disrespectful manner. That judge may judge you again, and will almost certainly have some good advice that you can carry on to future debates. There are very few bad judges. There are, however, many judges with whom debaters fail to communicate. We learn how to debate so that we can communicate with a wide range of people. Learn to communicate with your judges.

The purpose of this section is to provide advice for future and present debate judges. Debaters should also read this section for insights into the practice of judging. Before we begin, we should reiterate that there are as many ways of judging debates as there are ways of debating. Judges should work to cultivate their own styles and methods of evaluating debates. They should work with debaters, rather than in spite of them or around them, to create a learning community that will benefit everyone.

The Fine Art of Judging

When you judge a debate, you are usually asked to decide which team did the better debating and why. This team is said to have *won* the debate, usually through a combination of argumentation and presentation. It is important to remember that the team that wins the debate may not always be the better debate team—instead, they were the better debate team *in the debate that you watched.* Even the best world-class debate teams have critical slip-ups every now and again. You should try to be fair and judge each debate based on its own merits, rather than on gossip, speculation, past performances in debate rounds, or other factors.

It is easy to be intimidated by the enterprise of judging debates. You may feel unprepared or under-experienced, especially compared to the debaters, who may seem very professional and experienced. In reality, you are (no matter what your experience level) perfectly prepared to judge a debate. Even if you have never seen a debate before, you can still render a thoughtful and informed decision based only on your engaged participation. Parliamentary debate is meant to be entertaining and accessible to judges and audiences of all experience levels, so even if you are a novice judge, you will fit right in. You will also learn to be a better judge as you watch and judge more debates. You have to start somewhere, so don't be intimidated. All you have to do is make the best decision you can make.

Everyone recognizes, though, that some decisions are better than others are. Debaters have a tendency to be opinionated. Judges also hold opinions. In fact, just about everyone is likely to be opinionated about something. Holding opinions is normal, healthy, and in the interest of building lively communities. There is, however, a substantive difference between having opinions and forcing them on others at the expense of reasoned debate and discussion. We recommend that when you judge you make an effort to maintain an open mind about the arguments and examples used as evidence in the debate. Open-mindedness is not so much an issue of surrendering convictions as it is a matter of respecting the debaters' opinions and efforts. It is important to remember that parliamentary debate is switch-side debating. That means that, on occasion, you may have the opportunity to watch debaters defending a side contrary to what they (or you) might otherwise agree with.

What do we mean when we say that some decisions are better than others are? A good decision is one that relies on a consistent, fair method of deliberation. In order to judge fairly, you need to keep a few things in mind:

- **Identify your biases** and resist them rather than surrender to them.
- **Apply reciprocal standards** for evaluating arguments. In other words, don't identify an error made by one team and hold it against them when the other team or teams makes the same error. Make your judging standards relevant and fairly applied to all debate participants.

- **Presume that the debaters are acting in good faith.** Resist the temptation to read intention into their perceived mistakes. If a debater makes a factual error in the debate, she may not know that she is wrong. Do not assume, for example, that she is being deceitful or is in some way trying to put something over on you.

- **Be patient.** The debaters may, during the course of a given debate, do a good many things to annoy or otherwise irritate you. They are probably not doing these things on purpose.

- **Give debaters the benefit of the doubt** about their choices—they may not make the choices you would, but that's okay. Debate is an opportunity to create a rhetorical space where other bright critical thinkers can imagine, analyze, and innovate. If you do not give them the benefit of the doubt, you could end up stifling their creativity or substituting your sense of creativity for theirs.

- **Do not pre-interpret the topic.** Debaters get a topic for debate and then it is *their* task to interpret that topic. It is their interpretation that gets debated. When you hear the topic, you might think that the topic should be interpreted a different way. Do not impose your opinions about this issue on debaters. If they do not choose to interpret the topic in the manner you would have interpreted it, that should not be relevant to the outcome of the debate. If the opposition raises a different interpretation in a topicality argument, you should not be sympathetic to that argument simply because it matches up with your preconceptions about the topic.

Good decisions are reached fairly with appropriate and adequate deliberation on the issues and arguments that are presented in the debate. Good judges know and follow the rules of the particular format and tournament. As long as you make a concerted effort to be fair and respectful, you will quickly learn the practice of judging.

How should you conduct yourself in a debate? We have already told debaters that they should not treat the judge as if she were merely a passive info-receptacle propped up at the back of the room with a pen and a ballot. Just as the debaters should conduct themselves appropriately towards the judge, so too should you conduct yourself appropriately towards the debaters. The following is a list of "Don'ts" for aspiring and experienced debate judges:

- Do not talk during the debate for any reason, particularly to friends, about how the debate is going. Although you are a participant in the debate, your role should be primarily nonverbal until after it is finished.

- Do not, particularly in international debating, penalize debaters who speak in accents other than your own. Take into consideration that for some debaters, English may not be their native tongue.

- Do not usurp the role of the judge for personal whim or dictatorial edict (e.g., "you must use the words 'x, y, z' in the course of your speeches"; or "Tell an joke and I will give you 30 points"). The course and content of the debate is not yours to dictate.

- Do not engage in partisan participation during the event (e.g., heckling, introducing and sustaining arguments during speeches, making points of information, voting for a side based on your personal belief about the topic, etc.).

- Do not arbitrarily manufacture rules (e.g., "Points of information must be in the form of a question," "Parliamentary debaters are required to present a single value or criteria (sic)," "You need to have a plan and say the word 'plan,' in the first proposition speech," "New examples are prohibited in the rebuttal speeches.").

- Do not write the ballot during the rebuttal speeches. This practice conveys a total disregard for the competitors and for the integrity of the process. Wait until after the debate to make your decision and wait until after the debate to write the ballot.

- Do not "cut" speech time to hasten the process of the debate. The debaters expect and deserve the full allocation of time.

- Do not ignore the rules to suit your own preferences.

- Do not fail to be serious about the debate. Sometimes judges will demand simplicity (e.g., "too tired" to listen to complex argumentation; "just entertain me").

- Do not use marginalizing and discriminatory rhetoric or practice (anti-Semitic commentary; sexual harassment; voting against participants for fashion, hairstyle, body piercings, etc.). This rule should go without saying.

This list of "Don'ts" may seem long and foreboding, but it all boils down to a few basic suggestions: Be respectful of the debaters and be fair in your conduct and evaluation of the debate.

Before the debate begins, the debaters you are about to judge may want to ask you questions about your "judging philosophy" or how you plan to judge the debate. Keep your answers brief, and try to be as instructive as you can to the debaters, who are genuinely inquiring about your disposition towards arguments that may be advanced in the debate. Normally, this questioning time is not built into the time schedule for a tournament, so don't use a lot of time if the debaters want to talk to you before the debate. Avoid overly generic answers that do not provide meaningful information to the debaters: "I vote on the flow." (Yes, everyone says that about themselves.) "Entertain me." (Look, this isn't Vegas.) "I'm a policy maker." (Now, if only there were consensus about what that *means*.) "Rebuttals are important." (Well, duh.) If you can't say anything meaningful, don't say anything at all. In the USA, these pre-debate questioning periods have become increasingly tedious and uninformative. The time would be better used after the debate as an opportunity to educate the debaters.

When you go to judge a debate, you should always bring paper and pen. We encourage you to *flow* the debate, i.e., take notes in the stylized form described elsewhere in this book and adapted specifically to certain formats of parliamentary debate. Even if you do not flow in the traditional sense, you must still take notes. During the course of an average debate, many complex arguments are exchanged and refuted, and you will need notes to be able to follow and resolve these arguments for yourself and later in revealing your decision, either orally or on the ballot, to the debaters. No matter how reliable your memory, if you don't take notes, you risk missing some crucial example or answer that might aid in making the best possible decision. Good note taking will always help you decide who wins and how to best explain your decision.

Of course, the critical question is this: how *do* you decide who wins the debate? If we could offer a simple answer to this question, we would be out selling snake oil and certainly not laboring to produce a debate textbook. The best answer is that you should decide the debate based on the criteria offered by the debaters in the round. Every debate is about different issues, is conducted differently, and thus should be decided on its own merits. Different teams will offer different kinds of arguments. For example, not every opposition team will argue counterplans or disadvantages, so you should be careful of looking for specific tactics on the part of the debaters. You will have to decide whether or not the proposition team has made a case for endorsing the motion for debate. The opposition team will make arguments about why the proposition team's case is inadequate or dangerous or otherwise misguided. You will have to evaluate the merits of these arguments and decide whether the proposition team's rejoinders are adequate and satisfactory.

During the course of the debate, debaters may offer different criteria for your decision. They may even address you directly, saying that your vote should or should not be based on a particular argument set or on certain kind of arguments. They are not trying to order you around; rather, this is common practice. They are trying to assist you and influence you in your decision making process.

After the debate is over, you should use a separate piece of paper to figure out your decision. Even if you think, at the conclusion of the debate, that you know conclusively who has won and who has lost, you should still take some time to check your calculations and assumptions. One technique that may help you is to draw up a kind of balance sheet for the debate. List the most important arguments in the debate and then go through your flow to determine which side won those arguments and why. Then compare the arguments to each other.

Do not decide the debate based simply on the *number* of arguments won by each side. You will also need to evaluate the qualitative significance of each argument on the overall outcome of the debate. Take this common scenario: The proposition wins an advantage conclusively, while the opposition wins a disadvantage conclusively. Who wins? You can't decide based on the information we have given you. To answer this question, you need to know the relative significance of the advantage and disadvantage. This relative significance can have both quantitative and qualitative aspects. You may be tempted to decide based simply on the "biggest impact." For example, you may decide to vote for the proposition team because they claimed to avert a war, while the opposition team was "only" able to prove that the proposition team's proposal would cause the deaths of hundreds of children.

You also need to take into account questions of risk and probability when deciding who wins in complicated debates. In the above example, your decision would doubtless change if you decided, based on arguments advanced and won by the opposition team, that there was a very low probability that the proposition team's plan would be able to avert a war. However, this does not mean that you should interject your own risk calculation into the debate at this point. The debaters may have *weighed* the round for you—they may have made the best case as to why their arguments outweigh or are more important than or more instrumental to the decision than those of the other team. If the debaters do compare arguments to each other, you need to take that into account.

One common mistake that judges make is voting for the opposition team on the basis of partial solvency arguments. A partial solvency argument is an argument advanced by the opposition team that says the proposition team's case will not solve the problem *completely*, or that the harm or existing problem is not *quite* as bad as the proposition team claims it is. These are good defensive arguments for the opposition team, but they should *almost never* be reasons to vote for the opposition team. The only thing these arguments prove is that the proposition case is not as good as it was claimed to be. Big deal. It is rare indeed that arguments advanced in debates turn out to be just as triumphant as their authors predicted they would be. The proposition team can still win if their case can be shown to be *comparatively advantageous*, that is, if they can show that it is, on balance, better by some increment than the present state of affairs.

Don't vote based on your personal opinion on the topic. Sometimes, when the topic is announced, you may read it and think that you know what the debate will be about. Often, the proposition team will choose a case that may be different from one *you* would have chosen. This choice does not mean that you should then disregard their case or use the opposition's topicality argument as a thinly veiled excuse to vote against the proposition team's case. You may also have strong opinions about the subject matter of the topic. Perhaps you are a committed opponent of the death penalty and have to judge a debate about this subject. You may find that your personal presumption lies with the team that opposes the death penalty, but do not hold the other team to a higher burden of proof. The teams do not have to persuade you *personally* of the correctness of their position; *the debaters are debating each other and not you.*

Track arguments as they proceed and develop through the debate so you can evaluate the debate in the fairest way possible. Some judges make the mistake of deciding the debate more or less solely on the quality of the final rebuttal speech. This is a mistake because the proposition rebuttal needs to be evaluated both as a response to the opposition block's arguments and as a summation of the proposition team's final position. When deciding the debate, you need to figure out if the proposition rebuttalist dropped, or failed to answer, any opposition arguments. You then need to decide how to weigh those conceded arguments in the context of the other arguments in the debate.

Often you will have to consider dropped, or conceded, arguments and decide what to do about them. Some conceded arguments will not impact your decision. Others will. If an argument is conceded, it means you must assign the full weight of that argument to the side that argued it. This concession phenomenon should not mean that if a team concedes some arguments, they should automatically lose the debate. All arguments are not created equally. Some arguments can be safely ignored.

Other arguments may be introduced in the debate, only to have the team that introduced them later back down on their original claim. This is smart debating and is not a reason to look askance at a team. For example, an opposition team may advance a topicality argument in their first speech but not mention it again later in the debate. This behavior should be taken to mean that the opposition team has decided to admit (at least for this debate) that the proposition team's case is topical and concentrate their fire on other arguments. You should not then proceed to vote on topicality in this circumstance. If the opposition team has decided to drop this argument, you should drop it as well. It is common practice for opposition teams to argue a wider variety of arguments in their first speech than in their subsequent speeches. This tactic is called argument selection and is good debate practice. Do not penalize teams for not extending all of their arguments through the entire debate.

After the debate has concluded, you will have to decide who wins the debate and why. In American parliamentary debate, you will declare one side the winner and the other side the loser, based on the content of the arguments advanced in the debate.

In addition to deciding the winners of the debate, you will have to fill out your ballot and assign points and ranks to individual debaters. Speaker points are a measure of performance by individual debaters. Most tournaments give speaker awards, which are trophies given to individuals based on their aggregate point accumulation during the course of a tournament. Usually, you will be asked to rank the debaters on a 30-point scale, although there are other kinds of scales. You may choose to assign a *low-point win*. A low-point win is a circumstance where the team that won did not get the highest points. This circumstance arises occasionally, when judges feel that one team did the better job of speaking but did not win based on the arguments. We suggest the following guidelines for using these scales:

For a 30-point scale:

30 Almost no one should get a 30. A perfect score should happen every few years with a really brilliant speech.

28–29 Brilliant.

26–27 Strong, well above average.

25 Above average

23–24 Modest success as a debater

- Points below 23 should be reserved for people who are both unsuccessful as debaters and are also obnoxious and mean-spirited.
- Points should never drop below a 20, even if a debater was particularly bad. Lower points frequently exclude a debate team from elimination rounds, so if you give points below 20, you are saying that a debater has no chance of rehabilitation in any other debates.

For a 50-point scale:

50   See above regarding a 30. Should be reserved for the very best of the very best.

48–49 Incredibly brilliant.

45–47 Outstanding.

42–44 Well above average.

38–41 Good.

35–37 Good, but with one or more serious flaws.

30–35 Poor performance.

<30   Similar to receiving points below 20. See above.

After assigning points and ranking the debaters, you should write your ballot. We recommend that you use the space provided on the ballot to explain the reasons for your decision. Why did you vote the way you voted? What arguments were most persuasive to you? Why? Give advice and constructive criticism to the debaters you watched. What did they do well? How could they improve their performance or their arguments? Try to use as much of the ballot space as you can. Debaters and their coaches save ballots, and often refer back to them as references and resources. Do not use writing the ballot as an excuse not to deliver an oral critique, however brief, to the teams that you judge. Whatever interaction you have with the debaters after the debate will always be more valuable than the comments you write on the ballot.

A final issue therefore needs to be discussed: post-debate disclosure of your decision. You should disclose your decision and a brief explanation of the reason for your decision. Disclosure encourages accountable and ethical decision-making. In parliamentary debate, disclosure and post-round discussion serve an educational function. These practices offer the sole opportunity for new judges in attendance to consider the decision-making behaviors of experienced practitioners. This is a golden opportunity for judge training—it is lost when judges do not disclose. Judges do not have a sufficient chance to listen to peers critique a debate they have also witnessed. No space is created for the development of the critic's skills. This is akin to a hypothetical convention that would prohibit new and relatively inexperienced debaters from observing more experienced participants. As a new judge, you will find that disclosure will help you learn quickly.

Furthermore, nondisclosure is not really an option: it does not exist. Judges reveal decisions at tournaments selectively—to friends, regional teams, successful national competitors, in trade with judges evaluating their own teams, despite tournament rules and directors' admonitions. It is not disclosure versus nondisclosure. The real issue is whether the community should sustain selective, unequal, and unfair disclosure or support universal disclosure. We encourage you to disclose your decisions and discuss them with the debaters. The educational opportunity that disclosure affords is unparalleled.

Some object to post-debate disclosure on the grounds that there is not enough time in tournament schedules for such interaction to occur. To this argument, we suggest that tournaments have an obligation to adjust their schedule to accommodate interaction time between debaters and judges. The educational benefit accrued from five ten-minute critiques by judges during the course of a day of five debates is more than worth the investment of fifty extra minutes by the tournament participants. Disclosure benefits judges, who learn and improve from the process. Debaters also benefit, as they get direct education and exposure to the thoughts of their judge in ways simply not satisfied by a written ballot.

Sample American Parliamentary Debate Ballot

Name of Tournament _____

Round number _____

Location of Debate _____

Judge's Name _____

Motion _____

Proposition

Team Name or Code _____

Speaker 1 _____ Points _____ Rank _____

Speaker 2 _____ Points _____ Rank _____

Opposition

Team Name or Code _____

Speaker 1 _____ Points _____ Rank _____

Speaker 2 _____ Points _____ Rank _____

The decision is awarded to the (prop/opp) _____

Indicate low-point win _____

Judge's Name and Affiliation _____

Reason for Decision:

Chapter 15

Tournament Administration and Topic Selection

Debates are held in class, as well as in public settings for interested audiences, civic groups, business organizations, and corporations. Debate competitions are also available. Organized competitions include intramural scrimmages on a school campus, events featuring representatives from two schools, and tournaments with dozens to hundreds of teams.

Most people are familiar with the idea of a staged debate to inform or entertain an audience. The series of debates for presidential candidates, historically sponsored by the League of Women Voters, is a popular example. There are occasional debates on broadcast television and others sponsored by colleges and universities, which are also a more familiar form of debating. Perhaps the most common but least known format is the competitive debate tournament.

The debate tournament is an organized competition for debate teams representing schools, debating clubs, language societies, or regional and national organizations. Each year, many dozens of universities, high schools, debate organizations, nonprofit groups, corporations, and governments sponsor tournaments.

Tournament forms include select invitational tournaments; these events limit entry to a few debate teams. Select invitational tournaments include round robin tournaments and qualifying tournaments. Round robin tournaments are limited entry events at which each team debates all or most of the other competitors in the contest. Qualifying tournaments require entering teams to pre-qualify for participation by demonstrating success at other designated tournaments.

Debate tournaments may include instructional seminars. This type of event is often scheduled for novice participants by national and international

debate organizations in conjunction with debate and argumentation conferences, or by local debating clubs or leagues at the beginning of a competitive
debate season. Normally, seminars feature debater and judge training sessions, a demonstration debate, an open forum on debating art and practice,
and one or two competitive debates.

The most popular tournament form is the open invitational tournament,
in which any eligible debate team may enter. The overwhelming majority of
tournaments are open invitational tournaments.

Tournaments may sponsor debate divisions for competitors with differing
skills and debate experience; that is, they may sponsor a "senior" division for
experienced debates, as well as a novice division for those with less experience.

Tournament hosts design events to serve competitive and educational
needs. These goals can conflict. It is important that tournament hosts identify the appropriate goals for their events and design them accordingly.
Tournament hosts should schedule events, if practicable, in cooperation with
debate organizations and colleagues to minimize conflicts and increase debating opportunities for contestants.

Before the tournament

Debate tournaments may be simple affairs involving 10 to 15 debate teams
and judges. They may also be very complex conferences with hundreds of
competitors and additional hundreds of adjudicators and guests. Although
the scope of arrangements and resources will differ from event to event, the
minimum administrative arrangements are similar for all tournaments. A
tournament director's responsibilities seldom vary, despite the change in the
scope of her enterprise.

The following checklist includes the major elements of tournament administration and preparation:

Deciding to Host

The decision to host a debate tournament is a major undertaking for an individual or a small group. The decision should not be made lightly. Comprehensive planning, including prospective budgeting and tournament
administration, ought to be completed before making a public announcement
inviting debaters and adjudicators to attend an event. It is better to anticipate

problems, bottlenecks, and conflicts prior to a decision to host than to discover them at the time that guests are arriving at the airport, eager to participate in your tournament. Hosts should, of course, consider the cost of awards, ballots, staff, guest judges, site expenses, office supplies, food, entertainment, lodging, and miscellaneous expenses in the prospective budget.

Running a simulation of a debate tournament, including the administration of the debates using tournament tabulation software, is useful as a staff training opportunity.

Announcing the Tournament

- Acquire contact information
- Arrange for a date and site
- Draft an invitation

The tournament director should initially acquire contact information for prospective attendees. Such information can come from mailing lists from debate organizations, tournament participant lists from directors in the region, and addresses of debate "listservs."

The director will need to arrange for a site and date for the event. She should coordinate a date for the tournament with local debate organizations and colleagues in the region. Preliminary contacts regarding the tournament will reduce the likelihood that other area debate events will be scheduled on the selected date.

The director should select the tournament site and begin preliminary negotiations for access to this site on the selected tournament dates. She should anticipate the potential number of participants and make sure there are sufficient rooms for debates. She should make arrangements for room access (unlocking doors, etc.) and any additional administrative support that might be required to manage the site.

If required, the director or a member of the tournament staff should contact national or local debate organizations for support information and counsel and ensure compliance with any administrative rules or guidelines for the debate events.

The tournament director should draft a letter of invitation for the tournament, including relevant details for guests. The letter should be mailed to prospective attendees and debate listservs after the director completes the administrative tasks remaining in the tournament checklist.

Information for Tournament Guests

- Schedule
- Transportation information
- Lodging information
- Meal information

Tournament guests require specific information when making a decision to attend a debate tournament and arrange transportation to and from the event. Guests need to know the time they should arrive at and depart from the tournament. A tournament schedule is necessary for travel planning and should include the time for the opening ceremonies, first debate round, and the conclusion of the final, championship debate.

In our experience, too many debate tournaments are unable to complete events on schedule. The primary reason, it seems, is the tournament director's failure to set a reasonable schedule. Judges and debaters need time to move to and from the competition rooms. Some will get lost. If the tournament uses several buildings for the event, some individuals will get lost for each of the first two or three rounds of debate.

Directors would be wise to add 30 to 45 minutes to the schedule, particularly after the first or second round of debate, to account for such issues as longer-than-anticipated instructional question-and-answer sessions, difficulties in finding competition rooms, and registration queues.

Tournament schedules and policies should be fair to the needs of participants. In other words, a debate tournament should be designed to allow guests to attend the event and depart as quickly as possible after their elimination from the competition. Teams that have a four-hour trip home may be inconvenienced by a requirement to stay for an awards assembly that begins at 10:00 P.M. Guests may, of course, choose to remain at a tournament for the duration of the event.

A sample schedule for a debate tournament, with six preliminary debates and four elimination rounds, might be as follows:

Saturday

10:00AM–11:00AM	Registration
11:00AM–11:45AM	Judge Training and Seminar
12:00PM–1:30PM	Round 1

1:45PM–3:15PM	Round 2
3:30PM–5:00PM	Round 3
6:30PM–8:00PM	Round 4

Sunday

8:30AM–10:00AM	Round 5
10:30AM–12:00PM	Round 6
12:30PM–12:45PM	Announcements, Awards, and Elimination Rounds
1:00PM–2:15 PM	Octofinals
2:30PM–3:45PM	Quarterfinals
4:00PM–5:15PM	Semifinals
5:30PM–7:00PM	Finals

This schedule, designed for a two-team parliamentary debate format, allows approximately 90 minutes for each round. It would be difficult for the tournament to fail to meet this schedule for events. For example, a tournament debate would require 15 to 20 minutes for preparation time and 40 minutes for actual competition. The schedule includes an additional 30 minutes for judge deliberation, disclosure of the decision, and supplemental constructive commentary, including oral discussion with debaters and the completion of a written ballot.

Some directors host instructional seminars or an educational tournament, which often include some competitive debates. A schedule for such an event, typically offered in a single day, might be the following:

Saturday

8:30AM–9:00AM	Registration
9:30AM–10:30AM	Demonstration Debate and Evaluation
10:45AM–11:30AM	Instructional Small Group Session 1
11:30AM–1:00PM	Lunch
1:00PM–2:30PM	Round 1
2:45PM–3:30PM	Instructional Small Group Session 2
4:00PM–5:30PM	Round 2
6:00PM–6:30PM	Summation and Awards

In addition to schedule information, travelers will need to have information regarding any arrangements for transportation, lodging, and meals. Tournament directors need to inform guests of the proximity of airports, train, and bus stations, as well as the cost and preferred method of public transportation or taxi service from such locations to the tournament site. They also must provide walking, driving, and parking directions for those commuting to the site. If tournament hosts are able to arrange for discounted travel options (e.g., group airline discounts), they should include the necessary information, such as an airline or rail service discount code, in the tournament invitation.

Many debate events negotiate a discounted rate for conference guests with one or more local hotels. Special lodging offers should be included in the invitation. Tournament directors should make arrangements for special rates for dates prior to and after the tournament competition dates for those who need to stay extra days because of their travel arrangements.

Tournament hosts should explain what, if any, food service will be available at the tournament site. This information is not simply a courtesy, but a necessity for guests with dietary health concerns. Tournaments that provide meals to participants should consider the needs of all attendees, making an effort to offer vegan, vegetarian, and low-sugar options, as well as the standard full buffet for omnivores.

Tournament Operations

- Tabulating room staff
- Tabulating hardware and software
- Tournament office supplies
- Guest judging

The tournament director should identify experienced personnel to support tournament administrative tasks and debate tabulation. Experienced individuals may be at the hosting institution, but many experienced tournament tabulation staff and administrators are willing to provide advice or volunteer their time to assist at other sites. It is important to have sufficient personnel to manage tournament operations, *but* it is of equal importance to avoid a bloated tabulating room staff. Few things interfere with tab room efficiency more than an unwieldy and unnecessary bureaucracy to ensure a "responsible" job for each staff person. Some tasks are *not* better managed by several individuals when a single, capable person will do. A director should employ the minimum number of experienced or otherwise talented individuals for the tabulating staff.

There is free tournament tabulating software for Macintosh and PC computers for two-team events. The software is free and available on the Internet. (Please see Appendix 4: Resources.) Tournament directors should acquire the software that is appropriate for their computer system. The software should be downloaded and tested several weeks before the tournament.

Tournament software needs hardware. The tournament must have one or more computers and a printer. The tournament should have access to a photocopier, if this is at all practical. The director will need to acquire or purchase office supplies for tournament operations, including large envelopes or folders for registration packets and ballots, pens, paper, tape, and a stapler. Depending on the physical layout of the site, the tournament director may want to rent or purchase walkie-talkies (a relatively modest, one-time expense) for communication with tournament staff at other buildings at the tournament site. The director and other designated personnel should have a cellular phone for emergency communication with guests and site personnel.

Each debate requires one or more judges. The host should anticipate the number of judges required for the event and secure guest judges, as many attending teams will not have judges accompanying them to the event. Tournament directors may also choose to limit entries to those teams with accompanying judges, if it is difficult to secure a sufficient number of guest judges for the event.

Tournament Materials

• Registration packet
• Awards
• Ballots
• Instructional information
• Topic writing and selection

Tournaments work best when guests receive enough information to successfully navigate the physical site and the rules of the event. The tournament director should prepare a registration packet, which is a set of materials to deliver to participants at the time of team registration. The registration packet should include a receipt for entry fees and other tournament costs, copies of the tournament schedule, site and area maps, lists of interesting things to do in the area (if applicable), and contact information for the tournament tabulating room and director.

The tournament director should purchase awards for team and individual performers, if the tournament will present such awards. (Most events do.) The director should ensure the arrival of awards several days prior to the date of the event and examine the delivery for defective or missing items.

Debaters expect an accounting of their performances in an oral and written form. The tournament host should purchase or produce ballots for each judge for each round of debate. If the tournament has access to a photocopier, it is more convenient and decidedly less expensive to design and photocopy a tournament ballot. A sample ballot is included in this text. The tournament produces photocopies of the submitted ballot from each judge for each of the participating teams in the debate.

The host may choose to provide documents with competitor and adjudicator information. This information may include rules for the competition, guidelines for judging, and recommendations for assisting in the efficient operation of the tournament.

There are different kinds of debate motions, often categorized as limited preparation, closed and open. A limited preparation motion is announced anytime from several hours to several weeks prior to a tournament debate on the motion. Debaters are provided with some time to research materials and prepare arguments on the motion. A closed motion is most easily understood as a literal statement, one that should engage debaters in commonly accepted and obvious terms. An open motion describes a motion with more abstract or indirect language.

> **Limited preparation motion:** This House would limit civil liberties to promote national security.
>
> **Closed motion:** This House supports China's entry in the WTO.
>
> **Open motion:** This House would bury it.

A tournament director must decide which sorts of motions to include in the contest and the manner of positioning the motions in the tournament. Should the tournament offer a mix of categories? Should the tournament offer a single

category, e.g., only closed motions? Should the motions differ from preliminary debates to elimination round debates? Should motion categories vary
from round to round?

In a general sense, tournament directors currently try to encourage debate
on diverse topics, although this may be accomplished without using more than
one category of motions. It is possible, for example, to promote discussions
on a broad range of substantive issues and use only closed motions for debate.

A tournament host should consider the skills, experiences, and expectations of participants, as well as the purposes of the event. These factors will
influence the selection of the categories of motions, as well as the wording of
specific topics for debate. A host may decide to offer a variety of topic categories
at the event. The host might, for example, provide six preliminary rounds of
debate, selecting two each of limited preparation, closed, and open motions.

The tournament director, in this circumstance, can use the two motions
from the same category in following debates, beginning with the odd-numbered debate round. This format is not complicated and is particularly easy
to execute in two-team debates. In tournament contests with an even number
of preliminary debates, each team ought to debate the same number of proposition and opposition debates. In a tournament with six preliminary rounds,
each debate team would debate three times as the proposition and three times
as the opposition. In an odd-numbered debate, such as the first debate of the
tournament, a team could debate on either the proposition side or the opposition side. For example, in the first round of debating, half the entering teams
would be assigned to the proposition and they would be matched with opposition teams. In the even-numbered rounds, the teams switch sides. So, in the
second round, the teams which had just finished arguing on the opposition
side would now debate on the proposition side, while the former proposition
teams would switch, and argue for the opposition. This cycle is repeated in
each pair of debates in the preliminary debates, beginning with each odd-
numbered round of debate.

If the categories of motions are matched to the debate rounds in which
each debate team will argue both the proposition and opposition sides, participants are more likely to consider that the contest is fair. Each team, in the
example, would appreciate the opportunity to debate both the proposition
and opposition sides of limited preparation, closed, and open motions. If the
tournament director placed a limited preparation motion in the first and third

debates, rather than the first and second debates, it is likely that some teams would debate twice on the proposition or the opposition on this sort of motion. If limited preparation time provides an advantage to one side of the debate, it may be the case that the director's placement of categories of motions in debate rounds has given an unfair advantage to some teams in the tournament.

Some tournament directors might choose a single motion category for the entire event. A tournament organized at the time of a national election, for example, might select a series of limited preparation topics on election reform or the salient issues of candidates' or political parties' policies.

It may be the case that some tournament hosts might select a certain type of motion for the championship or grand final debate (so selected, for example, for a large public or broadcast audience available to watch the final tournament debate). It may be necessary to promote the event with an announcement of a specific topic or a topic area. In this circumstance, the director might use a limited preparation motion or closed motion. These motions might "preview" the subject of debate for targeted demographic groups likely to attend or view the debate.

There are, of course, a number of debate tournaments with an odd number of preliminary debates. If this is the case, the tournament director should reserve her most equitable or balanced motion for the last debate, as that will be the debate that will create an imbalance of argument sides for the contest. This final preliminary debate, in an odd-numbered round, will mean that teams debate more rounds on either the proposition or the opposition side.

Crafting Topics for Debate

Are there guides to the creation of effective motions for debate? Yes and no. There are guides that seem commonsensical. The motion ought to be interesting. It should be a matter in controversy (i.e., one should know that the matter is debatable). Participants should have some knowledge of the topic or the ideas and arguments suggested by it. The motion should be clearly worded. In most instances, the topic should be affirmatively, rather than negatively, worded. For example, it is better to avoid topics that begin "This House would not...."

These and similar aspirations might be satisfying to hosts and tournament guests ("I want topics that produce roughly equal arguments for the adversaries," "I want motions that will inspire an audience or cause it to swoon,"

"I want topics that will produce rigorous and challenging debate"). However, these are rather abstract and unhelpful critical guides and almost impossible to consistently use as standards for generating and constructing topic ideas. For example, the more one thinks about the issue of those matters that make a good motion, the more one produces standards for constructing them. The more standards for topic wording are generated, the more desirable it appears to apply the standards. The more one tries to apply multiple standards for evaluating a topic, the less likely it becomes that any topic will pass muster. It is something of a paradox.

We offer a simple guide for writing a motion: *Regardless of the category of the motion, keep the wording of the topic simple and direct.* There isn't enough preparation time prior to a debate for participants to figure out or imagine the inner workings of the topic author's peculiarities. Debaters should be able to take any motion and immediately (or within the first minute of the allotted preparation time) begin to work with the idea. In addition, it isn't necessary to force the hand of participants by including complex information in the actual motion for debate. The debaters will generate complex ideas from basically worded motions. They need to do so. This is the way they are more likely to win the debate.

In addition, simply worded motions provide due consideration to those participants debating in a second or third language. They assist novice or speech-apprehensive debaters, who are likely to be anxious about public speaking or the format and do not need to be confounded by the motion.

To clarify this point, we will offer two examples. First, a motion that is too complicated: "Feminism is not a girl, not yet a woman." This motion, used at a college tournament in the USA, is unnecessarily complicated. It is a reference to a Britney Spears song that not all debaters know of, let alone understand. The topic contains two negatives, making it difficult for both teams to negotiate. Also, this topic compares two things that do not genuinely contrast—there is no clear line between "girl" and "woman"; in fact, both terms can be used interchangeably. Although the topic might address interesting issues related to the ideological relevance of feminism in today's society, it could be more simply worded while still addressing the substantive issues at stake. For example, you might choose a topic like "Feminism has outlived its usefulness," or a more specific aspect of the topic: "The United States should adopt the Equal Rights Amendment."

Second, a motion that is simply worded: "This House supports a flat tax." This motion is brief and to the point. It clearly divides ground for debate between the proposition and the opposition and addresses the issue for debate in a straightforward manner.

Crafting a "simply worded motion" still requires time and care. It may not be so simple to design the motion with the quality of "simplicity." It is in the interest of a tournament director or topic designer to consider, from several perspectives (which may involve speaking to others about these matters, unless one prefers a schizophrenic or intellectually chaotic approach to idea formation), how debates will occur on the finished topics. There is a context for producing debate motions. The purpose of the motion is to promote debate. If experienced practitioners have considerable difficulty understanding the motion or applying interpretations of it to the context of a debate in a few minutes, the care, simplicity, investment of research and time, and other favorable features of the topic design method lose their relevance. The topic does not work and it should not be considered. This difficulty is not a reason to discard debate on the motion permanently. It may require testing in public or practice debates to begin working out the difficulties in its construction. The motion could then be used in later competitive events.

Here is an important, perhaps urgent, note: motions should be designed well in advance of the actual tournament date. Well in advance. They should be shared with other experienced topic authors for critical review and editing. The director should, quite obviously, draft at least as many motions as the number of rounds of debate. Actually, the director should draft more motions than required by the number of rounds for the event. There are circumstances in which fast-changing national and world events may moot selected topics. In the interim between the time when the topics are drafted, and the actual tournament, other debate tournaments may use some of the topics that were considered. It is sound to have several additional motions in appropriate categories available as substitutes for the ones that might be pre-selected for the tournament.

It can be argued, however, that categories of motions, as well as the wording of the motions themselves, are different from the substance, core elements, or "heart," of the debate. It isn't the case that appreciation of the motion carries the day. Few debates are won or lost when the motion is announced. Rather, debates are won on reasoning, evidence, and the persuasive skills of participants engaged in sophisticated argument on diverse issues related to the topic's interpretation. After all, any topic interpretation begets a host of arguments for a debate. It is these subsequently revealed issues, not the language of the motion itself, on which the outcome of a debate ultimately rests.

Ancillary Information

- Last-minute travel information
- Videotaping and broadcast preparation
- Confirmations

The host should update travelers with weather and travel information, particularly if transit delays or inclement weather are likely. This can be accomplished via email or by posting on a Web site or listserv.

The tournament host may choose to arrange to videotape debates or provide live Internet streaming of selected rounds. These plans should be completed well in advance of the tournament and several tests of audio/visual equipment or Internet configurations and connections should be completed by the date of the tournament. If appropriate, the tournament should provide appropriate waivers for individuals appearing on video or in broadcasts.

Prior to the tournament, the director should confirm all arrangements for the event. Participants should receive confirmation of their successful admission. Tournament service and support—room access, dining services, entertainment, etc.—should be confirmed. Efficient and timely planning will not matter much if there is a last minute error or oversight. It is best to check all the elements of successful tournament operations before guests arrive.

During the Tournament

The management of a debate tournament is a surprisingly uncomplicated affair if the host has completed the "before the tournament" tasks. Events ought to follow each other according to schedule. Experienced staff ought to be available to assist with difficulties. Tournament directors need to prepare for unlikely or untoward events.

Opening Events

- Registration
- Instructional sessions

The tournament director should prepare an orientation session to begin the event. This session may consist of documents supplied to participants at tournament registration, a video presentation, or an opening meeting. The orientation should include rules for the event, schedules, maps, and other resources to facilitate participation and avoid tournament delays. The documents or opening session may also include instructional information for debaters and judges.

Instructional information may include demonstration debates, seminars, training sessions, and support materials. Some contestants may have not participated in debates or in the particular debate format prior to the tournament. A seminar is an opportunity to assist participating debaters in understanding the intricacies of the rules and conventions of debate practice. It is also an opportunity to provide judges with information, instruction, and testing. This sort of judge training will both inform judges of practice standards for the tournament and also set consistent standards in deliberations and evaluations of debater performances.

Tournament Operations

- Announcements
- Tabulations
- Services: Meals, lodging, entertainment, awards
- Troubleshooting

The director should select a conveniently located common area for the public distribution of any announcements. Information that will be used throughout the tournament, e.g., an event schedule or directions to debate rooms, should be posted. Contact information for problems, as well as the location of the tabulating room, should be posted. The site should serve as a gathering place for tournament participants. Judges should secure and return ballots to this area.

The director should decide on a manner to announce each motion for debate. There are several popular forms, including a single common announcement, the private announcement by a judge or speaker, and the selection of the motion by the participants.

Many tournaments have a single public announcement of the motion for each round of debate. Tournament participants gather in a common area at an appointed time and the director of the event or a representative of the tournament-tabulating staff announces the motion. Typically, participants have approximately 15 to 20 minutes from the time of the announcement to the start of the debate.

Each tournament sets its own policy regarding preparation time between the announcement of the topic and the beginning of each debate. A sensible rule is that each team should have a minimum of 15 minutes to prepare for debates. If it requires five minutes to walk from the common announcement area to the furthest debating room, the tournament should provide 20 minutes of preparation time (15 minutes, plus a 5-minute walk to the debate site). This time frame provides all debaters a satisfactory minimum preparation time.

Other tournaments attach a copy of the motion to the debate ballot that judges receive prior to debates. After the teams and the judge arrive at their assigned room, the judge announces the motion and the teams have 15 minutes to prepare for the debate.

Another form of topic announcement for two-team debates uses a similar ballot attachment. The attachment to the ballot, however, has three motions for debate. The proposition team is able to strike or delete one of the motions from consideration and the opposition team is permitted to strike a second of the three motions. The remaining motion is the one used for the debate. Each team is allowed approximately one minute to make its choice of a topic strike and preparation time begins after the second topic is struck from consideration.

The results of debates are collected by the tournament administration and used to tabulate tournament results on a round-by-round basis. Tabulating software is available to assist this task. There are persons with experience with tabulating software. If the tournament director and tournament staff are not familiar with tournament tabulation methods or software, the director should identify one or more individuals to serve as tabulation directors or consultants. This procedure should ensure no problems or unnecessary delays in tournament operations. Quite obviously, accurate recording of the results of a competition is essential to its purpose and of great importance to guests, and the director needs to pay considerable attention to this detail of tournament administration.

After the announcement of the each preliminary debate, a member of the tournament staff should post the results of the debate tournament to that point. Tabulating software will produce the team records of each team in the contest. An alphabetical or rank order listing of the teams should be posted in a common area.

A public posting of the tournament results allows teams to verify the accuracy of tabulating room results. Debate teams are able to confirm the announced decision at the conclusion of the debate with the posted version by the tournament staff. Publicly posting results decreases the likelihood of tabulating room error and may avoid a serious matter, namely, the inadvertent exclusion of a qualifying team from the elimination round debates. It is also a convenient way to disseminate information to participants. After all, the results of each debate are hardly the proprietary information of the tournament tabulating staff.

The director must coordinate any receptions, meals, awards presentations, or other gatherings during the tournament. The host should prepare any speeches or announcements for these events well in advance. The director must have contact information for caterers, organizers, or other support staff for social events. Tournament staff should be assigned to manage these events, if necessary, as the tournament director may be involved with other matters at the time. All preparations for social and cultural events, awards, guest lodging, etc., should be confirmed with organizers and vendors prior to the date of the tournament.

The best planning will not necessarily guarantee a problem-free tournament. Inclement weather, hotel and catering company errors, locked classrooms or debating chambers, an insufficient number of judges, computer tabulating hardware and software difficulties, and more can disrupt an otherwise well-planned event. We have several suggestions for tournament directors and staff. These suggestions will not necessarily prevent problems but might assist in their amelioration.

In addition to posting event and contact information and providing guests with it in their registration materials, and having cellular telephones for staff communications, as previously suggested, the tournament host should appoint an assistant tournament director, with the full authority to make decisions regarding tournament operations, in the event that there are multiple difficulties occurring simultaneously and the director cannot attend to all of them personally.

The tournament should maintain a troubleshooting desk or make other arrangements for guest services. This part of tournament operations assists participants with legitimate but relatively minor concerns (i.e., those concerns that do not affect overall operations), including directions to debating rooms, lost and found items, schedule information, notes on dining options in the area, etc.

After the Tournament

Documentation

- Ballots and tabulation results
- Tournament Information
- Review and evaluation

The tournament host should collect the ballots from each judge for the preliminary and elimination round debates. Staff should organize and place ballots for each team or academic institution in folders or envelopes and make them available to guests at the point that guests are eliminated from the event. The tournament director should ensure that complete tabulation and awards results are included in each folder.

The tournament may choose to post the results of the contest on debate listservs and Websites. Full information for individual and team results may be e-mailed to listservs or forwarded to Website administrators. Some debate leagues or national organizations require that tournament results be forwarded to their offices for inclusion in national rankings for annual awards. The tournament director should promptly and completely deliver tournament tabulation results or a list of award recipients, as required.

The director should also post the motions used during the tournament to debate listservs and Websites. A topic list is an outstanding resource for competitors unable to participate in the contest. It provides a set of topics for practice debating. It familiarizes debaters with the issues considered controversial and appropriate for academic debates. It prevents the duplication of motions at subsequent tournaments.

One of the important functions of tournament administration is to establish an institutional history of the event. As a guide for colleagues, an efficient reference for the administration of future events, and a means to coordinate event publicity, a comprehensive tournament evaluation is a valued asset.

The director should prepare a comprehensive review of the tournament, including files of all invitations and announcements, schedules, support documentation, tabulation results, topics, and award recipients. The director should evaluate the event to anticipate her needs for subsequent tournaments and to provide a documentary history of tournament administration that will be available to future directors.

Publicity and Conclusion

The tournament staff should promote its successful event. Publicity may include press announcements to local and national media, broadcast of video-taped debates or tournament excerpts on the Internet, and announcements of future events to debate Websites and listservs.

The director has a final task, namely, to thank those individuals and institutions providing tournament support. A personal note, reference letter, Internet announcement, or thank-you on a Website should suffice to commend graciously the efforts of others, many of whom undoubtedly volunteered considerable time and skill to the endeavor.

Appendix 1: Sample Topics

All of the topics included below are actual topics that have been used in tournament competitions, both nationally and internationally, over the course of several years. In this list, you will find topics of all kinds. Some topics are better than other topics. Some of these motions are closed, while some are open. Some topics are metaphorical or idiomatic, and may thus be difficult for non-native English speakers. Other topics are specific to the internal affairs of particular nations, but can be easily modified to fit the needs of your nation or community.

This list can be an effective tool for teaching and practice. Debaters should use the topics for preparation—a good exercise would be to pick a few topics at a time and, for each topic, generate case ideas and topic interpretations linking the case to the motion. Teachers, trainers, and coaches should use the list to provide practice topics for their students. They may also choose to use topics from this list for tournaments or other kinds of scrimmages among debaters or debate squads. The most important function of this list, however, is that it serves to show the wide range of parliamentary debate topics.

Open Motions

This House would reject consensus.

This House would put pragmatism before its principles.

This House would heal the wound.

This House would rather be in than out.

This House would break the law.

This House supports the strong state.

Resistance is not futile.

This House would contemplate rather than act.

This House would mind the business of others.

This House believes that the Emperor is wearing no clothes.

This House should investigate the investigators.

This House would milk the cow dry.

This House would catch 'em all!

This House would be apathetic.

This House believes that the buck stops here.

That radical change is superior to incremental change.

The journey of a thousand miles begins with one step.

This House has got some nerve.

This House believes that once you start you can't stop.

This House believes that peace is undesirable.

This House approves of political inertia.

This House believes in order to get it you have to give it up.

This House believes love is foolish.

This House prefers second place to first.

This House would open its doors.

This House believes that the light at the end of the tunnel is an oncoming train.

This House would stop using cosmetics.

This House would expose the secrets.

This House would pull the plug.

This House would defend elitism.

This House would redistribute the wealth.

This House should recycle.

This House believes that good things come to those who wait.

This House believes that life imitates art.

This House believes you can judge a book by its cover.

This house believes that festivals are superior to competitions.

This House should teach an old dog a new trick.

This House should consider carefully that which seems initially successful.

This House should check its messages.

This House should change its locks.

How you play the game ought to be more important than winning the game.

The House would still the fires within.

This House would develop a strategy rather than a theory.

This House prefers cooperation to competition.

This House would hunt them down to the ends of the earth.

This House would reject dogma.

This House would rock the boat.

This House would balance the books.

This House believes the customer is always right.

Dramatic failure is more useful than mild success.

This House believes that silence means consent.

This House believes that the local is preferable to the global.

This House should balance its diet.

This House would lock its doors.

If at first you don't succeed, quit.

This House believes that it is more important to give than it is to receive.

This House would give it up.

This House would eliminate the subsidy.

Be it resolved that it is better to lead than to follow.

The loophole should be closed.

You don't need a weatherman to know which way the wind blows.

This House believes in competition.

This House believes that the whole is greater than the sum of its parts.

This House would make it up as we go along.

The ray of hope is a blinding light.

Just chill.

It is time to fish, or cut bait.

This House would upset the balance.

This House would turn the tables.

This House would follow them to the ends of the earth.

This House would unhitch the trailer.

This House believes in the survival of the fittest.

People should be accountable for their own rescues.

Apathy is more problematic than obedience.

This House believes that we should merge into one lane.

This House would repudiate patriotism.

This House would free the prisoners.

This House believes that deception is necessary.

This House would let the people decide.

This House would fail until it succeeds.

It is better to be safe than to be sorry.

This House would sell to the highest bidder.

This House would spend it.

Bury it.

This house would raise the bar.

This House believes that those who destroy should rebuild.

This House would trade swords for plowshares.

Resolved: that payments are always unbalanced.

You should build a fence around your house.

This House believes that it is better to stay parked than to jump on the accelerator.

This House would seek a simpler way.

No justice, no peace...

This House would seek a sinister way.

This House would hold its horses.

This House would go to the other extreme.

This House would come out of the closet.

This House would add fuel to the fire.

Freedom from is better than freedom to.

There is no place for personal privilege.

Railings only stop the foolish.

Resolved: You sell the sizzle not the steak.

This House would be guided by the youth.

This House prefers restraint to activism.

This House would bring back the boot camp.

Resolved: that what goes up must come down.

This House would break the glass ceiling.

This house believes that 9 out of 10 doctors are wrong.

High fences make good neighbors.

This House believes that the ends do not justify the means.

This House believes that the blind are leading the blind.

This House believes that the end is near.

This House would comfort the afflicted and afflict the comfortable.

This House would rather be poor than rich.

Cleanliness is not next to godliness.

This House would plan the perfect wedding.

This House supports the culture of openness.

This House would walk in a sacred manner.

This House would become a great mountain.

This House should increase access to information.

This House regrets devolution.

This House would uproot the cedar.

This House would rebalance the powers.

Liberty is more precious than law.

This House would put out the fire.

This House believes you can't handle the truth.

This House believes that well done is better than well said.

Science fiction will become science fact.

This House would take a walk on the wild side.

This House needs a miracle.

This House should break the silence.

This House would respond.

This House would get down and dirty.

This House would put the fat cats on a diet.

This House would have zero tolerance.

This House would rage against the machine.

This House would drop out.

This House believes that charity begins at home.

When in conflict, this house would rather be cheap than easy.

This House believes in playing favorites.

This House would go home.

Finish the job.

Give legitimacy to the union.

Our trust is misplaced.

Oops, this House did it again.

This House would revisit the 1970's.

This House would reach for the stars.

This House would remove government from the lives of the people.

This House would repudiate history.

Something can be true in theory but not in practice

Sometimes it is morally correct to be dishonest.

This House should spoil its children.

Resolved: The trend toward centrist politics is desirable.

This House would reveal its secrets.

This House would shred its documents.

In this instance, family members should exercise tough love.

This House believes that Shakespeare was right.

Resolved: Let it be.

This House believes that change is not progress.

This House will seek forgiveness later rather than permission now.

This House respects its elders.

This House believes in traditions.

This house prefers great taste to less filling.

This house would push the button.

This house believes that greed is good.

It is time to throw off the shackles of tradition.

This House would look to the past, not to the future.

This House believes that it's time for a change.

This House believes in the devolution of power.

This House would remain anonymous.

This House would let them in.

This House supports civil disobedience.

Resolved: Actions speak louder than words.

This House believes in the greatest good for the greatest number.

This House would stick to its principles.

This House believes in Right and Wrong.

This House would legislate, not liberate.

This House believes that divided we stand, united we fall.

The carrot is more effective than the stick.

This House would meet cruelty with kindness.

This House would reject big government.

This House would rather be public than private.

We don't believe that imitation is flattery.

The power of one is stronger than the power of many.

Obedience to authority is an excuse for cowardice.

True courage is demonstrated through passive resistance.

This House would throw caution to the wind.

This House would live outside the law.

This House would rather be beautiful than clever.

This House rejects a cost-benefit analysis.

This House would not vouch for vouchers.

This House doesn't believe these politicians.

Ignoring the fringe is better than engaging it.

This House believes that childhood is more important than adulthood.

This House should grease the wheels of justice.

This House believes that there are necessary illusions.

This House would repeat the mistakes of the past.

This House believes that fortune favors the foolish.

This House believes that it is better to be a middle of the roader.

This House believes that the people are wrong.

This House believes that we have never had it so good.

This House would let the majority rule.

This House believes in freedom from fear.

This House prefers justice to popularity.

This House should be a spiritual House.

This House should be a virtual House.

This House would support gridlock.

This House is in contempt of the court.

This House would assist those who wish to die.

The grass grows greener on the other side.

This House should save the family farm.

This House should resist the tyranny of principle.

Regulate the regulators.

This House would encourage saving our green.

This House believes it is better to stand alone.

This House would test its tires.

This House is sad, cold and lonely.

This House calls for grants, not loans.

This House will not survive.

This House would thwart the will of the majority.

This House should hide the truth.

This House believes the pen in mightier than the sword.

This House believes that there ought to be a law.

Corporate power has gone too far.

This House would burn the village to save it.

This House believes that fanaticism works.

This House believes that the truth is out there.

This House believes that old enemies can become new friends.

Resolved: This House believes there is no blank slate.

This House would boldly go where no House has gone before.

This House would rather be a tortoise than a hare.

This House would rather explode than implode.

This House believes that what costs little is of little worth.

This House would root for the underdog.

This House would watch the skies.

This House would watch the watchers.

This House would assassinate its enemies.

This House believes in painting the town red.

This House would cry over spilt milk.

This House would return the relics.

This House would repair the damage.

This House would not stand by her man.

This House would centralize.

This House would check it out.

This House would blame society.

This House should be forced to give up its vices.

This House would find the truth.

This House should forgive and forget.

This House would rather be East than West.

Taxation

Wealthy people's taxes should be raised and poor people's taxes should be lowered.

This House would use taxation to regulate behavior.

This House should replace the federal income tax with a federal sales tax.

Citizens should not be forced to pay taxes to finance Social Security.

The government should redistribute wealth by taxing some citizens in order to provide goods or services to others.

The government should be financed exclusively by voluntary contributions.

Citizens should be taxed to finance public education.

You can spend your own money more wisely than the government.

This House would give substantial tax relief to prevent a recession.

This House supports a flat tax.

This House would cut taxes.

In certain circumstances, a conscientious objection to paying taxes is justified.

This House would abolish direct taxation.

This House would increase taxes on the rich.

This House believes that taxation is theft.

This House believes that a fairer society needs higher taxation.

Criminal and Civil Justice

A victim's deliberate use of deadly force is justified as a response to domestic abuse.

In the criminal justice system, truth-seeking ought to take precedence over the rights of the accused.

This House believes in trial by jury.

The rights of the victim ought to take precedence over the rights of the accused.

This House would legalize prostitution.

This House would impose mandatory sentences for repeat offenders.

This House believes in "Three strikes and you're out"

This House would lock 'em up and throw away the key.

This House opposes the death penalty.

It should be legal to require criminal defendants to testify in their trials.

This House believes that crimes should have victims.

This House would eliminate due process of law.

This House believes that civil litigation should have the same requirements as criminal litigation.

That the means of police interrogation are less important that the ends.

This House should limit the type of evidence admissible in courts.

Resolved: This House believes rewards work better than punishments.

Be it resolved: Due process is overrated.

This House believes that convicted rapists are as bad as murderers and should be sent to prison for life.

Illegally obtained evidence should not be admissible in a criminal trial.

This House favors retribution over rehabilitation.

This House would limit the option of litigation.

This House believes that judges should be elected.

This House would chemically castrate sex offenders.

This House would publicize the whereabouts of sex offenders.

Resolved: That law enforcement agencies should be given greater freedom in the investigation and prosecution of crime.

This House would televise criminal trials.

This House believes that justice should be blind.

Resolved: Violent juvenile offenders ought to be treated as adults in the criminal justice system.

This House would crack down on petty crimes.

This House would extradite criminals to face the death penalty

This House should alter the system of jury selection.

This House should take a tougher stance toward criminals.

Drug Policy

This House would legalize all drugs.

This House believes that the war on drugs is inadvisable in a free society.

This House would legalize soft drugs.

This House would legalize hard drugs.

This House believes that the war on drugs is misdirected.

This House would ban all alcoholic drinks.

Political Systems and Philosophies

This House believes that only the elite can truly successfully manage national affairs.

This House believes in pacifism.

This House would use proportional representation to decide national elections.

This House would use force to make peace.

Resident non-citizens should be given the right to vote.

Special interest groups have too much influence in elections.

The government should take one or more actions to make it easier for citizens to vote.

The voting age should be set at 16.

This House would require that all candidates participate in mandatory, nationally televised debates in presidential elections.

This House would adopt a system of compulsory voting for all citizens.

Public campaign tactics should be limited in one or more ways.

This House believes that there are better alternatives to democracy.

This House believes state power is more important than federal power.

This House believes that the state has a duty to protect individuals from themselves.

This House would give Marxism another try.

This House favors a parliamentary form of government.

This House believes that strong dictatorship is better than weak democracy.

This House would reform the present system of checks and balances.

This House believes that one man's terrorist is another man's freedom fighter.

This House believes that the right wing is dead wrong.

This House would support a six-year presidential term of office.

Resolved: That politicians should be forgiven when leaving office.

This House has high hopes for third parties.

Be it resolved that the government that governs least governs best.

This House would reform the national campaign process.

This House believes that the judiciary should be popularly elected.

Resolved: That the power of the Presidency should be significantly curtailed.

The only proper function of government is to defend the individual rights of its citizens.

Resolved: that politics should be about the citizens and not the parties.

This House regards royalty as irrelevant.

This House believes that the government has forgotten its role.

This House supports campaign finance reform.

This House demands fully representative government.

This House would rather have a president than a monarch.

This House believes that the state should fund all political parties.

This House would ban all private donations to political parties.

This House calls for more use of the referendum.

This House believes that true democracy is direct democracy.

This House believes that negative political advertising is significantly detrimental to the democratic process.

This House believes that the public deserves the politicians it elects.

This House regrets the rise of career politicians.

This House believes that voting should be compulsory.

This House believes that it's a crime not to vote.

This House supports political advertising.

This House believes that there is a better way to elect the president.

This House opposes patriotism.

This House believes in term limits for federal officials.

This House should reform the political process.

This House would limit the cost of election campaigns.

This House believes in the two-party system.

Privacy and Individual Rights

This House believes danger is the price of liberty.

This House believes that the right to privacy is more important than the freedom of the press.

This House believes in the concept of intellectual property.

This House believes that freedom has been taken too far in the western world.

Resolved: That greater controls should be imposed on the gathering and utilization of information about citizens by government agencies.

This House believes in the right to die.

This House would introduce a National Identity Card.

This House believes the right to privacy has gone too far.

This House believes that the rights of the oppressed should be less important than the rights of the oppressors.

This House believes that security is more important than freedom.

This House believes that personal liberty must be restricted to reduce the threat of domestic terrorism.

The protection of public safety justifies random drug testing.

When in conflict, individual rights take precedence over government rights.

Laws that protect individuals from themselves are justified.

Resolved: that drug testing in the workplace should be abolished.

This House would restrict the liberty of people in order to prevent harm to their health.

Philososphy

Freedom of the individual is a myth.

It is possible to identify truths.

This House rejects all forms of violence.

This House believes that it is never right to take a life.

This House believes there is no such thing as a winnable war.

This House believes in absolute Truth.

This House deplores utilitarianism.

This House believes that conventionality is not morality.

This House values life over liberty.

Materialism will lead to the downfall of humanity.

This House believes that the ends do not justify the means.

Violence is an appropriate expression for the silenced.

Human beings are fundamentally good.

The fact that most people believe something is good makes it good.

Moral principles should be based on the requirements of human life, not commandments.

This House believes that collectivism is better than individualism.

When called upon by one's government, individuals are morally obligated to risk their lives.

This House regrets the decline of conventional morality.

Equality and Social Justice

This House would require prospective human parents to be licensed before having children.

This House would privatize the pension problem.

This House would address the concerns of an aging population.

The government should make reparations to black people and other abused minorities.

This House believes that the battle of the sexes is far from over.

This House would allow homosexual couples to adopt children.

_____ is the best way to protect rights of homosexuals.

The state should make inroads into parental rights.

This House would give money to beggars.

This House believes that charity begins with the homeless.

This House would help beggars become choosers.

Be it resolved that welfare be available only to persons over the age of 21.

Be it resolved that community service be a requirement of welfare payment.

This House would support positive discrimination.

Social responsibility should be compulsory.

Housing should be a basic human right.

The government should more actively protect the rights of persons with disabilities.

This House would end the war on poverty.

Be it resolved: The federal government ought to enact a policy to promote multiculturalism.

This House would reform the welfare system.

This House would support radical redistribution.

This House would give the young a voice.

This House believes that there is no such thing as universal human rights.

This House believes that a common culture is of greater value than a pluralistic culture.

This House supports same-sex marriage.

This nation should pay reparations for violating the human rights of its people.

This House would relax immigration laws.

This House would introduce hiring quotas.

This House believes that the 'melting pot' has failed.

This House would hold the military to a stricter standard on sexual harassment.

This House would put those on welfare to work.

This House would ration the old to nurture the young.

This House would spend less on the police and more on the people.

This House believes that the government must place the human interest above the national interest.

This House would end all classification by race.

This House would speak English.

This House would advocate color-blind justice.

The federal government should enact a policy to restrict entitlement programs.

This House deplores class warfare.

This House believes that the community is more important than the individual.

This House would pay a parent for staying home.

This House would reframe the urban future.

This House would establish a youth policy.

This House would restrict the rights of immigrants.

That violence and progressive dissent ought to be mutually exclusive.

The safety net should be mended.

This House believes in social unity over cultural diversity.

This House would adopt a superior alternative to affirmative action.

This House would adopt quotas.

This House believes that social welfare is the responsibility of local governments.

This House believes that equality is the benchmark of society.

This House would politely say "No" to reparations.

This House should close its borders.

This House supports open borders.

This House believes that good health is a human right.

The law discriminates against women and treats them worse than men.

This House believes that family values are over-rated.

Resolved: that affirmative action should focus on class, not race.

This House opposes affirmative action.

This House believes that the scales of justice are tilted.

This House supports discrimination.

This House would hold people responsible for the actions of their ancestors.

Peaceful and healthy immigrants should be allowed to cross the border freely.

Toleration is a virtue.

This House believes that racism can be controlled by legislation.

This House believes special protection creates special problems.

This House would means-test state benefits.

This House would abolish the welfare state.

This House believes the welfare state is a right, not a safety net.

Affirmative action should be used to even out differences between the sexes.

This House believes that minority privileges deny equality.

Labor and Economic Policy

This House believes that renewed strength of labor organizations is necessary for a progressive economy.

This House calls for a mandatory retirement age.

This House believes that the government should regulate the economy.

This House would increase consumer protection.

This House believes that accountants are to blame.

That House believes that we should subsidize traditional industries.

This House believes that multi-nationals are the new imperialists.

Capitalism is an immoral economic system.

This House would stabilize gas prices.

The government should subsidize some businesses and farms.

This House would increase partnerships between government and private enterprise.

This House would establish a living wage.

Capitalism is the only ethical economic system.

This House would increase the minimum wage.

This House would promote infrastructure development.

Resolved: That the government should nationalize the basic nonagricultural industries.

The recent mega-mergers of media companies will help competition more than they will hinder it.

This House would return to an unregulated free market.

This House regrets globalization.

This House supports the right to work.

This House believes that the right to strike should be given to all employees.

Wages should be raised 15 percent.

Small organizations are able to adapt to today's business environment better than large organizations.

This House believes you should invest in foreign markets.

That the work week should be shortened to 30 hours.

Enron reveals capitalism's moral bankruptcy.

This House believes in economic competition.

This House would end corporate welfare.

This House would re-nationalize the public utilities.

Resolved: That the federal government should establish a national program of public work for the unemployed.

Resolved: That the federal government should guarantee a minimum annual cash income to all citizens.

Resolved: That the federal government should adopt a program of compulsory wage and price controls.

This House would break up economic power.

The significance of consumer confidence has been overrated.

This House would stop the free exchange of currencies.

This House would get out of the stock market.

This House believes that equality and capitalism are incompatible.

This House would save the surplus.

Resolved: That the federal government should implement a program guaranteeing employment opportunities for all citizens in the labor force.

Resolved: That the federal government should significantly curtail the powers of the labor unions.

Resolved: That the nonagricultural industries should guarantee their employees an annual wage.

Resolved: That the requirement of membership in a labor organization as a condition of employment should be illegal.

Resolved: That labor organizations should be under the jurisdiction of anti-trust legislation.

This House would hold tobacco companies liable for the consequences of their products.

This House would set a maximum limit on salaries.

This House would bail out failing industries.

This House believes in supply-side economics.

Resolved: Labor should be given a direct share in the management of industry.

This House supports the power of labor unions.

This House believes that labor unions have outlived their usefulness.

Arts and Literature

This House believes that public monies should not finance art.

This House believes art is the essence of a nation's character.

Art is unnecessary for human progress.

This House believes in poetic license.

This House would let the language die.

This House would pay to go to a museum.

This House would abolish state funding of the arts.

Art is like a shark, it must move forward or it will die.

This nation should have an official language.

Art is permitted, but nature is forbidden.

This House would establish English as the official language.

Free Speech

Political correctness is the new McCarthyism.

This House believes any book worth banning is a book worth reading.

Communities ought to have the right to suppress pornography.

This House believes that censorship can never be justified.

This House would ban prisoners publishing accounts of their crimes.

Be it resolved: Hate speech ought to be banned.

This House believes that money is speech.

This House would give racists a platform.

This House would support a constitutional amendment to protect the flag from desecration.

The protection of domestic order justifies restrictions on free speech.

This House believes the press is too free.

Be it resolved that censorship of television, film and video materials be increased.

This House would be politically correct.

This House would legalize all adult pornography.

This House believes that a ban on flag burning better serves fascism than freedom.

Resolved: that the government should take a more active stance protecting free speech.

Resolved: A journalist's right to shield confidential sources ought to be protected by the First Amendment.

This House would restrict free speech.

Trade Policy

Be it resolved that the GATT system of international governance should be significantly revised.

The West will regret free trade.

This House will regret the trade bloc.

This House believes the WTO is a friend of the developing world.

This House believes that trade rights should be linked to human rights.

This House would expand NAFTA.

This House believes that NAFTA is a mistake.

That on balance, free trade benefits more than it costs.

This House would restrict non-tariff barriers.

Resolved: Something needs to be done about the WTO.

People are better off with tariffs than with complete free-trade today.

This House rejects the multilateral agreement on investment.

International Affairs and Policies

This House would test nuclear weapons.

This House believes that industrialization assures progress in the developing world.

In international relations, economic power is preferred to military power.

This House should adopt a more moderate stance toward Iran.

Resolved: That this nation's foreign policy toward one or more African nations should be substantially changed.

This House should apologize for its imperialistic past.

This House should end its foreign military operations.

This House believes that developing nations need strong dictatorship.

This House would be more realistic about humanitarian intervention by our military forces.

Let the world police itself.

This House would end the embargo with Cuba.

This House supports a Palestinian state.

This House would end unconditional aid to Israel.

This House would substantially reduce IMF and World Bank lending programs.

The debt of the third world should be forgiven.

This House believes that the poverty of the Third World is the fault of the First World.

This House has no business in Bosnia.

This House believes that the UN has failed.

This House would eliminate the veto power of the United Nations Security Council.

It is time to shun Arafat.

Iran should not be considered part of the "Axis of Evil."

Tony Blair should receive the Nobel Peace Prize.

This House believes we don't need Europe.

This House believes that the UN is a toothless watchdog.

This House would give the UN a standing army.

This House would reject a united Europe.

This House would give land for peace.

This House believes that the international community should start a dialogue with the Front for the Islamic Salvation of Algeria.

The Chemical Weapons Convention should not be ratified.

All foreign aid should be privately funded.

This House should enact a more aggressive foreign policy.

This House regrets humanitarian intervention.

This House fears China.

This House would end the arms trade.

This House believes that child labor is justifiable in the developing world.

This House believes that the assassination of dictators is justifiable.

Resolved: The possession of nuclear weapons is immoral.

This House fears Islamic fundamentalism.

Romania should be admitted to the European Union.

Romania should be admitted to NATO.

Protection of human rights justifies the use of military force.

This House supports the establishment of an international criminal court.

This House would ban all nuclear weapons.

This House believes in the right of any country to defend itself with nuclear weapons.

This House believes that economic sanctions do more harm than good.

This House would always prefer sanctions to war.

This House believes that terrorism is sometimes justifiable.

This House would take steps to substantially reduce nuclear proliferation.

Further debt relief for developing nations is needed.

This House would negotiate with terrorists.

What steps should the UN take to stop civil unrest in Africa?

This House believes war to be an unjustified response to aggression.

This House condemns the UN embargo of Iraq.

This House would make amends for the legacy of colonialism.

Sweden should abolish its monarchy and become a republic.

This house would shift its foreign policy focus to the western hemisphere.

This House would override national sovereignty to protect human rights.

The United Nations Charter should be substantially changed.

This House would expand NATO.

Resolved: That the federal government should substantially increase its development assistance, including increasing government-to-government assistance, within the Greater Horn of Africa.

Be it resolved that a permanent United Nations military force be established.

Be it resolved that international sanctions against Serbia be lifted.

Be it resolved that all east European countries be admitted into NATO.

Be it resolved that the Organization of American States should establish a regional drug interdiction military force to halt the flow of drugs in the Western Hemisphere.

On to Baghdad.

Adios, Latin America.

The United Nations should mandate and enforce an Israeli-Palestinian settlement.

This House would substantially increase population assistance in foreign aid programs.

This House would end financial aid to foreign nations.

Nationalism stands in the way of peace.

That carrots are better than sticks in foreign policy.

Resolved: A federal world government should be established.

This House would support the independence of Quebec.

This House should act against political oppression in the People's Republic of China.

This House would eliminate slavery in Africa.

This House believes that increased relations with China would be detrimental.

This House would intervene in Chechnya.

This House believes that international conflict is desirable.

It is immoral to use economic sanctions to achieve foreign policy goals.

This House would use economic sanctions to enforce a ban on nuclear weapons testing.

This House believes that the UN is dysfunctional.

This House welcomes a borderless world.

This House calls for a New World Order.

This House believes in the right of indigenous peoples to self-determination.

This House would rather live on a desert island than in the global village.

This House believes that human rights are a tool of Western foreign policy.

This House believes that aid to the Third World should be tied to human rights.

This House would manage ethnic conflict in Central Asia.

This House values human rights over state sovereignty.

This House would take policy action to support Kurdish self-determination.

Interference in the internal affairs of other countries is justified.

This House believes that Okinawa should be independent.

This House would increase support for the developing world.

This House would unite Ireland.

Environmental Policy And Philosophy

This House would substantially restrict visitors to the National Parks.

This House believes that the value of natural resources can be found only in their exploitation.

Be it resolved that the use of animals for public entertainment (zoos, circus acts, etc.) be illegal.

This House would restrict private car ownership.

Old growth forests should be logged.

This House believes that the lives of animals should not be subordinate to the rights of humankind.

This House would ban all experimentation on animals.

This House believes that meat is murder.

Resolved: That the federal government should adopt a comprehensive program to control land use.

Resolved: That the federal government should control the supply and utilization of energy.

This House would free the animals.

This House believes that we have no more right to risk the health of animals than of humans.

This House believes that animals have rights too.

This House would break the law to protect the rights of animals.

This House would ban hunting with hounds.

Privatizing all unused federal public land is a good protection for the environment.

Technology should be utilized to solve ecological problems.

This House believes that the value of natural resources is found in their exploitation.

When in conflict, This House values environmental protection over economic growth.

High petrol prices are a good thing.

Sustainability is not an achievable goal.

This House would act decisively to stop global warming.

This House believes that the government should take measures to substantially improve natural disaster relief.

Resolved: that the U.S. should begin immediately to phase-in measures to reduce the rate of increase in atmospheric CO_2 concentration.

The government should substantially reduce oil imports.

This House supports the international trading of pollution permits.

This house would save the dams, not the salmon.

This House would save the tropics.

This House would substantially reform farming.

This House would go forth and stop multiplying.

This House calls for increased population control.

This House would subsidize agriculture.

Overpopulation is the world's greatest threat.

This House believes that the Kyoto Summit didn't go far enough.

This House believes that global warming is the biggest international crisis.

This House would put the environment before economics.

This House would protect the lesser species.

This House believes spaceship earth is crashing.

This House would privatize national parks.

Popular Culture

This House believes American culture places too great an emphasis on athletic success.

Baseball is better than soccer.

This House should oppose the Olympics.

This House is resolved that there should be integration of the sexes in professional sports.

This House believes that dogs are better pets for humankind than cats.

This House believes our obsession with celebrities is harmful.

This House believes that there is too much money in sport.

This House applauds the Olympic ideal.

This House would blame Hollywood for the ills of society.

This House supports a national lottery.

This House would ban boxing.

This House would ban all blood sports.

This house believes the Super Bowl ain't that super.

This House condemns gambling of all forms.

This House believes that beauty pageants for children should be banned.

This House would restrict the movement of professional sports franchises.

This House believes that advertising is poison to society.

Be it resolved that drug testing be compulsory for all athletes involved in national and international competition.

This House would ban all tobacco advertising.

This House prefers Sega to Shakespeare.

Parents ought not purchase war toys for their children.

This House believes that music is more influential than literature.

State-run lotteries are undesirable.

This House believes that motion pictures are a reflection of society norms.

This House prefers country music to classical music.

This House believes that violence has no place in entertainment.

This House believes that commercialism has gone too far.

This House believes that the continued production of sport utility vehicles is undesirable.

This House believes that advertising degrades the quality of life.

Media And Television

This House believes that television destroys lives.

This House believes that journalistic integrity is dead.

This House believes that television is more significant than the computer.

This House believes that the media has gone too far.

This House believes that the news should be interesting rather than important.

This House supports domestic content quotas in broadcasting.

This House believes that the media has become too powerful.

Resolved: That the federal government should significantly strengthen the regulation of mass media communication.

Be it resolved that television is the major cause of increased violence in our society.

It is proper for the government to own the TV and radio airwaves.

This House would televise executions.

This House believes that the state should have no role in broadcasting.

This House would turn off the TV.

Science And Technology

This House would leave the planet.

This House thinks that Internet "junk mail" should be illegal.

The ethical costs of selling human eggs outweigh the potential benefits.

When in conflict, this House values scientific discovery over the welfare of animals.

This House would censor the Internet.

This House calls for further use of nuclear power.

This House believes that science is a menace to civilization.

This House believes that the march of science has gone too far.

This House fears the Information Age.

Resolved that the use of antibiotics should be significantly limited.

Resolved that genetic testing on human fetuses should be prohibited.

The federal government should significantly restrict research and development of one or more technologies.

This house would clone humans.

This House believes that research should be restrained by morality.

This House believes that space travel should be privatized.

This House should regulate on-line gambling.

This House would fear technology.

This House would ban genetic cloning.

This House believes computers are the answer.

This House would delete Microsoft.

That on balance, resources spent on space exploration would be better used if directed toward the exploration of earth.

This House would let the information superhighway run free.

This House calls for universal genetic screening.

This House would expand stem cell research.

This House believes that the benefits of genetic engineering outweigh its risks.

All software must be shipped with the source code.

This House would reduce applied research for basic research.

This House would ban genetic screening.

This House would test everyone for HIV.

This House would patrol the information superhighway.

Space research and development should be significantly curtailed.

Resolved: The Internet should be funded by government subsidies, as opposed to private investment.

Resolved: It is unethical for companies to track individuals' use of the Web without their knowledge.

That schools should use filtering software to prevent children from viewing restricted material on the Internet.

Genetically engineered food is the answer to feeding the world.

This House would buy every child a computer.

The Internet needs to be regulated.

Education Policy

This House believes that the students should run the school.

This House believes that public schools should forego freedom for safety.

This House believes that physically challenged people should not be separated in schools.

This House would eliminate letter grades.

This House believes that everyone should attend college.

Public education is necessary.

The government should institute mandatory arts education.

Resolved: Colleges and universities have a moral obligation to prohibit the public expression of hate speech on their campuses.

This House believes that vocational training is more important than liberal arts education.

Resolved: that charter schools erode public education.

This House would judge schools by their examination results.

This House would put Latin and Greek on the national curriculum.

This House would always educate boys and girls together.

Resolved: The use of grades in schools should be abandoned

This House would make the student pay back his debt to society.

This House believes that private schools are not in the public interest.

This House would reform education.

This House would make school sport voluntary.

Resolved: That the federal government should guarantee an opportunity for higher education to all qualified high school graduates.

This House rejects military recruiters at educational institutions.

Uniformity in education leads to mediocrity.

This House would revolutionize the educational system.

This House believes that every citizen has a right to a college education.

This House believes that women's studies should not include men.

This House would accept advertising in public schools.

This House would change its policy on funding education.

Resolved that the federal government should deny public education to illegal immigrants.

Teachers' salaries should be based on students' academic performance.

This House believes that it's better for the Japanese people to learn world history than Japanese history.

Tenure should be abolished in universities.

This House believes that schools should not prepare students for work.

This House believes that computers are the demise of education.

This House supports single-sex education.

This House rejects the business model for institutions of higher education.

This House believes that nursery education is a right, not a privilege.

This House would be allowed to leave school at 14.

This House would charge tuition fees for university students.

This House believes that a degree is a privilege, not a right.

This House would report violations by college students to their parents.

Institutional censorship of academic material is harmful to the educational process.

Access to higher education should be a right.

This House believes that to improve education, it is more important to raise salaries than standards.

The United States Of America

This House believes that the USA is more sinned against than sinning.

This House would denuclearize the USA.

Resolved: The Supreme Court of the USA should uphold substantive due process.

This House should honor its treaties with one or more Native American nations.

This House believes that "Homeland Security" should not be a cabinet level position.

This House rejects the American way of life.

This House would have a new song for America.

This House believes that the USA should repay its debt to the United Nations.

Resolved: That the USA should reduce substantially its military commitments to NATO member states.

Be it resolved that the USA should significantly increase its role in Russia's financial future.

This House believes that justice in America can be bought.

This House believes that America's right is wrong.

This house regrets the American response to September 11.

The USA should not abandon National Missile Defense.

A fully insured America is unrealistic.

This House wishes Plymouth Rock had landed on the pilgrims.

Racism contributes to United States' policy toward Africa.

The U.S.A. should change its foreign policy.

The Democratic Party is moribund.

This House would maintain United States military bases in Asia.

This House would curtail corporate puppetry of U.S. politics.

The United States is a terrorist network.

This House believes that the American dream has become a nightmare.

This House believes that, if America is the world's policeman, then the world is America's Rodney King.

This House regrets the influence of the USA.

Americans have too many rights and not enough responsibilities.

The USA ought to increase access to the political system.

The United States of America has overemphasized individual rights.

The USA should support bilingualism.

This House believes that the USA is a racist society.

This House believes that America's constitutional rights are being too harshly infringed.

This House believes that the US should take a tougher stance toward Israel.

The USA should significantly increase military spending.

Resolved: That the Congress of the USA should enact a compulsory fair employment practices law.

Resolved: That the USA should adopt a policy of free trade.

Resolved: That the USA should significantly increase its foreign military commitments.

Resolved: That the USA should discontinue direct economic aid to foreign countries.

Resolved: That the Congress of the USA should be given the power to reverse decisions of the Supreme Court.

The USA should punish China for its human rights abuses.

This House believes the Electoral College is still necessary.

Resolved that the U.S. has overplayed the sanction card.

This House believes that America is blinded by the light.

Be it resolved that the U.S.A. should significantly reduce its superpower role.

Be it resolved that the U.S.A. should withdraw from NAFTA.

Be it resolved that the U.S.A. should significantly revise its trade status with Japan.

The government of the United States of America should reduce due process protections in one or more areas.

This house believes the Supreme Court has gone too far.

Be it resolved that the U.S.A. should take a greater role in the Israeli/Palestinian peace process.

Be it resolved that the U.S.A. should significantly increase its ties to China.

Be it resolved that the U.S.A. should lift the embargo against Cuba.

Be it resolved that the federal government of the USA should expand its role in educating America's youth.

Be it resolved that the federal government of the United States of America should fund the relief efforts of faith-based organizations.

This House believes that the First Amendment applies to the Internet.

Jesse Ventura is right.

Be it resolved that hegemony by the USA is detrimental to world stability.

This House believes you can go to the mall and see America.

This House believes that the USA should be less involved in world affairs.

The American media works against the best interests of the public.

This House would dramatically increase funding for the National Endowment for the Arts.

This House is resolved that President Bush should sign the Ottawa Treaty to ban the production and export of land mines.

This House would treat America's youth like adults.

We believe that America's safety net catches more than it misses.

Be it resolved: That the federal government should substantially increase its support to the arts of America.

This House would abolish "Don't ask, don't tell" policies.

This House is resolved that a global marketplace is good for the USA.

This House would not have named Washington National Airport after Ronald Reagan.

The Supreme Court should expand executive privilege.

This House would eliminate the Department of Education.

This House would induct the 51st state.

This House believes that Miranda rights favor the guilty.

The United States of America should mind its own business.

This House believes that the U.S. government should stop subsidizing farmers.

This House would grant political independence to Washington, D. C.

This House would repeal Title IX.

The federal government of the United States of America should substantially change its nuclear waste policy.

The USA should increase its trade agreements with Africa.

There should be additions to Mount Rushmore.

Resolved that parental notification of abortions by minors be mandatory in the USA.

Resolved that testing for performance-enhancing drugs be implemented in all NCAA Division I sports.

Resolved that California reinstate affirmative action in all public universities.

Litigation has replaced legislation in America.

This House believes that country music reflects a decline in American culture.

Be it resolved that the United States of America should adopt the Nuclear Test-Ban Treaty.

The United States of America should reform Social Security.

The Congress of the USA should enact reparations for descendants of slaves.

This House would eliminate the CIA.

Resolved: that Medicare is worse than no care at all.

This House believes that the USA should apologize to Latin America.

This House believes that the IRS needs to be abolished.

This House believes that American automobiles are a better bargain than European automobiles.

The European Union

This House believes that the European Community ought to expand now.

Europe should take deliberate steps to stop Russia's siege of Chechnya.

This House believes that the single European currency will fail.

This House believes that Europe should be the next USA.

This House would join a European defense alliance.

This House welcomes European federalism.

This House believes that a wider Europe is not in Britain's interest.

This House welcomes the Euro.

This House believes that the Eurovision song contest is the role-model.

Health Care

This House believes that basic medical care is a privilege, not a right.

Be it resolved that national comprehensive health care would fail.

The government should provide universal health care.

Capitalism impairs health delivery systems.

This House would significantly reform the health care system.

This house would standardize health care.

This House would protect the patient.

This House believes that the markets and health make poor bedfellows.

Modern medicine over-emphasizes prolonging life.

The rich will always be healthier than the poor.

United Kingdom

This House is resolved that the British monarchy is the best system of government the world has ever known.

This House would tax the monarchy.

This House would give Britain a written constitution.

This House would limit the terms of MPs.

Resolved: That the government should adopt a program of compulsory health insurance for all citizens.

This House would tear up the Act of Union.

This House calls for the disestablishment of the Church of England.

This House would allow 18 year-olds to be MPs.

This House believes that MPs should represent their constituents, not lobby groups.

This House would introduce proportional representation in Britain.

This House has no confidence in Her Majesty's Government.

This House would provide complementary medicine on the NHS.

This House believes that Britain's licensing laws are outdated and draconian.

This House believes that New Labor is Old Tory.

This House believes that the "first past the post" system is undemocratic.

This House would privatize the BBC.

This House believes that Britain has failed its responsibilities to refugees.

This House would privatize the NHS.

This House would buy British.

This House would abolish the Commonwealth.

This House believes that, if the Commonwealth didn't exist, no one would think of mentioning it.

This House would dissolve the House of Lords.

This House would abolish the A-level.

This House would remove the privileges of Oxbridge students.

Former Soviet Union

This House is resolved that communism was better than capitalism for Russia.

This House mourns the demise of the Soviet Union.

Military Affairs

Military conscription is superior to a volunteer army.

The military limits freedom of expression too much.

This House believes that military justice is an oxymoron.

This House believes that military spending is detrimental to society.

This House would lift the ban on gays in the military.

Gun Control

Resolved: That the government should adopt a policy of mandatory background checks for the purchasers of firearms.

That possession of handguns should be made illegal.

This House should increase regulation of firearms.

This House believes in the right to bear arms.

Gun manufacturers should be held liable for gun-related deaths.

This House would mandate gun safety education in all schools.

Resolved: The government should substantially increase restrictions on gun manufacturers.

Citizens should have the right to carry concealed guns.

Be it resolved that an armed society is a polite society.

Reproductive Rights

This House believes that the unborn child has no rights.

That public money should not be used to pay for abortions.

Women should have the right to have an abortion if they so choose.

This House believes that abortion is justifiable.

This House would allow surrogate motherhood.

Abortion must be outlawed.

This House believes that contraception for teenagers encourages promiscuity.

Other Public Policy Issues

This House would re-introduce National Service.

This House would continue to prosecute World War II criminals.

This House would legalize voluntary euthanasia.

That the draft should be abolished and replaced by professional military forces.

This House would impose a curfew on children under 10.

This House would make tobacco companies pay compensation to the individual.

This house would put limits on the issuance of credit cards to anyone less than 25 years old.

Be it resolved that new drivers will be issued a restricted license, and that these restrictions will apply for one year.

This House would ban smoking.

This House would ban smoking in public places.

Public transport is more convenient than cars.

Emergency action for earthquakes and typhoons should be improved.

The automobile is the ultimate cause of urban decline.

Family Matters

This House would make divorce easier.

This House demands new family values.

This House believes that marriage is an outdated institution.

Marriage and government should be divorced.

This House would get married for the sake of the children.

Australia

Australia is an old economy country.

It is morally justifiable to bury nuclear waste in Western Australia.

Australian foreign policy has contributed to Indonesia's unrest.

Canada

Be it resolved that native Canadians be given the right to self-government.

Be it resolved that it is essential for Canada to maintain its military presence in Somalia.

Be it resolved that spraying for mosquitoes in Winnipeg is in the best interest of the public.

Be it resolved that capital punishment be reinstated for premeditated murder.

Be it resolved that the burning of stubble by Manitoba farmers be restricted.

Be it resolved that the trial period for Sunday shopping be extended.

Be it resolved that gambling be illegal in Manitoba.

Be it resolved that the City of Winnipeg take the responsibility of financing a new arena, to be located within the city limits.

Be it resolved that Quebec should separate from Canada.

Be it resolved that Canada's military role shall be only in self -defense.

Be it resolved that Canada shall privatize its medical system.

Be it resolved that taxpayer money no longer be used for the support of the Winnipeg Jets.

Appendix 2: British Format Debating

The British Format — Eight-Person Debating

In the British format, two teams represent each side of the topic for debate. Each team has two people. This means that eight debaters participate in any given debate. Every speaker gives one speech, and debaters may attempt points of information during all speeches, rather than only in the constructive speeches (as in the American format). The British format is an exciting and engaging format for parliamentary debating. You will find that having eight competitors makes the debate particularly fun, and we encourage you to try this style of debating in your classes, clubs, and meets.

Of the two teams on the same side of the motion, one is designated first proposition and the other as second proposition. The same is the case for the opposition teams: teams are listed as first or second opposition. The first proposition team and the first opposition team function in the same way as American debaters do in the constructive speeches. They establish an argument for the motion, dispute it, and defend it. The second proposition team provides an **extension** of the original case of the first proposition team, and expands the debate to new areas. The second opposition team refutes this new argument direction. The final speakers for each team in the debate are like the rebuttalists in the American format, as their job is to summarize the winning points of the debate for their respective side.

There are eight speeches in the debate. Each speaker delivers a single speech. Each speech is the same duration, usually either five or seven minutes. There is no preparation time for speakers during the debate.

In the British format, a proposition team opens the debate and an opposition team closes the debate. The speeches are in this order:

First proposition, first speaker

First opposition, first speaker

First proposition, second speaker

First opposition, second speaker

Second proposition, first speaker

Second opposition, first speaker

Second proposition, second speaker

Second opposition, second speaker

Points of information play a particularly important role in this format and are available after the first minute and before the final minute of all eight speeches. Because each speaker only has a single stand on the floor, it is important for each debater to make his or her presence known at other portions of the debate. For example, the opening speakers will not be heard for the remaining 45 minutes of the debate if they do not successfully make points of information during their opponents' speeches. Likewise, the latter speakers will not play a role in establishing the debate's foundational issues if they fail to make informational points at an early stage of the debate.

Managing points of information is a particular challenge in this format. Because of the importance of making points, debaters are more likely to make them in the British than the American format. In addition, a speaker holding the floor faces four respondents, rather than two, able to make points of information. It is very challenging to present organized, winning material and at the same time manage the distractions and interruptions from the other side.

As in the four-person format, there may be one or more than one judge for the debate. In the American format, each judge deliberates in private to decide the outcome of the debate. The team that does not win the debate loses the debate. The judge also provides individual marks for each of the four debaters. Because there is private deliberation and voting by judges, it is necessary to have an **odd number** of judges for each debate.

However, in the British format, judicial decision making is by consensus, much the way juries decide trials. After their deliberation at the conclusion of the debate, the judge or judging panel issues a single decision. The debate decision ranks the four teams in the round of debate from first to fourth places. Each judge also provides individual speaker marks for the participants. It is possible to have an odd number or even number of judges for each debate.

In order to succeed, debate teams must not only defeat the two teams on the opposing side but must also outperform the debate team assigned to the same side of the motion. Teams do not coordinate information or otherwise work together during preparation time in these debates. Each team prepares individually and must show some loyalty to the team on its side while at the same time showing that they are superior to that team. Debaters are penalized for failing to support the debate team on their side of the motion.

We will discuss the differences in speaker roles between the American and British debate formats. Many of the roles, particularly for speakers opening and closing the debate, are nearly identical to speaker roles in the American form. As in the American format, after the opening proposition case, British format debaters advance new issues and challenge the ideas of their opponents.

First speaker, first proposition   The first speaker in the British debate format has a nearly identical role to the first speaker for the proposition in the American format. The speaker interprets the motion and makes a convincing case for it. The case should provide opportunities for serious debate and for argument extension. (See the role of the first speaker, second proposition, below.)

First speaker, first opposition   Same as the first speaker, opposition, in the American format.

Second speaker, first proposition   This is extraordinarily similar to the second speaker, proposition, in the American format. This speaker should amplify the arguments of her partner and initiate at least one new argument in the debate.

Second speaker, first opposition   Same as the second speaker, opposition, in the American format. This speaker should amplify the arguments of her partner and initiate at least one new argument in the debate.

First speaker, second proposition   At last, a serious point of departure between the British and American formats. The second proposition team's first speaker must establish an *extension* of the case presented by the first proposition team's opening speaker. The case extension may not simply repeat the ideas of the opening speaker of the debate, nor may the speaker offer yet another example for the same argument. While showing loyalty to the opening proposition team, the first speaker of the second proposition team must subtly shift the discussion to a new area of investigation or amplify an opening team's examples, themes or underlying assumptions. This speaker then follows the form of the opening speaker, establishing a case for the motion. The case includes three or four main lines of argument constituting a logical proof for the second proposition team's interpretation of the motion.

Because the second proposition team shares a side of the motion with the first proposition team, it is important for the second team to offer a position that is consistent with the initial argument claims. To do otherwise, that is, to undermine the arguments of the opening proposition team, is to figuratively stab colleagues in the back. When this undermining occurs, the second proposition team is said to "knife" the first team. "Knifing" is almost always held against a second proposition team. It is so disfavored by judges that it is difficult for a team engaging in the practice to receive a rank higher than fourth place. Consider that parliamentary debate's roots lie in governing bodies, which frequently involve coalition governments of more than one party. When one party rejects the claims of its supposed partner, it is in effect disbanding the coalition.

First speaker, second opposition   Same as the first speaker, opposition, in the American format. This speaker must rebut the case presented by the second proposition team's first speaker.

Second speaker, second proposition   This speech is very much like a rebuttal in the American format. The speaker summarizes the debate, making the necessary points for a winning conclusion for her team.

Second speaker, second opposition   Same as the second speaker, opposition, in the American format, or second speaker, proposition, in the British format.

Appendix 3: Logical Fallacies

Logical Fallacies

A logical fallacy is simply a failure of logic. When we say that an argument is *fallacious*, what we mean is that the argument is a logical failure. Debaters need to learn to spot logical fallacies. The ability to point out holes in your opponents' reasoning is a very powerful tool in debates. Many of us hear and agree with faulty arguments all the time. In fact, many arguments that are fallacious or otherwise fatally flawed are widely accepted. The argument type we call the *slippery slope*, for example, appears repeatedly in public policy speeches. Once you understand more about logical fallacies and learn to identify them, you may be surprised at how often they turn up in commonly accepted arguments.

- **Appeal to force**. This fallacy occurs when you tell someone that some kind of misfortune will happen to them if they don't agree with you, e.g., "If you don't believe that our utopia is ideal, then I guess we'll have to release the hounds."

- **Appeal to the crowd**. Sometimes called the "bandwagon" or "*ad populum*" (Latin for "to the people"), this fallacy occurs when the arguer contends you will be left out of the crowd if you don't agree: "All of the cool kids smoke cigarettes these days."

- **Appeal to ignorance**. When an argument has not been disproved, it does not therefore follow that it is true. Yet the appeal to ignorance works a surprisingly large amount of the time, particularly in conspiracy theories: "No one has yet proven that aliens have *not* landed on Earth; therefore, our theory about ongoing colonization should be taken seriously."

- **Appeal to emotions**. This fallacy is what it sounds like. Speakers routinely try to play on the emotions of the crowd instead of making real arguments. "I know this national missile defense plan has its detractors, but won't someone *please* think of the children?"

- **Appeal to tradition**. Often a substitute for actual argument, the appeal to tradition happens when a speaker tries to justify her arguments by reference to habits, e.g., "We should continue to discriminate against the poor because that's what we've always done."

- **Appeal to authority**. While it is often appropriate and even necessary to cite credible sources to prove a point, the appeal to authority becomes fallacious when it is a substitute for reasoning or when the cited authority's credibility is dubious. "Well, I guess I'll buy this luxury car because nine out of ten dentists recommend it."

- **Ad hominem**. Sometimes, arguers will attack the person making the argument rather than the argument itself. This is an *ad hominem* (Latin for "to the man") attack, e.g., "I don't know how my opponent found the time to research this issue, since plainly he doesn't even have time to bathe."

- **Begging the question.** Begging the question occurs when the conclusion assumes what it tries to prove: "Of course he tried to fix the boxing match, since he was one of the people who stood to gain by fixing the boxing match."
- **Red herring.** An old favorite, the red herring happens when the arguer diverts attention to another issue and then draws a conclusion based on the diversion. "The candidate has a weak stand on education. Just look at what she says about foreign policy."
- **Hasty generalization.** This fallacy occurs when a conclusion is drawn based on a non-representative sample, e.g., "Most Americans oppose the war. Just ask these three peace demonstrators."
- **False cause, or "*post hoc, ergo propter hoc.*"** This fallacy is just what it sounds like. In the English, at least: "After this, therefore because of this." Sometimes, speakers will draw a faulty link between premises and a conclusion such that the link depends upon a causal connection that probably does not exist: "The sun rises every time I get out of bed. Therefore, by getting out of bed, I make the sun rise." It is important to remember that correlation does not imply causality, and neither does chronology imply causality.
- **Equivocation.** In this fallacy, the meaning of a critical term is changed through the course of an argument. Lewis Carroll in *Alice's Adventures Through the Looking Glass:* "'You couldn't have it if you **did** want it,' the Queen said. 'The rule is jam tomorrow and jam yesterday—but never Jam today' 'It must come sometimes to Jam today,' Alice objected. 'No, it can't,' said the Queen. 'It's jam every *other* day: today isn't every *other* day, you know.'"
- **Slippery slope.** One of the more popular logical fallacies, particularly in political circles, the slippery slope argument contends that an event will set off an uncontrollable chain reaction when there is no real reason to expect that reaction to occur. "If we start regulating carbon dioxide, the next thing you know the proposition team will be telling you what to eat for breakfast."
- **Weak analogy.** While argument by analogy is a very strong, common form of argumentation, the weak analogy fallacy occurs when an argument's conclusion rests on a nonexistent similarity between two examples, e.g., "Well, if it worked in a college term paper, it'll work in American foreign policy."
- **False dichotomy.** This fallacy occurs when the premise of an argument presents two alternatives, and suggests that it is impossible to do both, e.g., "It's either free school lunches or nuclear war;" "Either you let me go to the concert or my life will be ruined."
- **Fallacy of composition.** This fallacy happens when the conclusion of an argument depends on falsely transferring some characteristic from the parts to the whole: "Jake likes fish. He also likes chocolate. Therefore, he would like chocolate covered fish."
- **Fallacy of division.** The opposite of the fallacy of composition, the fallacy of division occurs when the conclusion of an argument depends on the faulty attribution of a characteristic from the whole to its parts: "The average American family has 2.3 children. The Jones family is an average American family. Therefore, the Jones family has 2.3 children."

- **Complex question**. Used in questioning, this fallacy occurs when a single question is really two or more questions: "Do you still cheat on your tests?"; "How long have you been smoking banana leaves?"
- **Scarecrow**. Formerly called the "straw man" fallacy, this kind of argument is a diversionary tactic where a speaker exaggerates or mischaracterizes his or her opponent's position and then proceeds to attack this caricature. This is a common tactic used in advertising campaigns: "Worried about your family getting leprosy? Better use our disinfectant."
- **Scapegoating**. This fallacy is similar to the scarecrow fallacy. The term "scapegoating" comes to us from the Judeo-Christian tradition. In the Old Testament book of Leviticus, Aaron confessed the sins of his people over a goat and sent the goat away, thereby absolving the sins of his community. In contemporary rhetorical theory, we say someone is scapegoating when he or she attributes a current situation to a group of people who may or may not be responsible for the problem. Some politicians are notorious for scapegoating minority groups for broad social problems. In America, for example, illegal immigrants are often convenient scapegoats for budget or social services problems.
- **Non sequiturs**. The Latin phrase *non sequitur* means "it does not follow." Thus, reasoning that is *non sequitur* is composed of arguments that are irrelevant to the topic. As a debater, you should insist that your opponents' reasoning stick strictly to the topic(s) at hand.
- **Common cause**. Often, two things will occur together so regularly that you are tempted to assume that they are cause and effect. However, sometimes those two events are the cause of a third factor, which must be taken into consideration to make the reasoning complete. For example, noticing that there are many dead fish in a river and that the river's water is poisoned, you might conclude that the dead fish caused the poisonous water. If you drew this conclusion, you might miss that an industry is dumping into the water, and has caused both the pollution and the dead fish.

Appendix 4: Resources

Sample American Parliamentary Debate Ballot

Name of Tournament_____

Round Number _____

Location of Debate _____

Judge's Name_____

Motion _____

Proposition

Team Name or Code_____

Speaker 1 _____ Points _____ Rank _____

Speaker 2 _____ Points _____ Rank _____

Opposition

Team Name or Code_____

Speaker 1 _____ Points _____ Rank _____

Speaker 2 _____ Points _____ Rank _____

The decision is awarded to the (prop/opp) _____

Indicate low-point win_____

Judge's Name and Affiliation _____

Reason for Decision:

Sample British Parliamentary Debate Ballot

Name of Tournament_____

Motion _____

First Proposition Team	*First Opposition Team*
Rank (circle) 1 2 3 4	Rank (circle) 1 2 3 4
Speaker 1_____ Score____	Speaker 1_____ Score____
Speaker 2_____ Score____	Speaker 2_____ Score____
Second Proposition Team	*Second Opposition Team*
Rank (circle) 1 2 3 4	Rank (circle) 1 2 3 4
Speaker 1_____ Score____	Speaker 1_____ Score____
Speaker 2_____ Score____	Speaker 2_____ Score____

Judges' Names _____

Tournament Director's Responsibilities

Before the Tournament

Announcing the tournament
- Acquire contact information
- Arrange for a date and site
- Draft an invitation

Information for tournament guests
- Schedule
- Transportation information
- Lodging information
- Meal information

Tournament operations
- Tabulating Room Staff
- Tabulating Hardware and Software
- Tournament Office Supplies
- Guest judging

Tournament materials
- Registration packet
- Awards
- Ballots
- Instructional Information
- Topic Writing and Selection

Ancillary information
- Last Minute Travel Information
- Harassment and Legal Information
- Videotaping and Broadcast Preparation
- Confirmations

During the Tournament

Opening events
- Registration
- Instructional Sessions

Tournament operations
- Announcements
- Tabulations
- Services: Meals, Lodging, Entertainment, Awards
- Troubleshooting

After the Tournament

Documentation
- Ballots and Tabulation Results
- Tournament Information
- Review and Evaluation

Publicity and Conclusion

Websites

Debate Support

American Parliamentary Debate Association
http://www.apdaweb.org/
This is the official site of the American Parliamentary Debate Association, a student-administered competitive debate organization sponsored by parliamentary debate societies at more than 40 colleges and universities, primarily on the East Coast. The site includes rules, tournament schedules, and contact information.

Australasian Intervarsity Debating Association
http://www.debating.net/aida/
Comprehensive information on the Australasian format, guides to effective practice, and tournament information are available on this official site for 3-on-3 debating in Australia and the South Pacific.

British Debate (English Speaking Union)
http://www.britishdebate.com/
The English Speaking Union hosts this site, which provides substantial information about debating in Britain and Ireland.

The site includes contact information, tournament calendars, tournament results, guides to debating and adjudication, and links to debate organizations throughout the world.

Canadian University Society for Intercollegiate Debate
http://www.cusid.ca/
The virtual home of the organization administering university debating in Canada, the CUSID site provides tournament information and discussion forums for debating in Canada and at the North American Championship (administered with the American Parliamentary Debate Association.)

Debate Central
http://debate.uvm.edu/
A comprehensive site on debate formats worldwide, with information on parliamentary debate, American policy debate, Lincoln-Douglas debate, Karl Popper debate, and a number of other formats. There are links to debating listservs, national debate organizations, and individual debate

programs. The site includes a video lecture series on parliamentary (American and British formats) and policy (American format for high school and college) debating. Sample video debates are also included on the site.

Estonian Debate Society
http://www.debate.ee/English/EngIndex.html
This is the home site of the Estonian Debate Society, an NGO. The site provides support information for effective participation in parliamentary debate, Karl Popper debate, public speaking, and mock trial, including dates, locations, and contacts for events in Estonia.

European Debating Council
http://www.debating.net/EUCouncil/
The European Debating Council (EDC) governs the European Championship. The site provides information on the parent organization (EDC) and its constitution. It also provides site information, rules, tournament results, and motions for the European Championship.

International Debate Education Association
http://www.idebate.org/
The virtual home of the International Debate Education Association (IDEA), an international NGO sponsoring debate and youth education programs, the site unites more than 70,000 secondary school and college teachers and students from 27 countries.

The site includes information on debating practice (primarily the Karl Popper format), youth democracy promotion and civic education, language training, and critical communication skills. It features the debate reference site, Debatabase, a searchable argument database on political, philosophical, economic, social, and cultural affairs.

The website contains information on IDEA's international conferences and publications, member tournaments and workshops, listservs, and resources for teachers and students. Much of the material is available in English and Russian.

Japan Parliamentary Debate Association
http://www.asahi-net.or.jp/~cj3m-lbky/parlidebate.html
A resource for parliamentary debate for secondary school and university students, the JPDA site includes debate rules, guides for tournament organization, and contact information and links to debate organizations in Japan and Korea.

National Parliamentary Debate Association
http://www.bethel.edu/Majors/Communication/npda/home.html
The official site of the largest parliamentary debate organization in the United States, it lists organizational rules, membership forms, sample motions, and competitive tournament results.

World Debating Web Page
http://www.debating.net/flynn/colmmain.htm
Comprehensive information on international debating, including debate and adjudication rules for the World Universities Championship, world championship registration and results links, and links to national organizations, listservs, debate clubs, online and video sample debates, and news and tournament invitations.

Tournament Software

Baylor University
http://www.baylor.edu/~Richard_Edwards/Software.html
Richard Edwards, Baylor University
Debate Tab Room for the Mac
Debate Tab Room for PC

Wheaton College
ftp://ftp.wheaton.edu/pub/debate/
Gary Larson, Wheaton College
Smart Tournament Administrator (for Windows)

International Debate Education Association
http://www.idebate.org/files/easy.asp
Marjan Stojnev, International Debate Education Association
IDEA Easy Tournament Administration (for Windows)

Appendix 5: Argumentation and Debate Glossary

ad hominem An attack on the advocate of an argument rather than on the content of the argument itself.

Ad populum An appeal to the people or other majoritarian sentiment as the basis for a claim.

advantage The claimed benefits of the proposition team's plan.

affirmative The side in a debate that supports the resolution.

agent counterplan A counterplan that argues that the plan that the proposition team would implement through one agent of action should instead be implemented through another agent of action.

agent of action The persons or institutions responsible for implementation of policy directives.

alternate causality A circumstance in which more than a single cause may result in a particular effect.

analogy A similarity or likeness between things in some circumstances or effects, when the things are otherwise entirely different.

appeal to tradition A fallacy of reasoning; an appeal to historical behavior as the basis for continuing to act in a certain manner.

apriorism The claim of a presumptive truth or condition.

argument A reason or reasons offered for or against a proposition or measure.

assertion An unsupported statement; a conclusion that lacks evidence for support.

audience The listening, reading, or viewing individual or group reached by a performative or communicative act.

authority A position of power, credibility, or special function, attained by qualities of experience, insight, and skill.

backlash A response to campaigns for social or political change, involving efforts to discredit and undermine that change.

ballot 1) Literally, the piece of paper filled out at the end of a debate by a judge that says who won, who lost, and what speaker points. 2) Figuratively, what debaters are trying to win in each debate, so that they can be said to "collect" ballots through the course of a tournament, i.e., "We have three ballots, so I think we're going to *clear.*"

begging the question An argumentative fallacy offering repetition of a claim as a proof for a claim.

bias A prejudiced attitude on the part of the source of evidence quoted in a debate. It is often argued that when sources are biased, their testimony is questionable and sometimes unacceptable.

bracket The arrangement of teams in elimination rounds whereby teams debate each other according to seeding.

break To advance to the *elimination rounds* of a tournament. (See also *clear.*)

break rounds Preliminary rounds in which a team's ability to *clear* and advance to elimination rounds is at stake. At most tournaments, teams will need a certain record to advance to the elimination rounds, such as 3-2 or 5-3.

brief The outline of an argument, including claims, supportive reasoning, and evidence.

brink An element of a disadvantage which claims that the policy action of the plan is a sufficient condition to alter current institutions in a way to produce a dangerous or counterproductive consequence. A *brink* is the point at which a disadvantage begins to happen: It may be said that the plan would push us "over the brink" into the abyss of the *impact.*

burden of proof The responsibility of the person, upon introducing an argument, to provide sufficient reasoning and detail for the argument that the opponent is obliged to take the issue into consideration.

canon   A set of works described as essential for the national literary culture.

case   The proposition team's argument for the motion; usually a reference to the arguments presented in the opening constructive speech by the proposition team.

case list   A list kept by a squad and by individual teams that tracks what plans and advantages are being run by other teams.

case-side   Issues that relate to the stock or core issues of a proposition team's case, including the demonstration of the ongoing nature of a problem (inherency), the qualitative and/or quantitative measure of a problem (significance), and the availability of a potential remedy for a problem (solvency). Also referred to as "on-case" arguments.

causal principles   An expression of multiple principles, such as that every event has a cause, that the same cause must have the same effect, and that the cause must have at least as much reality as the effect.

civil society   The nongovernmental aspects of modern society, e.g., religious, economic, and voluntary associational relations.

clash   The direct and indirect opposition between the arguments made by each side in a debate.

clear   "to clear" To advance to the *elimination rounds* of a tournament. (See also *break*.)

closure   A sense of formal completeness or clear outcome.

comparative advantage   An argument, usually employed by the proposition team, that says that even if the proposition's case does not completely solve the harm, that case is still advantageous compared to the status quo.

competitiveness   An argument for evaluating the legitimacy of a counterplan in formal debate. The presence of the counterplan should force a choice for the decision maker between the policies advocated by the plan and the counterplan. Competition is the quality of a policy that makes it a reason to reject another policy.

Classically, competition was measured solely by means of *mutual exclusivity*. Now, however, competition is largely defined in terms of *net benefits* so that when we say a counterplan is *competitive* or *net beneficial*, we mean that it is better alone than the plan or any combination of the whole plan and all or part of the counterplan. (See also *permutations, net benefits, counterplan, mutual exclusivity*.)

concede   To admit that an opponent is right about a certain argument or set of arguments. (See also *grant*.)

conditional   Arguments advanced in debates that may be dropped at any time without repercussion to their advocates. Usually this phrase is used in the context of *conditional counterplans*, which can be dropped if undesirable without forfeiture of the debate.

consequentialism   A doctrine that the moral rightness of an act or policy depends entirely on its outcome or consequences.

constructive speeches   The foundational, opening speeches of a formal debate, in which the participants establish the major arguments that will be subject to analysis, refutation, and revision in the debate's subsequent stages.

consultation counterplan   A counterplan that argues that another relevant actor should be consulted as to whether or not the proposition team's plan should be implemented. That alternate actor is therefore given a kind of veto power over the adoption of the proposition team's plan. If the alternate actor says yes, the plan is adopted. If, on the other hand, the alternate actor says no, the plan is not adopted.

contentions   Also known as "observations," these are the outlined arguments of the opening proposition constructive speech.

contextual definitions   A defining interpretation of the resolution that incorporates many or all of the terms of the topic.

cooption   The influence of outside parties hampering an agent's efforts to carry out his instructions.

counterplan: 1) *Noun* A policy proposed by the opposition. The policy must offer a reason to reject the affirmative plan in the debate. Generally, the counterplan will either try to solve the case harms in a more beneficial way, e.g., by "avoiding" (not linking to) disadvantages accrued by the proposition's plan. Traditionally, it was thought that counterplans had to be both non-topical and competitive. These days, topical counterplans are more accepted as the emphasis shifts to *net benefits* and policy comparison and away from abstract theoretical concerns. Counterplans may also have *advantages*, which are similar to affirmative advantages in that they are benefits accrued by the counterplan. 2) *Verb* To run a counterplan.

counterposition See *counterplan*.

criteria Standards for decision making in a debate.

criticism Any or all of the activities of evaluation, description, classification, or interpretation of language and text.

critiquing This is a method of criticism in formal debate that focuses on the language, reasoning, underlying assumptions, expert testimony, interpretations, and proofs of the opponent. The argument form is often referred to as a "critique" or "kritik," meaning a type of argument that uncovers the fundamental assumptions of a team, case, word, or argument, and uses criticism of those fundamental assumptions to win the debate.

cross-examination The question-and-answer period following constructive speeches in formal policy debates.

debatability A standard, usually found in topicality debates, that says that as long as a definition provides fair grounds for debate, it should be accepted.

debate format The order of speeches and the speaking time limits for each speech.

decision-making theory The investigation of the rational decision processes of persons and institutions in government and politics.

deductive reasoning The act of reasoning from known principle to an unknown,

from the general to the specific.

delay counterplan A counterplan that suggests that the judge or audience withhold implementation of the proposition team's plan until a specific time or condition named by the opposition team.

deontology The view that duty is a primary moral notion and that at least some of our duties do not depend on any value that may result in fulfilling them. In some circumstances, the justification of duties is an appeal to absolute rule, e.g., an opposition to the taking of life.

disadvantage (also known as a "DA" or "dis-ad") The bad thing that will happen when a plan goes into effect. In formal debates, opposition teams run disadvantages when they want to show that adoption of the government's plan will lead to far greater undesirable than desirable consequences. To win a debate on a disadvantage, the opposition team must generally prove at least three basic things: that the disadvantage *links* to the plan; that it is *unique* to the plan; and that the *impact* of the disadvantage is sufficiently undesirable to *outweigh* the advantages.

disco A charming, somewhat old-fashioned term used to describe a debate strategy where a team takes advantage of the interrelationship among arguments in the debate. Usually, one team will strategically *concede* large portions of their opponents' arguments, hoping that this tactic will allow the debate to re-focus favorably on their arguments. Often this strategy is used to capitalize on mistakes or contradictory arguments made by the other team.

dispositional counterplan A counterplan which, if proven disadvantageous or noncompetitive, can be dismissed from consideration.

double turn In answering a disadvantage, a double turn takes place when a team argues a *link turn* ("You produce that problem") AND an *impact turn* ("That problem is actually a benefit") on the same disadvantage. When this happens, the proposition is saying that supporting their side of the debate would stop a good thing.

effects topicality A type of topicality standard that contends that the proposition's case is only topical by *effect* rather than by mandate. In these debates, it is often said that the proposition has failed to present a *prima facie* case or that they have *mixed burdens*—in this case, the burdens of solvency and topicality.

elimination rounds The single-elimination rounds that occur after the preliminary rounds at most tournaments. These rounds are usually *seeded*, using a *bracket* whereby the top seed (the team with the highest preliminary record) debates the bottom seed, etc.

empirical evidence Evidence or proof that is based on past examples or statistical studies.

empiricism Any theory emphasizing experience rather than reason as the basis for justifiable decision making.

essentialism The belief that there are essential features, or universal foundations, of human nature.

evidence Expert testimony, in the form of quotations from literature, broadcasts, the Internet, etc., used to support a debater's reasoning. Broadly, evidence is also reasoning used to prove a point.

example A sample that is selected to show the qualities or characteristics of a larger group.

extensions Arguments that occur in response to opponents' arguments, extensions elaborate upon and develop the original arguments.

externalities The costs and benefits of economic activity that are not incurred or enjoyed by the person or group performing it.

extra-topicality Government plans that contain planks or actions not specifically called for by the motion.

fallacy A mistaken inference or an erroneous conclusion based on faulty reasoning.

false dichotomy Also known as a *false dilemma*, an argument fallacy that falsely analyzes a circumstance as a choice between only two possible alternatives.

federalism 1) A political concept, critical in the framing of the Constitution of the USA and elsewhere, that divides labor between the states and the federal government. 2) A disadvantage, sometimes run in conjunction with the *states counterplan*, which usually argues that the proposition team's plan is an abuse of federal power, i.e., it violates the federalist doctrine, and that is bad.

feminism Any of the varieties of analysis of the exploitation and manipulation of women; some of these analyses provide proposals for social reform and transformation.

fiat A term used to describe the process that allows debate of the plan as if it were already adopted.

flow A system of note taking for debates that includes systematized guides for multiple speakers and tracking multiple issues.

flow sheet Also known as *flow*, the transcription of a debate; the notes used by debate participants to track arguments from speech to speech.

funding plank The part of the plan naming or listing those sources from which the plan will receive its funding.

generic arguments Arguments, usually used by the opposition, that are general and can be made to apply to a wide range of cases or plans.

grant out of To concede some of the other team's arguments in order to back off of a position a debater had previously taken. For example, an opposition speaker might concede the proposition team's "no link" argument to render their own disadvantage irrelevant.

hasty generalization A claim that an example, or set of examples, is insufficient to prove a more generalized proposition.

impact Most generally, the consequence of an idea that is presented in a debate. The consequence may be expressed in terms of the qualitative or quantitative significance of an issue or the role that an idea will play in the outcome of the debate. Typically, impacts are the bad or good events that happen as a result of an affirmative case, counterplan, or disadvantages.

individualism An understanding of human social life through the behavior of individuals. As the basic unit of society, individuals (not groups or nations) have rights that serve as the basis for moral reasoning.

inductive reasoning The act of reasoning from the specific to the general.

inherency 1) An explanation of the reason or reasons for the failure of current decision makers to make policy moves in the direction of implementation of the plan. In formal debates, the issue of inherency functions to establish the probability of unique advantages. 2) The reason why someone is not doing something about a plan right now; the cause of a problem's existence.

invisible hand An expression by Scot economist Adam Smith to describe his belief that the actions of individuals in a free marketplace taken for their own economic benefit are guided in a manner to provide benefits for the society as a whole.

irony A mode of expression in which one thing is said and the opposite is meant.

jargon Specialized or technical language. In formal debate, jargon describes the use of terms not readily discernible to a lay audience, e.g., "fiat," "competitiveness," "effects topicality," "off-case," "permutation," etc.

judging philosophy A method or practice a judge uses to decide the outcome of a round. Although few judges have explicit philosophies or ironclad *paradigms* anymore, it is possible to guess their judging philosophy through careful observation and experience.

lay judge A term applied to persons who judge debates but who are not formally trained in debate (i.e., are not coaches or debaters or former debaters). Treat with respect.

limiting standards Any of the evaluations of the definitions of the terms of a formal debate motion that establish a hierarchical system and demonstrate a preference for precise, conservative, and "limited" interpretations of the terms.

Lincoln-Douglas debate A debate format in which two individuals debate each other, using a time format of 6-3-7-3-4-6-3 (six minute opening affirmative constructive speech, three minute cross-examination, seven minute negative constructive speech, three minute cross-examination, four minute affirmative rebuttal, six minute negative rebuttal, three minute closing affirmative rebuttal).

linearity The ratio of the degree of policy action to a degree of beneficial or undesirable consequences.

link A causal relationship. In formal debates, a link is the relationship of one's argument to the opponent's position and the internal chain of reasoning in a complex argument. More specifically, links are how disadvantages or advantages apply to an proposition team's case. Note: Since disadvantages often employ chains of causal reasoning, we may speak of different levels of link. An "initial link" is the one that applies directly to the proposition team's plan or advantages, while the "internal links" are links in reasoning or causality that bridge the gap between the initial link and the impact.

Marxist criticism An approach to criticism that relates literature to the political, economic, and social circumstances of its production.

metaphor A reference to one object in terms of another, so that the features of the second are transferred to the first. Metaphor is claimed to be the central process by which humans construct the world through language.

mixing burdens A term from the antiquated concept of stock issues, that describes when a proposition team uses one stock issue to prove another. This tactic is said to be unfair because the proposition team has to prove each issue independently. The only way this term is currently used is in debates about *effects topicality*, where the opposition may argue that a proposition team is using their solvency to prove they are topical. This is said to be bad because the proposition's case should have to be a topical example in order to allow the opposition a fair chance to clash with the proposition.

multiple causations The claim that no one factor can account for the outcome of a particular event and that there are many factors that lead to its occurrence; these factors interact and cannot be considered independently in assessing the outcome of a behavior.

mutual exclusivity A claim that it is impossible for the proposition team's plan and the counterplan to coexist and an historical test for the competitiveness of a counterplan in formal debates. For example, an proposition team's plan that calls for the USA to increase and modernize its NATO forces and a counterplan that calls for the USA to withdraw from NATO are said to be "mutually exclusive."

narrative A presentation that has the qualities and form of a story.

narrative fidelity The plausibility or credibility of a story, how likely the elements of a story are true.

natural law A foundation for human law, natural law refers to embedded principles in human society or the rules of conduct or innate moral sense inherent in the relations of human beings and discoverable by reason or recognized by historical developments. It is contrasted with statutory or common law.

natural rights A theory of human rights that argues that rights arise from the nature of human and social existence.

negative The side of a formal debate that opposes the affirmative's proofs for the resolution.

net benefits One standard of counterplan competition. A counterplan is said to be "net beneficial" when it alone is a policy option superior to the whole plan and all or any part of the counterplan; in other words, the counterplan forces a choice between the policies advanced by the affirmative and negative teams in the debate.

nihilism A theory that rejects traditional values, such as the belief in knowledge,

metaphysical truth, and the foundation of ethical principles.

normal means A term usually applied to proposition team plans used to describe the specifics of how the plan might be funded, implemented, or enforced. For example, a team's plan might say at the end: "Funding and enforcement through normal means." Often what is meant is: "However a plan like ours might normally be done, that is how this plan will be done." Proposition teams usually say they employ this phrase to avoid confusion; however, it serves a strategic purpose in plan design. Do not assume that there is general agreement over what "normal means" means. In the case of funding, for example, there are many ways that governments fund their programs (borrowing, re-allocation, new spending, etc.).

objectivism One or more theories that claim that a given subject matter contains objects existing independently of human beliefs and attitudes.

off-case In a formal debate, the opposition argumentation (in limited circumstances, supplemental proposition team argumentation) that does not directly refute the foundational arguments of the case proper, i.e., the first affirmative constructive arguments. "Off-case" generally refers to the forms of indirect refutation by the negative, e.g., topicality arguments, counterplans, disadvantages, and critiques. This term used to mean the arguments made in a debate that linked to the *plan*, as opposed to those that linked to the *case*. These days, it refers to arguments that are being debated on pieces of paper other than those devoted to the affirmative case. These arguments should be labeled as "off-case" arguments in the opposition speaker's roadmap, where she or he will say something like "I'm going to present two 'off-case' arguments, and then I'll be debating the proposition team's advantage and solvency."

off-case flow The notes transcribing the off-case arguments.

on-case In a formal debate, the argumentation that is directed to the foundational or stock issues of the affirmative case, i.e., the issues of inherency, significance, and solvency. (See also *case-side.*)

opportunity cost   The sacrifice made when selecting one policy over another.

paradigm   A systematic and rational appraisal of debate that identifies the preferred features of the event and suggests models of analysis and deliberation. In contemporary policy debate, the most common paradigmatic approaches have included policy making, hypothesis testing, gaming, and performance. Although paradigms are usually conflated with judging philosophies, debaters can and often do have paradigms. (See also *judging philosophies.*)

paradox   A contradictory statement from which a valid inference may be drawn.

parliamentary debate   A format for extemporaneous debate. Parliamentary debate involves two-person or three-person teams. Formats include two or four competing teams in a single debate. Debate is on a topic announced some 15 to 20 minutes before each debate. Limited parliamentary procedures (points of information or other parliamentary points) are used in the contests, varying by tournament guideline.

permutation   A test of the competitiveness of a counterplan, a permutation is an argument that explains how the plan and counterplan are complementary. More practically, a permutation is a type of argument used by proposition teams to illustrate the noncompetitiveness of counterplans. Proposition teams argue that if it is possible to imagine the coexistence of the plan and the counterplan, and if such an imagined example would be net beneficial, then the counterplan does not provide a reason to reject the proposition team's plan. (See also *net beneficial.*)

philosophical competition   A now-defunct standard of competition for counterplans that argues that since the two plans are philosophically different, they are exclusive of one another.

policy debate   A format of formal debate that calls for implementation of a policy directive or course of action. The common format for policy debate involves team debate with constructive speeches of eight or nine minutes and rebuttal speeches of five or six minutes for each of the participants. There is usually a three-minute cross-examination period following each of the constructive speeches.

policy making   A paradigm that says debate rounds should be evaluated from the perspective of a pseudo-legislator weighing the advantages and disadvantages of two conflicting policy systems. (See also *paradigm.*)

post hoc ergo propter hoc: Literally, "after this [fact], therefore because of this [fact]." A fallacy of reasoning that presumes a specific causal relation for two or more conditions because one of the events followed the other event.

pragmatism   The claim that the meanings of propositions lie in their possible effects on our experiences; a test of the validity of concepts by their practical effects.

preemption or **preempt**   An argument designed to respond to another argument that has not been made, but which is anticipated.

preparation time   Also known as "prep time," a period of time given to individuals or teams to prepare their speeches during a debate.

present system   A description of current governmental, corporate, social, and cultural institutions or policies.

presumption   A corollary of burden of proof, the argument that accords an advantage to the attitudes, institutions, and practices that currently exist. In other words, "presumption" is the assumption that a system should be kept unless there is a clear reason to change it. Although this term comes from law, in debate it is usually understood to mean that the judge should presume for the status quo unless the proposition team provides a clear and convincing reason to change. (See also *burden of proof, status quo.*)

prima facie   Literally, "at first appearance," the responsibility of the advocate of a debate resolution to offer a proof for the proposition in the opening presentation, such that an opponent is obliged to answer the major elements of the case proper.

procedural arguments The arguments that establish the way the elements of a debate will be conducted; determinative issues that are contested in a debate regarding debate practice and the method of appropriate decision making and distinguished from the substantive issues of the proposition.

proof That which reduces uncertainty and increases the probable truth of a claim. Evidence is transformed into proof through the use of reasoning, which demonstrates how and to what extent the claim is believable. Proof is, of course, a relative concept, ranging from probability to certainty.

proposition Also known as a "topic" or a "motion," a subject to be discussed or a statement to be upheld. Usually, a proposition is a fact, value, or policy that the proposition team is obligated to support. The motion is generally understood to focus debate.

rationalism A theory advancing reasoning as the basis for making moral judgments and acquiring knowledge.

rebuttal Refutation of an opponent's argument; also, the summary speeches of a debate.

reductio ad absurdum Literally, a "reduction to absurdity," a proof of a proposition by showing that its opposite is absurd or a disproof of a proposition by showing that its logical conclusion is impossible or absurd.

refutation The overthrowing of an argument, opinion, testimony, etc. Refutation is a direct and specific response to an opponent's argument.

resolution See *proposition*.

sandbag To preserve important parts of an argument for use in a later speech.

scarecrow Formerly known as a "straw man," this is a fallacious argument that identifies a weak argument of an opponent and falsely characterizes all of the opponent's arguments as equally deficient.

scenario An outline of a real or imag-ined case study of a proposed course of action. Usually, a scenario is a picture, explained through specific examples, of what would occur if an advantage or disadvantage were to happen. (See also *story*.)

scouting The practice of knowing what arguments are being made by other teams, scouting is necessary for adequate preparation. Scouting includes, but is not limited to, keeping a case list. (See also *case list*.)

second line Additional evidence for presentation in rebuttals or constructive extensions.

self-fulfilling prophecy The principle that events occur as anticipated, not because one is able to predict a potential effect, but rather because one will behave in a manner that will inexorably produce the effect.

self-serving bias The claim that people will tend to deny responsibility for failure and take credit for success.

severance permutation A permutation that contains only part of (rather than all of) the proposition team's plan.

shift To abandon an original position and take up a different one.

significance An expression of qualitative or quantitative dimension of a problem or condition; often listed as a "stock issue" in formal debate. Traditionally used as a measure of the need claimed by the affirmative or proposition team.

slippery slope Widely recognized as a logical *fallacy*, this type of argument says that a particular course of action sets in motion an unstoppable chain of events whereby an undesirable result becomes inevitable. One example of this argument is often made in debates about assisted suicide—"If we allow some so-called mercy killings, what's to stop the state from calling other bigoted policies mercy killings as well?" (See also *fallacy*.)

snowball An argument very similar to the *slippery slope*, which states that a small action can become much bigger through time. Imagine a snowball rolling downhill, collecting more snow as it goes.

social contract The duty to obey the government and the law and the right of the government to make the law arises from the contractual relationship, explicit or implied, between the government and the governed.

socialism   A variety of theories emphasizing that the social or collective nature of economic production serves as the justification for public action regarding the distribution of economic goods and services.

solvency   A stock issue that expresses the ability to successfully implement a suggested policy directive. Solvency is the ability of the affirmative plan or negative counterplan to solve the problem.

spread   The rapid introduction of multiple arguments in a formal debate.

standards   A hierarchy or ranking system to evaluate arguments presented in a debate, usually an evaluation of the merit of definitions of key terms of the resolution in a topicality argument. A set of rules that allows the judge to decide which argument is better. Usually employed in topicality debates or counterplan competition discussions.

states counterplan   A specific type of counterplan. Opposition teams often counterplan with sub-federal action, saying the 50 states (in the USA) or other provincial, decentralized governments would be a superior policy option. This counterplan is often run with net benefits such as the federalism disadvantage. These disadvantages, in order to be considered net benefits, would have to argue that federal action in the area of the plan was bad. Frequently, opposition teams running this counterplan will also claim that their policy is better suited to *solve* the affirmative harm area because states are better positioned (via efficiency, experimentation, enforcement, or whatever) than the federal government. (See also *counterplan, federalism, net benefits.*)

status quo   Literally, "the way things are." An understanding of current institutions and policies; the current state of affairs. Usually, the proposition team tries to prove that a world with their plan would be better than the status quo.

stock issues   The core elements of a log-

ical proof of an proposition case, including the key elements of inherency, significance, and solvency.

story   Debaters often use stories to prove their points. When a debater tells a *link story*, she or he is using narrative to explain how a link might play itself out in real life. In debate, stories and scenarios are concrete examples of more abstract concepts and arguments. Stories and scenarios make arguments specific and tangible. (See also *scenario.*)

study counterplan   A variety of generic counterplan that says that instead of acting in the specified area of the proposition or the proposition team's case, we should instead study the problem to find the most desirable course of action.

subpoints   Supporting points of arguments, often used to structure larger arguments.

take out   Any argument in refutation that undermines, or "takes out," an opponent's position; usually refers to an argument that eliminates the link or relevance of an opponent's argument.

text   Anything that signifies in any medium.

threshold   The degree of change necessary to precipitate a particular outcome; usually, the degree of change of a plan from current policy that will trigger undesirable consequences (disadvantages).

time frame   The amount of time it takes for something, usually an impact, to occur.

topicality   The issue that establishes the relation of the plan to the language of the topic; the proof that the proposition team's argument is a representation of the motion. Also known as "T."

turn   An argument that reverses the position of an opponent. Turns usually come in two kinds: *link turns* and *impact turns.* Link turns are arguments that attempt to reverse a link established by the other team. For example, an opposition team might run a disadvantage that said the plan hurt economic growth. The proposition might argue a *link turn* by saying that the proposition actually helped economic growth. An impact turn is an argument that tries to reverse an established impact. In this same example, the proposition team might argue that economic growth is actually bad, thereby *turning* the impact of the disadvantage. Also known as a "turnaround," or, historically, as "turning the tables."

uniqueness The claim that any benefit or cost is relevant to the advocacy of one side of a debate and can be used to decide favorably for that side or unfavorably against the other side. Uniqueness is the part of a disadvantage that proves that the proposition's plan and only the proposition's plan could trigger the impacts. The proposition team's advantages can also have a burden of uniqueness: If their harm is being solved now, then there is no unique need for the plan.

utilitarianism Any of a variety of consequentialist views that claim to maximize good or minimize evil.

values Principles, acts, customs, and qualities regarded as desirable by individuals or groups.

voting issues The arguments in a formal debate that are used to decide the ultimate outcome of the debate.

weighing the issues A comparative analysis of all the issues in a debate; an evaluation of their relative probability and impact conducted in order to determine which are most important, and thus, who wins. Rebuttalists usually weigh the issues, saying things like "Well, the plan may increase crime a little bit, but that's a small price to pay to safeguard our constitutional rights," thereby comparing the impact of the negative's crime disadvantage to the impact of their racial profiling advantage.

whole resolution An argument in formal debate suggesting that the proposition side must responsibly maintain a proof for all the possible interpretations, not a single instance or set of examples of the proposition.

workability A condition whereby a proposal could actually operate to solve a problem if implemented as legislation.

zero-sum Circumstances in which the interests of one or more parties are advanced at the direct and reciprocal expense of the interests of one or more other parties.

Appendix 6: Sample Debate Transcripts

The following is a sample of the opening speeches of the first proposition and first opposition speeches in an American parliamentary debate on the motion "This House should return the goods."

First Proposition Constructive: "Thank you very much. I believe that debate is a vigorous discourse in which we should discuss important and controversial issues. Keeping that in mind we turn to the topic: "This House should return the goods." We're talking about return of stolen cultural artifacts—art objects. We have a worldwide phenomenon of systematic theft by imperialist nations of cultural artifacts, and they are now being held with impunity. What we would advocate, on the side of the government, is that these artifacts should be returned when we can identify the rightful owners. And so, there are several reasons why we would advocate this issue. The first one is that we need to move beyond Western conceptions of law, because the current way the legal system works is that we allow countries to act tyrannically. We allow them to steal cultural artifacts, to use their political or physical power to prevent their return, and then, after a certain period of time, then they just say 'Well, now the statute of limitations gives us immunity on this issue, and we're no longer liable, and you can't have them back.' So what we need to do is create a specific exemption to the statute of limitations that would allow for the return of cultural artifacts. We've had this tyrannical action with the stealing of the Parthenon frieze, with Nazi art, with Native American artifacts, and we would advocate the return of these as well as other stolen cultural artifacts.

"It goes beyond that. What we also need to do is establish an appropriate relationship between states. The theft of cultural artifacts is a way to assert cultural dominance by one country over another country. In fact, this is what the British Museum is. The British Empire went out around the world and collected...well, collected is a nice way to say it. One might aptly say that they stole cultural artifacts from around the world and now their culture is able to subsume all other cultures—within their culture, they subsume all other cultures and that makes them the superior culture. And only with the return of these artifacts..." [Opposition speaker rises]

Opposition speaker: "Point of information."

First Proposition speaker: "Hold on, I'll get to you in one second. Only with the return of these artifacts can we start down the path of an equitable relationship between states. Yes?"

Opposition speaker: "What about cases where the rightful owner is unclear?"

First Proposition speaker: "Well, it's unclear, Andrea. It's unclear. As I said, we needed to return these when the rightful owner could be determined. Now, if the rightful owner can be determined, then it wouldn't be unclear. I think in the examples that I've given, such as the case of the Parthenon frieze, the ownership is very clear. There is historical record establishing what happened. In fact, Lord Elgin *sold* the Parthenon frieze to the British Museum. In the case of Nazi art, the Nazis were very organized. This caused many deaths, but also resulted in specific records about who stole what art. These records are just now becoming available. That's why we need to provide for an exemption within the statute of limitations to allow for the return of these artifacts. When we cannot establish a rightful owner we will, of course, not return them. That's an interesting point you bring up.

"Before I got off on that tangent of Andrea's very pointed question, I was talking about why we need to establish an equitable relationship between states. The reason why is if we can establish an equitable relationship between states, we can increase peace, stability, and harmony between nations. Just as if you can establish a more equitable relationship with your brother, you start fighting less if he gives you back all of the toys he has stolen. It's the same sort of idea on a larger and more important scale.

"The last important reason for the return of cultural artifacts is that we need to move beyond our own ideas about what the role of cultural artifacts actually is. What we need to do is look at an example of one cultural artifact in the USA, which would be the Declaration of Independence. What do we do with the Declaration of Independence?"

[Opposition speaker rises, crosses arms]

"We stick it under a piece of plastic laminate, we enclose it in gas, we put two armed guards beside it, and then we install a three million dollar video camera created by NASA's Jet Propulsion Laboratory to make sure that no one steals it. It must, by the way, be one hell of a camera for that price. In any case [gestures to standing opposition speaker], and you're going to get called on any minute now, so you can stop shifting around..."

[Standing opposition speaker appears to jog, almost imperceptibly, in place]

"We come to believe that anyone who *fails* to take these kinds of precautions is failing in their duty to respect cultural artifacts, just as [gestures to standing opposition speaker again] Nate is failing in his duty to respect me as a speaker by doing this sort of little dance [turns to opposition speaker]. But I'll take your question anyway."

Opposition speaker: "So what should we do with the Declaration of Independence? Everyone should be able to touch it and fold it and write on it? Tell me: What should we do?"

First Proposition speaker: "No, I'm saying that what we do with the Declaration of Independence is fine, but we should recognize, in fact, that this treatment frequently destroys the religious, cultural, or political significance that other, distinct cultures place upon their cultural perspective. Look at the Igbu tribe, who deliberately allow their objects to decay because they need to preserve the desire to re-create. In fact, they value deterioration as an aesthetic virtue. There's nothing wrong with our aesthetic perspective, that we want to preserve this from decay, but we should also respect other aesthetic perspectives because your aesthetic perspective dictates how you view yourself and how you view others. It goes down to the fundamental consideration of what you view as beautiful. Once you allow people to co-opt the abilities of other people to make these critical determinations, once you take an Igbu artifact and place it under a glass case and destroy that distinct aesthetic perspective, you strike at the very heart of what it means to be human. So to prevent that and to correct for that, I would urge a proposition ballot. Thank you very much."

═══════════

First Opposition Speaker: "I'd like to thank everyone for coming. Let's talk about the ridiculous assumptions behind this case. First of all, they say that we're only interested in returning these things, quote, 'when the rightful owner can be determined.' We ask them 'When can that happen?' They say: 'We provide very good examples of that. We've provided the example of the Parthenon frieze and the example of Nazi art.' Well, the Parthenon frieze was built using stolen funds and marble that Athens actually appropriated from other countries in the year circa 400 B.C. So who owns the Parthenon frieze? Is it the people who actually owned the objects that were amalgamated into the Parthenon? Or is it the Greeks, who stole those things and used them to build the Parthenon? Let's look at the example of Nazi art. Let's say that the Nazis are stealing several things from the museums of the Vichy government in France. Which were, in turn, stolen from the Germans during the wars over the French Revolution. Who owns those pieces of art?"

Proposition speaker, rising: "Will you take a point?"

Opposition speaker: "The simple fact is that it's not as simple as looking at the last time an artifact was stolen because the history of cultural artifacts is one of theft, and you can't avoid this. There is no clear-cut case, as Judd would have you believe, in any situation where the rightful owner can be determined. It's never like their example of some kid stealing another kid's shoes. On that point?"

Proposition speaker: "So do you deny that there are explicit records of Nazi art that trace back the legitimate owners?"

Opposition speaker: "No, I'm not denying that. I'm saying that there are legitimate records tracing back legitimate ownership in the sense that that legitimate ownership was, in fact, still a stolen cultural artifact. There is never any art artifact that is produced without theft. If you think about even the most basic art artifact, it is produced using the labor of a lower class in order to sustain a class of elite intellectuals and artists who then use that elitism to create these art objects. Art is a world of theft, and it's implicated in theft, and you cannot blindly assume, as the government has, that this does not happen."

[Proposition speaker rises]

Opposition speaker: "Sit down, please. Now, then they say: 'Well, we're viewing art wrongly.' We ask for an example of this. They offer the example of the Declaration of Independence. We say: 'What should we do with the Declaration of Independence?' They say: 'Well, actually, that's fine, but the problem is the Igbu tribe.' Let's look at the Igbu tribe. Now, I don't know too much about them, but just based on what the speaker said, if the Igbu tribe creates things and they like those things to decay, then why are they objecting to us taking those things and putting them into our museums?"

Proposition speaker, rising with hand outstretched: "On that point."

Opposition speaker: "Clearly, they have no investment in having these things for their own personal use because they want them to decay. Please sit down. Now, here are two questions. Number one: Are they talking about art? Are they interested in the benefits of art? If they are, they need to realize that there's no one context to art. Art can mean many different things to many different people. Just because you don't belong to the Igbu tribe doesn't mean that you can't appreciate them from your own aesthetic perspective."

Proposition speaker: "Point of information."

Opposition speaker: "No, thank you. Sit down."

Proposition speaker, taking his seat: "You don't have to get so upset."

Opposition speaker: "Okay, I know I don't have to get upset, but how about you stay sitting for more than 30 seconds?"

[Proposition speakers both stand up]

Opposition speaker: "That's great. Please, both of you, sit down. Secondly, they say: 'Well, we need to move beyond Western conceptions of law.' But where have they gotten these very mystical and Eastern conceptions? From the involvement with and investigation of these art artifacts. That's what gives them these other perspectives. That's what allows them to make these arguments. Additionally, you need to consider the care of this art. It's a simple fact that most of these societies do not have the ability to maintain this art because they are developing societies and, quite frankly, they have other priorities. Look at the Parthenon frieze. The two marbles that have been left on the Parthenon frieze are in a state of extreme decay, whereas the Parthenon marbles that are in the British Museum are in a state of remarkable artistic effectiveness. Or, they could be talking about the people. They may not want to help the art: They may instead want to help the people."

[Proposition speaker rises]

Opposition speaker: "Please sit down. Let's talk about reparations in terms of war. They say that when there's a war and people steal art, we have an obligation to return that art. But there's a limited amount of political capital in terms of reparations. It's not like everyone in Germany is running around stumbling all over themselves to pay billions of dollars back to the French. That's not a movement in Germany. In fact, it happens only with great amounts of political capital and at a tremendous political expense. You need to ask yourself: What is the most effective use of that political capital? Is it to restore art objects, something that the top one percent of the top one percent of the people use, create, and experience? Or is it in industrial, environmental, and medical reparations—things that affect the lives of the vast majority of these countries?

"All that their proposal does is extinguish these symbols of imperialism. They say, and this is a quote: 'We need to establish an appropriate relationship between states.' I agree. But you don't simply do that by closing your eyes and erasing all of the history of imperialism. There is a system that exists right now whereby certain countries, most notably Western countries, are far more powerful than countries around the world. One of the major signs of that power disparity is the fact that these artifacts exist in locations other than where they were produced. When you move those artifacts back, you don't change the situation. You don't make those countries equal. Don't let them fool you into believing that. What you do is just eliminate the *sign* of that inequality. You eliminate the fact that all of us can, for example, talk about this. Why is this a debatable issue? Because we have been made aware that there is inequality in international relations through the existence of these art objects in disparate locations. When you move the art objects back, you will deny the same lesson to other people. After the objects are returned there will be no sign of inequality, no sign for us to determine whether we should be changing our policies as they relate to the rest of the world. For all these reasons, we beg to oppose."